Envisioning BYU

VOLUME 1

Foundations and Dreams

Envisioning BYU

VOLUME 1

Foundations and Dreams

Edited by

John S. Tanner

BRIGHAM YOUNG UNIVERSITY

PROVO, UTAH

Produced and published by BYU Brand & Creative, Provo, UT 84602, create.byu.edu.

Library of Congress Control Number: 2022945498
ISBN: 978-0-8425-0095-1 (hardback)
ISBN: 978-0-8425-0096-8 (paperback)

PRINTED IN THE UNITED STATES OF AMERICA
10 9 8 7 6 5 4 3 2 1

To all those who have believed in and
contributed to BYU's inspired mission—
and to those who will yet do so.

— John S. Tanner

Contents

ACKNOWLEDGEMENTS

I AM GRATEFUL for the help of many people in publishing this volume:

To Kevin Worthen and Shane Reese for inviting me to revise the Norton and Welch volume, *Educating Zion*, in connection with BYU's sesquicentennial.

To BYU Brand & Creative, especially to Jeff McClellan for overall direction, to Lena Harper Primosch for her work as managing editor, to Bruce Patrick for his work as senior graphic designer, to Natalie Miles for typesetting the book, and to Ashley Young, who was my primary editor for the project. As an English professor and occasional editor myself, I have long said that everyone needs a good editor. Ashley proved the validity of this statement for me in her invaluable and unfailingly pleasant work on this project.

To the BYU English Department for providing me an office, copy machines, and student secretarial help in the person of Melanie Black Hemsley.

To Justin Collings, who read and gave suggestions on early drafts of the project.

Above all, I am indebted to my wife, Susan, for her help and support. Susan has the mission of BYU in her soul.

— JOHN S. TANNER

FOREWORD

WITH BRIGHAM YOUNG UNIVERSITY approaching its sesqui-centennial, the administration invited me to update *Educating Zion*. I am honored to do so. For over a quarter of a century, this classic compilation of speeches has been an invaluable source of inspiration and perspective for me and for many others. I thank the previous editors, John W. Welch and Don E. Norton, for their groundbreaking work.

For this volume, I have retained many speeches from the original collection. I have also adhered to the former editors' decision to limit new selections to "key speeches delivered at BYU by Church and university authorities."[1] Yet even with these limitations, I could include only a fraction of key mission-centric discourses. To keep my revision to a reasonable size, I am publishing it in more than one volume, and I have edited some selections for length. However, the complete text and audio of most speeches herein are available online at speeches.byu.edu/envisioning-BYU.

I have tried to make this anthology browser friendly by providing brief introductions for my entries and by grouping the selections into thematic units. Admittedly, the items in these thematic units are somewhat loosely unified; many speeches could fall under multiple headings. Nevertheless, I hope that this new format improves readability and highlights intertextual connections.

A brief word about the selections in this volume. I begin with a talk that I gave to BYU graduate students discussing key scriptures about education. This talk serves as a preface, as these scriptures are featured in "Foundations" and elsewhere in these volumes. The first section, "Foundations," gathers what may be regarded as canonical texts—speeches repeatedly cited as authoritative statements about BYU. The second section is drawn from a remarkably rich vein of "Dreams, Prophecies, and Prayers" about BYU. The final section, "Education in Zion," includes two talks introducing an impressive permanent exhibit on campus, which I hope that readers will be prompted to visit. It concludes with a moving talk by President Russell M. Nelson given at the dedication of the BYU Life Sciences Building.

The title *Envisioning BYU* is intended to signal the aspirational and BYU-centric focus of the collection. Much more than most universities, BYU exists as a spiritual idea as well as a physical institution. It consists not only of a tangible campus but of intangible ideals and ardent aspirations. It lives—as does the idea of Zion—on the horizon of the hopes and dreams that many Latter-day Saints hold about what a Church university ought to be. As I once told the faculty:

> [Brigham Young University] *is built of brick and mortar. It comprises libraries and laboratories, classrooms and cafeterias, well-groomed grounds and cluttered faculty offices. It is built of impressive financial resources and of remarkable human capital. But, above all, BYU is and ever has been built of dreams and ideals. Our house of learning is also a house of dreams.*[2]

The speeches collected herein overwhelmingly speak to BYU's institutional vision. They are remarkably consistent both in how they understand this vision and in how they call on BYU to live up to it. In this sense, these speeches are more hortatory than laudatory. This is as it should be, for "institutions and individuals [are] better off when they are animated by a vision of the good rather than a belief that they possess it."[3] The high expectations that have enveloped BYU since its founding offer little occasion for self-congratulation but much opportunity for self-reflection and self-correction. We look back on the hopes and dreams of those who have gone before in order, Janus-like, to look forward to a future worthy of their sacrifices and aspirations. I hope that this volume will help faculty, students, and staff more fully understand and embrace BYU's mission.

Never mind that BYU's reach should exceed its grasp. This is unavoidable when prophets have set such high expectations for the university, as did President Spencer W. Kimball on the cusp of BYU's second century when he said, "We expect (we do not simply hope)" for BYU to become "an 'educational Everest,'" "a leader among the great universities of the world," and, at the same time, "a unique university in all of the world"—one that "must not be made over in the image of the world."[4] Excelling academically while remaining distinctive spiritually may seem like an unattainable dream, but this, too, is as it should be. For as President Kimball also observed, "Ideals are like stars; you will not succeed in touching them with your hands. But like the seafaring man on the desert of waters, you choose them as your guides, and following them you will reach your destiny."[5] Or as Karl G. Maeser remarked in a similar vein, "The mariner is guided by the stars of heaven, although he does not get there with his ship."[6] Readers may glimpse herein the stars that have guided BYU's mariners, as well as the seas—both smooth and turbulent—through which the good ship BYU has sailed for 150 years. May BYU ever steer by the stars.

—John S. Tanner

NOTES

1. John W. Welch and Don E. Norton, eds., *Educating Zion* (Provo: BYU Studies, 1996), vii.

2. John S. Tanner, "A House of Dreams," BYU annual university conference address, 28 August 2007.

3. John Churchill, "Is Postmodern Community Possible?" *Liberal Education* 83, no. 1 (Winter 1997): 27; quoted in John S. Tanner, "'One of the Great Lights of the World': Seeking Learning by Study and Faith at BYU," BYU annual university conference address, 23 August 2005.

4. Spencer W. Kimball, "The Second Century of Brigham Young University," BYU devotional address, 10 October 1975; see also Harold B. Lee, "Be Loyal to the Royal Within You," BYU devotional address, 11 September 1973.

5. Carl Schurz, address in Faneuil Hall, Boston, 18 April 1859; quoted in Kimball, "Second Century."

6. Karl G. Maeser, *School and Fireside* (Provo: Skelton, Maeser, 1897), 84.

PREFACE

The purpose of this preface is to explain the primary scriptural injunctions for education. It thus provides an introduction to this first volume of *Envisioning BYU*. It is also a personal credo, outlining views that have animated me over the years. This preface was originally delivered as a talk, titled "A Gospel Ground for Education: An Academic Credo," to BYU graduate students at the Faith and Scholarship Symposium on February 16, 2005.

I AM HONORED to speak about the relationship between faith and scholarship, knowing that so many of you embody a seamless unity of these values in your own lives. When hearing of this topic, you likely envision a talk on the *horizontal* relationship between faith and scholarship: that is, how they complement or conflict with one another. However, I want to take a different tack. I want to address the *vertical* relationship between faith and scholarship: specifically, how faith—or, more broadly, religious belief—undergirds and grounds education. I have called my remarks "A Gospel Ground for Education."

By "gospel ground for education," I mean the theological basis for education. I recognize that this is an inherently abstract topic— about as appetizing as dry toast without butter. So I shall try to make my views more palatable by focusing on two familiar foundational instances in the scriptures: the two great commandments in the New Testament[1] and the Olive Leaf revelation in the Doctrine and Covenants.[2] The first allows me to comment on the broad Christian underpinning for education; the second allows me to consider its specifically Latter-day Saint basis.

Both of these scriptural texts contain commandments; they express religious imperatives. This focus is intentional, for I believe that education is a religious duty: God expects us to use our minds to love Him and our neighbor. Since education is based on eternal imperatives, what follows is not just an analysis but also an academic credo of sorts—a statement of what I believe the Lord expects of me as a believer. Hence my subtitle, "An Academic Credo," in which *credo* means "I believe."

THE TWO GREAT COMMANDMENTS

I believe that the mind is a divine gift and that we are fashioned to love and serve God intelligently—as Thomas More says in Robert Bolt's play *A Man for All Seasons:*

> *God made the **angels** to show him splendour—as he made animals for innocence and plants for their simplicity. But Man he made to serve him wittily, in the tangle of his mind!*[3]

This sentiment is similar to what William Shakespeare's Hamlet exclaims:

> *Sure he that made us with such large discourse,*
> *Looking before and after, gave us not*
> *That capability and godlike reason*
> *To fust* [mold] *in us unused.*[4]

Likewise, the Lord affirms the mind as a divine gift in His great charter of Christian discipleship—the so-called "great commandments" to love God and neighbor.

The first commandment explicitly sanctions the mind as a means of worship. It is telling that Jesus added *mind* when He reformulated Deuteronomy 6:5 as "the first and great commandment," saying, "Thou shalt love the Lord thy God with all thy heart, and with all thy soul, and with all thy mind."[5] *Mind* occurs in all three versions of this commandment in the Gospels.[6] What is more, *mind* also appears in similar formulations found in modern revelation. There are at least ten more such instances in Latter-day Saint scripture containing similar lists that include *mind.*[7]

Let me draw out some implications from this remarkable emphasis on the mind by focusing on several words in the first commandment.

Mind

First, of course, is *mind.* As I have already stated, I believe that the inclusion of *mind* is both deliberate and deeply significant. The first commandment dignifies the intellect as a vehicle with which to worship God and honor His creations. Some religious traditions disparage the intellect because of its potential for misuse. By contrast, the first commandment recognizes that the mind is fundamentally holy, on a par with the heart or the soul. To be sure, there are spiritual dangers associated with the intellect, but these are perils from the misuse of a good gift, not from any inherent evil in the gift itself. "To be learned is good," Jacob affirms, "if they hearken."[8] This gets it just right. The Lord expects scholars to hearken; scholars are not exempt from obedience or meekness. At the same time, the Lord expects them to use their minds to love Him and to understand His creations.

Love

We often think of loving God as something we do solely or mainly with our hearts and with our hands in service. The first commandment obligates us to *love* the Lord with our *minds.* What a powerful idea, that the mind can be an instrument of love! I believe that God expects us to love Him thoughtfully, attentively, and studiously. We demonstrate our love for God by learning about Him and His creations. The first commandment reminds us that there is a relationship between learning and loving. To love with the mind describes my deepest experience as a learner, as a student not only of sacred but of secular matters. For me, learning at its best is an intense form of loving, culminating in delight.

All

We are commanded to love God with *all* our minds. Given this injunction, I believe that it is improper to segment our minds into hermetically sealed spheres, such as "sacred" and "secular," as if all truth were not ultimately one. To love God with *all* our minds means that our views on the academic disciplines must be informed by our discipleship. The first commandment calls us to intellectual wholeness or integrity.

Heart, Soul, and Strength

Similarly, the first commandment links the mind with other faculties: *heart, soul,* and *strength.* Like the emphasis on *all,* this list suggests an integrated approach to matters of the mind. It implies that the mind ought to be integrated with our other faculties. We are not simply minds in a vat; we are embodied beings who are commanded to love God with the totality of our being.

God

The first commandment focuses on loving *God.* What does it mean to bring our minds to the love of God? Does this enjoin us to study only religious subjects? I think not. Rather, I believe that the command to love God with our minds invites us to contemplate not only the Creator but His wondrous creations. To love God with our minds implies understanding His handiwork. In the Doctrine and Covenants we read that anyone who has looked up into the starry sky "hath seen God moving in his majesty and power."[9] Those in former times spoke of God's revealing Himself in two books: the book of scripture and the book of nature. I believe that the first commandment invites us to read the testimonies of the Divine inscribed in both books.

First

In one Gospel, Jesus states that "this is the first commandment."[10] In another Gospel, He calls it "the first and great commandment."[11] This priority is crucial. To me, *first* signifies that the love of God must claim precedence as our highest love; properly, the love of God orders and subordinates all other loves. This is to say that the first commandment obligates believers to engage in the academic disciplines as disciples.

Love of Neighbor

Now let me turn to the second commandment. The second commandment calls us to love our neighbors as ourselves.[12] This, too, has important implications with respect to a gospel ground for education. I believe that the imperative to love our neighbors implies an obligation to *understand* our neighbors—their culture, history, language, science, and so forth. For how can I love someone "as myself" whom I do not understand?

I also believe that the second commandment implies a responsibility to understand and care about our neighborhoods, which shape the soul for good and ill. As Kenneth A. Myers has written:

> *Fulfilling the commands to love God and neighbor requires that we pay careful attention to the neighborhood: that is, every sphere of human life where God is either glorified or despised, where neighbors are either edified or undermined. Therefore, living as disciples of Christ pertains not just to prayer, evangelism, and Bible study, but also our enjoyment of literature and music, our use of tools and machines, our eating and drinking, our views on government and economics, and so on.*[13]

Love of neighbor thus requires thoughtful engagement with the world, including serious reflection on the academic disciplines, which serve as repositories of the world's wisdom.

Together, the two great commandments call us, as disciples, to seek wisdom in light of our discipleship. All of us who embrace these divine injunctions live under a religious imperative to learn—about God and His mighty creations as well as about neighbors and neighborhoods in which Christian love must be practiced.

THE OLIVE LEAF

I also believe that modern revelation makes our duty to learn, as latter-day Christians, even more explicit and concrete. The revelation given to Joseph Smith known as the Olive Leaf, found in Doctrine and Covenants 88, sets forth an expansive vision of education for Latter-day Saints. According to President Dallin H. Oaks, the Olive Leaf, "which defined the objectives of the School of the Prophets," still serves as "the basic constitution of Church education."[14] Let me briefly describe how this constitutional revelation articulates the *how*, *what*, and *why* of a gospel ground for education.

How

In the Olive Leaf, the Lord enjoins His people to "diligently . . . seek learning, even by study and also by faith."[15] This counsel, which is repeated three times in the Doctrine and Covenants,[16] describes *how* Latter-day Saints should approach education. The key commandment as to how we should learn is likely familiar to all of you. We should learn by diligent study and by faith. Note that both study *and* faith are divinely sanctioned means of learning. I believe in a holistic pursuit of wisdom, which embraces such dichotomies as intellect and spirit, reason and revelation, and head and heart.

I also believe that we should approach learning "diligently." Modern revelation frequently uses the adverb *diligently* to describe how the Saints are to seek and search. I find it telling that, at root, *diligent* connotes not only strenuous effort but delight. *Diligence* derives from the Latin *diligere*, meaning to esteem highly, love, choose, and take delight in. *Diligently* thus captures not only the rigor and assiduousness that should attend our study but also the joy and excitement that should characterize gospel-grounded learning.

What

The Olive Leaf also articulates *what* should be studied. It sets forth a broadly inclusive curriculum. Early Latter-day Saints were to "be instructed more perfectly in theory, in principle, in doctrine."[17] They were to learn

of things both in heaven and in the earth, and under the earth;
things which have been, things which are, [and] *things which must*
shortly come to pass; things . . . at home . . . [and] *abroad;* [and]
the wars and the perplexities of the nations.[18]

They were further commanded to seek wisdom "out of the best books"[19] and to "study and learn, and become acquainted with . . . languages, tongues, and people."[20]

To my knowledge, these injunctions have never been revoked or rescinded. Therefore we, just like the early Saints, ought to understand the broad domains of human knowledge. For me, this is not only a daunting but a thrilling prospect. It invites me to indulge my intellectual curiosity. It is an antidote to intellectual sloth, narrow-mindedness, and self-satisfaction. And it is an injunction to never cease learning and to ever seek to learn from those in every walk of life, not just from those in my narrow area of expertise.

The stunning scope of the Lord's curriculum in the Olive Leaf lends support to the proposition that the gospel embraces all truth. So wide is the expanse of things the Lord would have His Saints know!

This breadth may also bespeak the fact that ideas have consequences. The Lord knows that ideas in the academic disciplines can deeply affect discipleship, for good and ill. Hence disciples in every generation must be "wise as serpents."[21] They must take the measure of the philosophy, science, art, culture, and technology of their age if they are to "be prepared in all things" to proclaim the gospel.[22] What the age *propounds* affects how disciples must *expound* the gospel to their neighbors. Therefore, disciples have a double obligation to the disciplines: disciples have much to learn *from* the disciplines, and disciples bring an important perspective *to* the disciplines.

Why

Finally, modern revelation describes *why* believers are to seek learning—its *telos* or purpose. Traditionally, two competing reasons are adduced to justify learning: instrumental value and intrinsic value. The Doctrine and Covenants ascribes both *instrumental* and *intrinsic* value to learning.

The early Saints were commanded to seek learning so that they would "be prepared in all things . . . to magnify [their] calling" as witnesses.[23] That is, they were to seek learning for the sake of a world they were called to serve and save. This implies that learning is an *instrumental* good, one that helps disciples act more effectively in the world.

In addition, however, the Saints were to seek intelligence to become more like God. To this end they were taught that "the glory of God is intelligence, or, in other words, light and truth."[24] This doctrine implies that learning truth is an *intrinsic* good, a good in and of itself, for it is an attribute of the Divine.

I cannot conceive a more powerful argument for the intrinsic value of learning than this, nor a more inspiring incentive to learn all the truth we can—even while in this life. For we have this promise:

> *Whatever principle of intelligence we attain unto in this life, it will rise with us in the resurrection.*
> *And if a person gains more knowledge and intelligence in this life through his diligence and obedience than another, he will have so much the advantage in the world to come.*[25]

Intelligence makes us more like God. Obviously, intelligence is not coterminous with knowledge of academic subjects, but I suspect there is some overlap, since "truth is knowledge of things as they" were, are, and will be.[26] Further, the habits of truth-seeking by study and faith will also rise with us in the Resurrection and aid us in our quest for perfection and eternal life.

This is, finally, the true goal of education. The ultimate end of true education is to help us become more like God. As John Milton says in *Of Education:*

> *The end then of learning is to repair the ruins of our first parents by regaining to know God aright, and out of that knowledge to love him, to imitate him, to be like him.*[27]

CONCLUDING THOUGHTS

I have offered an academic credo regarding the gospel ground for learning—a credo founded on the great commandments and on modern revelation. I have focused on our religious obligation to learn. If, however, I were to reduce my academic credo to a sentence, I would state it as follows: *I believe that as disciples we have a religious duty to learn truth, to love truth, and to live truth.*

I have focused almost exclusively on our duty to learn truth. This, however, is only the beginning of a disciple's duty. It is not enough merely to learn truth; we must love it. And it is not enough only to love truth; we must live it. Loving and living truth constitute higher obligations than learning truth, but to explore them would clearly require another lecture. May you found your scholarship on your faith.

— John S. Tanner

NOTES

1. See Mark 12:29–31.
2. See Doctrine and Covenants 88, section heading.
3. Robert Bolt, *A Man for All Seasons: A Play in Two Acts* (London: Heinemann Educational Books, 1960), act 2, page 74; emphasis in original.
4. William Shakespeare, *Hamlet*, act 4, scene 4, lines 36–39.
5. Matthew 22:38 and 37. Deuteronomy 6:5 says, "And thou shalt love the Lord thy God with all thine heart, and with all thy soul, and with all thy might." See also 2 Kings 23:25.
6. See Matthew 22:37–39; Mark 12:29–31; Luke 10:27.
7. See 2 Nephi 25:29; Mosiah 2:11; Alma 39:13; Moroni 10:32; Doctrine and Covenants 4:2; 11:20; 20:31; 33:7; 59:5; 98:47.
8. 2 Nephi 9:29.
9. Doctrine and Covenants 88:47.
10. Mark 12:30.
11. Matthew 22:38.
12. See Matthew 22:39; Mark 12:31; Luke 10:27.
13. Kenneth A. Myers, "About Mars Hill Audio," Mars Hill Audio, accessed December 2004, marshillaudio.org/about/aboutmha.asp (webpage discontinued); also published at "Mars Hill Audio Incorporated: Mission," GuideStar, Candid, guidestar.org/profile/54-1525723.

14. Dallin H. Oaks, "A House of Faith," BYU annual university conference address, 31 August 1977, 8.

15. Doctrine and Covenants 88:118.

16. See Doctrine and Covenants 88:118; 109:7, 14.

17. Doctrine and Covenants 88:78.

18. Doctrine and Covenants 88:79.

19. Doctrine and Covenants 88:118.

20. Doctrine and Covenants 90:15.

21. Matthew 10:16.

22. Doctrine and Covenants 88:80.

23. Doctrine and Covenants 88:80.

24. Doctrine and Covenants 93:36.

25. Doctrine and Covenants 130:18–19.

26. Doctrine and Covenants 93:24.

27. John Milton, *Of Education* (1644).

FOUNDATIONS

Ye are called to do this by prayer and thanksgiving, as the Spirit shall give utterance in all your doings…in the school of the prophets, that it may become a sanctuary, a tabernacle of the Holy Spirit to your edification.

— Doctrine and Covenants 88:137

Brother Maeser, I want you to remember that you ought not to teach even the alphabet or the multiplication tables without the Spirit of God.

— Brigham Young

The Basic Constitution of Church Education

* *Excerpts from Doctrine and Covenants 88, 90, and 93,*
  1832–1833

INTRODUCTION

President Dallin H. Oaks called Doctrine and Covenants 88 "the first and greatest revelation of this dispensation on the subject of education" and "the basic constitution of Church education. It defines Brigham Young University's role in the kingdom" ("A House of Faith," BYU annual university conference address, 31 August 1977). As BYU's basic constitution, Doctrine and Covenants 88—which Joseph Smith named the Olive Leaf—reminds us that the university's spiritual origins predate the founding of Brigham Young Academy in pioneer Utah.

The Olive Leaf links BYU to the Prophet Joseph, with his extravagant thirst for knowledge, and to similar revelations he received affirming that "the glory of God is intelligence" and admonishing the Saints to "become acquainted with all good books, and with languages, tongues, and people"; with "history," "countries," and the "laws of God and man" (Doctrine and Covenants 90:15; 93:36, 53). The Olive Leaf links BYU to the School of the Prophets, which placed learning among Latter-day Saints on spiritual foundations, and to the University of the City of Nauvoo, with its ambitious Olive Leaf–inspired curriculum and with the high hopes Joseph had to found a university that would become "one of the great lights of the world"

(Joseph Smith, Sidney Rigdon, and Hyrum Smith, "A Proclamation to the Saints Scattered Abroad," *Times and Seasons* 2, no. 6 [15 January 1841]: 274). These and many other educational currents flow from the Church in Joseph's day to BYU today.

But above all, the Olive Leaf links BYU to the Church's first temple and to Latter-day Saint temples generally. Verses from this revelation, including the oft-repeated injunction to "seek learning, even by study and also by faith" (Doctrine and Covenants 88:118), were quoted in the dedicatory prayer of the Kirtland Temple (see Doctrine and Covenants 109:7). The overlap between Doctrine and Covenants 88 and 109 bespeaks deep continuities and homologies between school and temple in Latter-day Saint history and doctrine. Church schools were originally housed in temples. Today they often stand beside temples. And they share with temples a mandate to become houses of faith, learning, and the Spirit (see Doctrine and Covenants 88:119, 137).

The following excerpts from the Olive Leaf and from Doctrine and Covenants 90 and 93 illustrate foundational principles of Church education regarding truth, learning, and schools:

- **Truth:** God is the source of truth and light; His light quickens the understanding; He gives law to all things; His creations reveal His majesty.
- **Learning:** To comprehend light, learners must be clean and sanctify themselves, having eyes and minds single to God; they are to seek learning diligently, both by study and by faith; they are to teach one another not only doctrine but broadly of things in heaven and in earth so as to be prepared in all things.
- **Schools:** Church schools are to be temple-like houses of learning and faith; in them, teachers and students are to learn from each other such that all are edified of all; in them, all gather as brothers and sisters in the bonds of love, remembering their covenants and determined to walk in the commandments.

: ⚜ :

DOCTRINE AND COVENANTS 88

Verses 6–7

H<small>E THAT ASCENDED</small> up on high, as also he descended below all things, in that he comprehended all things, that he might be in all and through all things, the light of truth;

Which truth shineth. This is the light of Christ. As also he is in the sun, and the light of the sun, and the power thereof by which it was made.

Verses 11–13

And the light which shineth, which giveth you light, is through him who enlighteneth your eyes, which is the same light that quickeneth your understandings;

Which light proceedeth forth from the presence of God to fill the immensity of space—

The light which is in all things, which giveth life to all things, which is the law by which all things are governed, even the power of God who sitteth upon his throne, who is in the bosom of eternity, who is in the midst of all things.

Verses 36–37

All kingdoms have a law given;

And there are many kingdoms; for there is no space in the which there is no kingdom; and there is no kingdom in which there is no space, either a greater or a lesser kingdom.

Verses 40–47

For intelligence cleaveth unto intelligence; wisdom receiveth wisdom; truth embraceth truth; virtue loveth virtue; light cleaveth unto light; mercy hath compassion on mercy and claimeth her own; justice continueth its course and claimeth its own; judgment goeth before the face of him who sitteth upon the throne and governeth and executeth all things.

He comprehendeth all things, and all things are before him, and all things are round about him; and he is above all things, and in all things, and is through all things, and is round about all things; and all things are by him, and of him, even God, forever and ever.

And again, verily I say unto you, he hath given a law unto all things, by which they move in their times and their seasons;

And their courses are fixed, even the courses of the heavens and the earth, which comprehend the earth and all the planets.

And they give light to each other in their times and in their seasons, in their minutes, in their hours, in their days, in their weeks, in their months, in their years—all these are one year with God, but not with man.

The earth rolls upon her wings, and the sun giveth his light by day, and the moon giveth her light by night, and the stars also give their light, as they roll upon their wings in their glory, in the midst of the power of God.

Unto what shall I liken these kingdoms, that ye may understand?

Behold, all these are kingdoms, and any man who hath seen any or the least of these hath seen God moving in his majesty and power.

Verses 63–69

Draw near unto me and I will draw near unto you; seek me diligently and ye shall find me; ask, and ye shall receive; knock, and it shall be opened unto you.

Whatsoever ye ask the Father in my name it shall be given unto you, that is expedient for you;

And if ye ask anything that is not expedient for you, it shall turn unto your condemnation.

Behold, that which you hear is as the voice of one crying in the wilderness—in the wilderness, because you cannot see him—my voice, because my voice is Spirit; my Spirit is truth; truth abideth and hath no end; and if it be in you it shall abound.

And if your eye be single to my glory, your whole bodies shall be filled with light, and there shall be no darkness in you; and that body which is filled with light comprehendeth all things.

Therefore, sanctify yourselves that your minds become single to God, and the days will come that you shall see him; for he will unveil his face unto you, and it shall be in his own time, and in his own way, and according to his own will.

Remember the great and last promise which I have made unto you; cast away your idle thoughts and your excess of laughter far from you.
Verses 77–80

And I give unto you a commandment that you shall teach one another the doctrine of the kingdom.

Teach ye diligently and my grace shall attend you, that you may be instructed more perfectly in theory, in principle, in doctrine, in the law of the gospel, in all things that pertain unto the kingdom of God, that are expedient for you to understand;

Of things both in heaven and in the earth, and under the earth; things which have been, things which are, things which must shortly come to pass; things which are at home, things which are abroad; the wars and the perplexities of the nations, and the judgments which are on the land; and a knowledge also of countries and of kingdoms—

That ye may be prepared in all things when I shall send you again to magnify the calling whereunto I have called you, and the mission with which I have commissioned you.
Verses 118–138

And as all have not faith, seek ye diligently and teach one another words of wisdom; yea, seek ye out of the best books words of wisdom; seek learning, even by study and also by faith.

Organize yourselves; prepare every needful thing; and establish a house, even a house of prayer, a house of fasting, a house of faith, a house of learning, a house of glory, a house of order, a house of God;

That your incomings may be in the name of the Lord; that your outgoings may be in the name of the Lord; that all your salutations may be in the name of the Lord, with uplifted hands unto the Most High.

Therefore, cease from all your light speeches, from all laughter, from all your lustful desires, from all your pride and light-mindedness, and from all your wicked doings.

Appoint among yourselves a teacher, and let not all be spokesmen at once; but let one speak at a time and let all listen unto his sayings, that when all have spoken that all may be edified of all, and that every man may have an equal privilege.

See that ye love one another; cease to be covetous; learn to impart one to another as the gospel requires.

Cease to be idle; cease to be unclean; cease to find fault one with another; cease to sleep longer than is needful; retire to thy bed early, that ye may not be weary; arise early, that your bodies and your minds may be invigorated.

And above all things, clothe yourselves with the bond of charity, as with a mantle, which is the bond of perfectness and peace.

Pray always, that ye may not faint, until I come. Behold, and lo, I will come quickly, and receive you unto myself. Amen.

And again, the order of the house prepared for the presidency of the school of the prophets, established for their instruction in all things that are expedient for them, even for all the officers of the church, or in other words, those who are called to the ministry in the church, beginning at the high priests, even down to the deacons—

And this shall be the order of the house of the presidency of the school: He that is appointed to be president, or teacher, shall be found standing in his place, in the house which shall be prepared for him.

Therefore, he shall be first in the house of God, in a place that the congregation in the house may hear his words carefully and distinctly, not with loud speech.

And when he cometh into the house of God, for he should be first in the house—behold, this is beautiful, that he may be an example—

Let him offer himself in prayer upon his knees before God, in token or remembrance of the everlasting covenant.

And when any shall come in after him, let the teacher arise, and, with uplifted hands to heaven, yea, even directly, salute his brother or brethren with these words:

Art thou a brother or brethren? I salute you in the name of the Lord Jesus Christ, in token or remembrance of the everlasting covenant, in which covenant I receive you to fellowship, in a determination that is fixed, immovable, and unchangeable, to be your friend and brother through the grace of God in the bonds of love, to walk in all the commandments of God blameless, in thanksgiving, forever and ever. Amen.

And he that is found unworthy of this salutation shall not have place among you; for ye shall not suffer that mine house shall be polluted by him.

And he that cometh in and is faithful before me, and is a brother, or if they be brethren, they shall salute the president or teacher with uplifted hands to heaven, with this same prayer and covenant, or by saying Amen, in token of the same.

Behold, verily, I say unto you, this is an ensample unto you for a salutation to one another in the house of God, in the school of the prophets.

And ye are called to do this by prayer and thanksgiving, as the Spirit shall give utterance in all your doings in the house of the Lord, in the school of the prophets, that it may become a sanctuary, a tabernacle of the Holy Spirit to your edification.

And ye shall not receive any among you into this school save he is clean from the blood of this generation.

DOCTRINE AND COVENANTS 90

Verse 15

AND SET IN order the churches, and study and learn, and become acquainted with all good books, and with languages, tongues, and people.

DOCTRINE AND COVENANTS 93

Verses 36, 53

THE GLORY OF God is intelligence, or, in other words, light and truth. And, verily I say unto you, that it is my will that you should hasten to translate my scriptures, and to obtain a knowledge of history, and of countries, and of kingdoms, of laws of God and man, and all this for the salvation of Zion. Amen.

Brigham Young's 1876 Charge to Karl G. Maeser

Reinhard Maeser

* *In* Karl G. Maeser: A Biography by His Son, *1928*

INTRODUCTION

Brigham Young's famous founding charge to Karl G. Maeser—that he "ought not to teach even the alphabet or the multiplication tables without the Spirit of God"—is well known (page 14). It is BYU's prime directive. Maeser himself referred to the charge as the "one thing constant" and "the mainspring of all her labors" ("History of the Academy," page 21).

The version here has been excerpted from Reinhard Maeser, *Karl G. Maeser: A Biography by His Son* (Provo: Brigham Young University, 1928), 76–80; the text has been modernized.

"Teach nothing, do nothing, without the Spirit of God." Oh, how in the years that followed, this holy admonition became the very guiding star of his life.

— Reinhard Maeser

: ⚘ :

IN THE SPRING of 1876, just prior to the April conference, a terrific explosion of powder occurred on Arsenal Hill near the present site of the Utah State Capitol. Several lives were lost and extensive damage was done to adjacent property, such as the breaking of window glass and crashing of roofs by the large boulders. Nearly all of the plaster was shaken from the ceiling of the Twentieth Ward schoolhouse, where Professor Maeser was teaching. Immediately he started in search of his bishop, John Sharp. He found the bishop at the president's [Brigham Young's] office and reported to him what had just happened, adding that the school would have to be dismissed until the house could be repaired.

But at this point, President Young interrupted the conversation with the remark, "That is exactly right, Brother Maeser; I have another mission for you."

"Yes," said the president, "we have been considering the establishment of a Church school and are looking around for a man—the man to take charge of it. You are the man, Brother Maeser. We want you to go to Provo to organize and conduct an academy to be established in the name of the Church—a Church school."

[Brother Maeser] knew full well there would be perplexing problems to solve, difficult situations to meet, and soul-trying times to endure, when he would have to go up to his Gethsemane to seek relief. This struggle continued within him for several days. At last he decided that he must accept the appointment or, coward-like, back out. He went to President Young, whom he found in his office, busy on important matters. Addressing the president, he said, "I am about to leave for Provo, Brother Young, to start my work in the academy. Have you any instructions to give me?"

The president looked steadily forward for a few moments, as though deep in thought, then said: "Brother Maeser, I want you to remember that you ought not to teach even the alphabet or the multiplication tables without the Spirit of God. That is all. God bless you. Good-bye."

But what did the words of the prophet mean? Brother Maeser at first felt that he had received but a stone where he had asked for bread, but as time rolled on, he realized more and more that the very bread of life had been given him. "Teach nothing, do nothing, without the Spirit of God." Oh, how in the years that followed, this holy admonition became the very guiding star of his life.

History of the Academy

KARL G. MAESER

* *Brigham Young Academy Founders Day Address,*
  October 16, 1891

INTRODUCTION

This address was delivered at Brigham Young Academy's first Founders Day exercises. President Maeser recounted how Brigham Young Academy began with the revelation to Brigham Young of "the necessity for the establishment of a new kind of educational institution for Zion" (page 19). The new educational system was not merely to duplicate existing models, for "following . . . in the old grooves would simply lead to the same results" (page 20). Brigham Young Academy was to be unique. At BYA "neither the alphabet nor the multiplication tables should be taught without the Spirit of God" (page 20). "The spirit of the latter-day work" was to go through the academy "like a golden thread" (page 21). Karl G. Maeser served as president of Brigham Young Academy from 1876 to 1892. This speech was originally printed in *Karl G. Maeser: A Biography by His Son* by Reinhard Maeser (Provo: Brigham Young University, 1928), 128–32.

Amid the ever-changing scenes of development… there must go through it all, like a golden thread, one thing constant: the spirit of the latter-day work.

— Karl G. Maeser

: ❧ :

WHEN, AT THE April conference 1876, President Brigham Young appointed me as principal of the educational institution that has been established in Provo and bears the name of its illustrious founder, it was with no comprehension of the magnitude of the work that the appointee laid out the plans for his new mission.

Adding another experimental term to one conducted by his predecessor, he found premises inadequate, facilities limited, students few in number and poorly prepared, and financial conditions exceedingly discouraging. To make matters still worse, there were many even among the influential men in the community who not only had no confidence in the stability of the new venture but openly opposed it by using their influence against it. Yet there were not wanting some prophetic signs of a more prosperous future—in the growing enthusiasm of the students, in the spreading influence outside the schoolroom, in the unqualified support of President Abraham O. Smoot, and in the approval of the presidency of the Church. This was the condition of affairs when, in August of the same year, the first term of the first academic year was commenced.

The two experimental terms had demonstrated the fact that the strength of Brigham Young Academy was not in her financial condition; nor could her aims be to enter, for the present, into competition with institutions of higher education in our country; nor was her distinguishing characteristic to be sought in the professional efficiency of her teachers alone, for all of these advantages have been claimed and enjoyed by schools of learning before. And yet the necessity for the establishment of a new kind of educational institution for Zion had been revealed by the Lord to the prophet Brigham Young. The lack of what element created that necessity? It has been said that the Saints will be saviors upon Mount Zion, that they are destined to redeem the world. Redeem the world from what? From the thralldom of sin, ignorance, and degradation! In order to do this, Zion will have to take the lead in everything and consequently also in education. But there is much education already, much science, much art, much skill, and much so-called civilization—in fact, so much that this generation is fast getting into the notion that they can get along without a God, like the Titans of old who wanted to storm the heavens by piling one mountain on top of another.

A glance over the conditions of mankind in this our day, with its misery, discontent, corruption, and disintegration of the social, religious, and philosophic fabrics, shows that this generation has been put into the balance and has been found wanting. A following, therefore, in the old grooves would simply lead to the same results, and that is what the Lord has designed shall be avoided in Zion. President Brigham Young felt it in his heart that an educational system ought to be inaugurated in Zion in which, as he put it in his terse way of saying things, neither the alphabet nor the multiplication tables should be taught without the Spirit of God.

Thus was started this nucleus of a new system. When, years after, a certain person could find no other fault with it than that it should have started some twenty years before, I thanked God that it hadn't; for if it had been thus started without teachers to comprehend its aims, without boards to enter into its spirit, and without students to feel its necessity, unavoidable failure would have postponed a successful commencement for a generation or more.

All the above-mentioned adversities of the infant institution were blessings in disguise. Without means, by relying upon the liberality of her patrons, the academy engendered a growing interest among the people in its aims. Without teachers sufficiently devoted to its sacred cause to labor for a mere nominal salary, the academy was forced to create a Normal Department, composed of volunteers, to raise her own teachers. Without a board of members experienced in educational affairs, they went through an empirical training in having their attentions turned gradually from the primitive conditions of the beginning to the more complex organization of the school's further advancement.

If, amidst all these changing scenes, clouds of discouragement did occasionally darken the horizon of our vision, they were always dispelled by the voice of the Spirit whispering, "O ye of little faith."

Amid the ever-changing scenes of development which Brigham Young Academy has passed through—whether holding forth in one single room under makeshift arrangements or enjoying the benefits of more suitable facilities; whether in rented premises, fitted up for the time being, or in her own palatial habitation; whether laboring according to the humble program of the primary and intermediate grades or aspiring to academic or collegiate honors—there must go through it all, like a golden thread, one thing constant: the spirit of the latter-day work. As long as this principle shall be the mainspring of all her labors, whether in teaching the alphabet or the multiplication tables or unfolding the advanced truths of science and art, the future of Brigham Young Academy will surpass in glory the fondest hopes of her most ardent admirers.

The Charted Course of the Church in Education

J. Reuben Clark Jr.

❖ *BYU Summer School Address, August 8, 1938*

INTRODUCTION

 Concerned about rising secularism in Church education, J. Reuben Clark Jr., first counselor in the First Presidency, gave this address to Church seminary and institute leaders at the BYU summer school in Aspen Grove. It has been called "the most influential address to seminary and institute teachers in the history of Church education" (*By Study and Also by Faith: One Hundred Years of Seminaries and Institutes of Religion* [Salt Lake City: The Church of Jesus Christ of Latter-day Saints, 2015], 101). While President Clark focused on seminary and institute teachers, the talk also implied the university's need to hire Latter-day Saint faculty in all disciplines who were fully converted, for "our Church schools cannot be manned by unconverted, untestimonied teachers" (page 33). President Packer admonished BYU faculty that "The Charted Course" "should be read by every one of you every year. It is insightful; it is profound; it is prophetic; it is scripture" ("The Snow-White Birds," page 230). So it is included among BYU's founding documents even though its focus is on seminaries and institute teachers.

23

May He give you entrance
to the hearts of those you
teach and then make you
know that as you enter there,
you stand in holy places.

—J. REUBEN CLARK JR.

: 🌿 :

As a schoolboy, I was thrilled with the great debate between the
two giants Daniel Webster and Robert Y. Hayne. The beauty of
their oratory, the sublimity of Webster's lofty expression of patriotism,
and the forecast of the civil struggle to come for the mastery of freedom over slavery all stirred me to the very depths. The debate began
over the Foot Resolution concerning the public lands. It developed
into consideration of great fundamental problems of constitutional
law. I have never forgotten the opening paragraph of Webster's reply to
Hayne, by which Webster brought back to its place of beginning this
debate that had drifted so far from its course. That paragraph reads:

> *Mr. President, when the mariner has been tossed for many
> days in thick weather, and on an unknown sea, he naturally avails
> himself of the first pause in the storm, the earliest glance of the sun,
> to take his latitude, and ascertain how far the elements have driven
> him from his true course. Let us imitate this prudence, and, before
> we float farther on the waves of this debate, refer to the point from
> which we departed, that we may at least be able to conjecture where
> we now are. I ask for the reading of the resolution before the Senate.*[1]

Now I hasten to express the hope that you will not think that I
think this is a Webster-Hayne occasion or that I think I am a Daniel
Webster. If you were to think those things—either of them—you
would make a grievous mistake. I admit I am old, but I am not that old.
But Webster seemed to invoke so sensible a procedure for occasions
in which, after wandering on the high seas or in the wilderness, effort
is to be made to get back to the place of starting, that I thought you
would excuse me if I invoked and in a way used this same procedure
to restate some of the more outstanding and essential fundamentals
underlying our Church school education.

The following are to me those fundamentals:

The Church is the organized priesthood of God. The priesthood can exist without the Church, but the Church cannot exist without the priesthood. The mission of the Church is, first, to teach, encourage, assist, and protect the individual member in his striving to live the perfect life, temporally and spiritually, as laid down in the Gospels by the Master: "Be ye therefore perfect, even as your Father which is in heaven is perfect."[2] Secondly, the Church is to maintain, teach, encourage, and protect, temporally and spiritually, the membership as a group in its living of the gospel. Thirdly, the Church is militantly to proclaim the truth, calling upon all men to repent and to live in obedience to the gospel, for "every knee [must] bow, and every tongue confess."[3]

In all this there are for the Church—and for each and all of its members—two prime things which may not be overlooked, forgotten, shaded, or discarded:

First, that Jesus Christ is the Son of God, the Only Begotten of the Father in the flesh, the Creator of the world, the Lamb of God, the Sacrifice for the sins of the world, and the Atoner for Adam's transgression; that He was crucified; that His spirit left His body; that He died; that He was laid away in the tomb; that on the third day His spirit was reunited with His body, which again became a living being; that He was raised from the tomb a resurrected being, a perfect being, the First Fruits of the Resurrection; that He later ascended to the Father; and that because of His death and by and through His Resurrection, every man born into the world since the beginning will be likewise literally resurrected. This doctrine is as old as the world. Job declared:

> And though after my skin worms destroy this body, yet in my flesh shall I see God:
> Whom I shall see for myself, and mine eyes shall behold, and not another.[4]

The resurrected body is a body of flesh and bones and spirit, and Job was uttering a great and everlasting truth. These positive facts, and all other facts necessarily implied therein, must all be honestly believed, in full faith, by every member of the Church.

The second of the two things to which we must all give full faith is that the Father and the Son actually and in truth and very deed appeared to the Prophet Joseph in a vision in the woods; that other heavenly visions followed to Joseph and to others; that the gospel and the Holy Priesthood, after the Order of the Son of God, were in truth and fact restored to the earth from which they were lost by the apostasy of the primitive Church; that the Lord again set up His Church through the agency of Joseph Smith; that the Book of Mormon is just what it professes to be; that to the Prophet came numerous revelations for the guidance, upbuilding, organization, and encouragement of the Church and its members; that the Prophet's successors, likewise called of God, have received revelations as the needs of the Church have required and that they will continue to receive revelations as the Church and its members, living the truth they already have, shall stand in need of more; that this is in truth The Church of Jesus Christ of Latter-day Saints; and that its foundation beliefs are the laws and principles laid down in the Articles of Faith. These facts, each of them, together with all things necessarily implied therein or flowing therefrom, must stand unchanged, unmodified, and without dilution, excuse, apology, or avoidance; they may not be explained away or submerged.

Without these two great beliefs, the Church would cease to be the Church.

Any individual who does not accept the fulness of these doctrines as to Jesus of Nazareth or as to the Restoration of the gospel and the holy priesthood is not a Latter-day Saint. The hundreds of thousands of faithful, God-fearing men and women who compose the great body of the Church membership do believe these things fully and completely, and they support the Church and its institutions because of this belief.

I have set out these matters because they are the latitude and longitude of the actual location and position of the Church, both in this world and in eternity. Knowing our true position, we can change our bearings if they need changing; we can lay down anew our true course. And here we may wisely recall that Paul said:

> But though we, or an angel from heaven, preach any other gospel unto you than that which we have preached unto you, let him be accursed.[5]

Returning to the Webster-Hayne precedent, I have now finished reading the original resolution.

♦ ♦ ♦

As I have already said, I am to say something about the religious education of the youth of the Church. I shall bring together what I have to say under two general headings—the student and the teacher. I shall speak very frankly, for we have passed the place where we may wisely talk in ambiguous words and veiled phrases. We must say plainly what we mean, because the future of our youth, both here on earth and in the hereafter, and also the welfare of the whole Church are at stake.

The youth of the Church—your students—are in great majority sound in thought and in spirit. The problem primarily is to keep them sound, not to convert them.

The youth of the Church are hungry for things of the Spirit; they are eager to learn the gospel, and they want it straight, undiluted.

They want to know about the fundamentals I have just set out, about our beliefs; they want to gain testimonies of their truth. They are not now doubters but inquirers, seekers after truth. Doubt must not be planted in their hearts. Great is the burden and the condemnation of any teacher who sows doubt in a trusting soul.

These students crave the faith their fathers and mothers have; they want it in its simplicity and purity. There are few indeed who have not seen the manifestations of its divine power. They wish to be not only the beneficiaries of this faith but also want to be themselves able to call it forth to work.

They want to believe in the ordinances of the gospel; they wish to understand them so far as they may.

They are prepared to understand the truth, which is as old as the gospel and which was expressed thus by Paul (a master of logic and metaphysics unapproached by the modern critics who decry all religion):

> *For what man knoweth the things of a man, save the spirit of man which is in him? even so the things of God knoweth no man, but the Spirit of God.*
>
> *Now we have received, not the spirit of the world, but the spirit which is of God; that we might know the things that are freely given to us of God.*[6]

> *For they that are after the flesh do mind the things of the flesh; but they that are after the Spirit the things of the Spirit.*[7]

> *This I say then, Walk in the Spirit, and ye shall not fulfil the lust of the flesh.*
>
> *For the flesh lusteth against the Spirit, and the Spirit against the flesh: and these are contrary the one to the other: so that ye cannot do the things that ye would.*
>
> *But if ye be led of the Spirit, ye are not under the law.*[8]

Our youth understand, too, the principle declared in modern revelation:

> *Ye cannot behold with your natural eyes, for the present time, the design of your God concerning those things which shall come hereafter, and the glory which shall follow after much tribulation.*[9]

> *By the power of the Spirit our eyes were opened and our understandings were enlightened, so as to see and understand the things of God. . . .*
>
> *And while we meditated upon these things, the Lord touched the eyes of our understandings and they were opened, and the glory of the Lord shone round about.*
>
> *And we beheld the glory of the Son, on the right hand of the Father, and received of his fulness;*

And saw the holy angels, and them who are sanctified before his throne, worshiping God, and the Lamb, who worship him forever and ever.

And now, after the many testimonies which have been given of him, this is the testimony, last of all, which we give of him: That he lives!

For we saw him, even on the right hand of God; and we heard the voice bearing record that he is the Only Begotten of the Father—

That by him, and through him, and of him, the worlds are and were created, and the inhabitants thereof are begotten sons and daughters unto God. . . .

And while we were yet in the Spirit, the Lord commanded us that we should write the vision.[10]

These students are prepared, too, to understand what Moses meant when he declared:

But now mine own eyes have beheld God; but not my natural, but my spiritual eyes, for my natural eyes could not have beheld; for I should have withered and died in his presence; but his glory was upon me; and I beheld his face, for I was transfigured before him.[11]

These students are prepared to believe and understand that all these things are matters of faith, not to be explained or understood by any process of human reason and probably not by any experiment of known physical science.

These students (to put the matter shortly) are prepared to understand and to believe that there is a natural world and there is a spiritual world; that the things of the natural world will not explain the things of the spiritual world; that the things of the spiritual world cannot be understood or comprehended by the things of the natural world; and that you cannot rationalize the things of the Spirit—first, because the things of the Spirit are not sufficiently known and comprehended, and second, because finite mind and reason cannot comprehend nor explain infinite wisdom and ultimate truth.

These students already know that they must be "honest, true, chaste, benevolent, virtuous, and [do] good to all men" and that "if there is anything virtuous, lovely, or of good report or praiseworthy, we seek after these things"[12]—these things they have been taught from very birth. They should be encouraged in all proper ways to do these things which they know to be true, but they do not need to have a year's course of instruction to make them believe and know them.

These students fully sense the hollowness of teachings that would make the gospel plan a mere system of ethics. They know that Christ's teachings are in the highest degree ethical, but they also know that they are more than this. They will see that ethics relate primarily to the doings of this life and that to make of the gospel a mere system of ethics is to confess a lack of faith, if not a disbelief, in the hereafter. They know that the gospel teachings not only touch this life but the life that is to come, with its salvation and exaltation as the final goal.

These students hunger and thirst, as did their fathers before them, for a testimony of the things of the Spirit and of the hereafter, and knowing that you cannot rationalize eternity, they seek faith and the knowledge which follows faith. They sense, by the Spirit they have, that the testimony they seek is engendered and nurtured by the testimony of others and that to gain this testimony which they seek for— one living, burning, honest testimony of a righteous, God-fearing man that Jesus is the Christ and that Joseph was God's prophet—is worth a thousand books and lectures aimed at debasing the gospel to a system of ethics or seeking to rationalize infinity.

Two thousand years ago the Master said:

> Or what man is there of you, whom if his son ask bread, will he give him a stone?
> Or if he ask a fish, will he give him a serpent?[13]

These students, born under the covenant, can understand that age and maturity and intellectual training are not in any way or to any degree necessary to communion with the Lord and His Spirit. They know the story of the youth Samuel in the temple, of Jesus at twelve years confounding the doctors in the temple, of Joseph at fourteen seeing God the Father and the Son in one of the most glorious visions ever beheld by man. They are not as were the Corinthians, of whom Paul said:

> I have fed you with milk, and not with meat: for hitherto ye were not able to bear it, neither yet now are ye able.[14]

They are rather as was Paul himself when he declared to the same Corinthians:

> When I was a child, I spake as a child, I understood as a child, I thought as a child: but when I became a man, I put away childish things.[15]

These students as they come to you are spiritually working toward a maturity which they will early reach if you but feed them the right food. They come to you possessing spiritual knowledge and experience the world does not know.

So much for your students and what they are and what they expect and what they are capable of. I am telling you the things that some of you teachers have told me and that many of your youth have told me.

*   *   *

May I now say a few words to you teachers? In the first place, there is neither reason nor is there excuse for our Church religious teaching and training facilities and institutions unless the youth are to be taught and trained in the principles of the gospel, embracing therein the two great elements that Jesus is the Christ and that Joseph was God's prophet. The teaching of a system of ethics to the students is not a sufficient reason for running our seminaries and institutes. The great public school system teaches ethics. The students of seminaries and institutes should of course be taught the ordinary canons of good and righteous living, for these are part, and an essential part, of the gospel. But there are the great principles involved in eternal life—the priesthood, the Resurrection, and many like other things—that go way beyond these canons of good living. These great fundamental principles also must be taught to the youth; they are the things the youth wish first to know about.

The first requisite of a teacher for teaching these principles is a personal testimony of their truth. No amount of learning, no amount of study, and no number of scholastic degrees can take the place of this testimony, which is the *sine qua non* of the teacher in our Church school system. A teacher who does not have a real testimony of the truth of the gospel as revealed to and believed by the Latter-day Saints and a testimony of the Sonship and Messiahship of Jesus and of the divine mission of Joseph Smith—including, in all its reality, the First Vision—has no place in the Church school system. If there be any such, and I hope and pray there are none, he should at once resign; if the commissioner knows of any such and he does not resign, the commissioner should request his resignation. The First Presidency expects this pruning to be made.

This does not mean that we would cast out such teachers from the Church—not at all. We shall take up with them a labor of love, in all patience and long-suffering, to win them to the knowledge to which as God-fearing men and women they are entitled. But this does mean that our Church schools cannot be manned by unconverted, untestimonied teachers.

But for you teachers, the mere possession of a testimony is not enough. You must have, besides this, one of the rarest and most precious of all the many elements of human character—moral courage. For in the absence of moral courage to declare your testimony, it will reach the students only after such dilution as will make it difficult, if not impossible, for them to detect it, and the spiritual and psychological effect of a weak and vacillating testimony may well be actually harmful instead of helpful.

The successful seminary or institute teacher must also possess another of the rare and valuable elements of character, a twin brother of moral courage and often mistaken for it. I mean intellectual courage—the courage to affirm principles, beliefs, and faith that may not always be considered as harmonizing with such knowledge, scientific or otherwise, as the teacher or his educational colleagues may believe they possess.

Not unknown are cases in which men of presumed faith, holding responsible positions, have felt that, since by affirming their full faith they might call down upon themselves the ridicule of their unbelieving colleagues, they must either modify or explain away their faith or destructively dilute it or even pretend to cast it away. Such are hypocrites to their colleagues and to their coreligionists.

An object of pity (not of scorn, as some would have it) is that man or woman who, having the truth and knowing it, finds it necessary either to repudiate the truth or to compromise with error in order that he may live with or among unbelievers without subjecting himself to their disfavor or derision as he supposes. Tragic indeed is his place, for the real fact is that all such discardings and shadings in the end bring the very punishments that the weak-willed one sought to avoid. For there is nothing the world so values and reveres as the man who, having righteous convictions, stands for them in any and all circumstances; there is nothing toward which the world turns more contempt than the man who, having righteous convictions, either slips away from them, abandons them, or repudiates them. For any Latter-day Saint psychologist, chemist, physicist, geologist, archeologist, or any other scientist to explain away or misinterpret or evade or elude or, most of all, repudiate or deny the great fundamental doctrines of the Church in which he professes to believe is to give the lie to his intellect, to lose his self-respect, to bring sorrow to his friends, to break the hearts of and bring shame to his parents, to besmirch the Church and its members, and to forfeit the respect and honor of those whom he has sought, by his course, to win as friends and helpers.

I prayerfully hope there may not be any such among the teachers of the Church school system, but if there are any such, high or low, they must travel the same route as the teacher without the testimony. Sham and pretext and evasion and hypocrisy have, and can have, no place in the Church school system or in the character building and spiritual growth of our youth.

Another thing that must be watched in our Church institutions is this: It must not be possible for men to keep positions of spiritual trust who, not being converted themselves, being really unbelievers, seek to turn aside the beliefs, education, and activities of our youth, and our aged also, from the ways they should follow into other paths of education, beliefs, and activities that (though leading where the unbeliever would go) do not bring us to places where the gospel would take us. That this works as a conscience-balm to the unbeliever who directs it is of no importance. This is the grossest betrayal of trust, and there is too much reason to think it has happened.

* * *

I wish to mention another thing that has happened in other lines as a caution against the same thing happening in the Church Educational System. On more than one occasion, our Church members have gone to other places for special training in particular lines. They have had the training which was supposedly the last word, the most modern view, the *ne plus ultra* of up-to-dateness; then they have brought it back and dosed it upon us without any thought as to whether we needed it or not. I refrain from mentioning well-known and, I believe, well-recognized instances of this sort of thing. I do not wish to wound any feelings.

But before trying on the newest-fangled ideas in any line of thought, education, activity, or whatnot, experts should just stop and consider that however backward they think we are and however backward we may actually be in some things, in other things we are far out in the lead, and therefore these new methods may be old, if not worn out, with us.

In whatever relates to community life and activity in general; to clean group social amusement and entertainment; to closely knit and carefully directed religious worship and activity; to a positive, clear-cut, faith-promoting spirituality; to a real, everyday, practical religion; or to a firm-fixed desire and acutely sensed need for faith in God, we are far in the vanguard of on-marching humanity. Before effort is made to inoculate us with new ideas, experts should kindly consider whether the methods used to spur community spirit or build religious activities among groups that are decadent and maybe dead to these things are quite applicable to us and whether their effort to impose these upon us is not a rather crude, even gross, anachronism.

For example, to apply to our spiritually minded and religiously alert youth a plan evolved to teach religion to youth having no interest or concern in matters of the Spirit would not only fail in meeting our actual religious needs but would tend to destroy the best qualities which our youth now possess.

I have already indicated that our youth are not children spiritually; they are well on toward the normal spiritual maturity of the world. To treat them as children spiritually, as the world might treat the same age group, is therefore and likewise an anachronism. I say once more, there is scarcely a youth who comes through your seminary or institute door who has not been the conscious beneficiary of spiritual blessings or who has not seen the efficacy of prayer or who has not witnessed the power of faith to heal the sick or who has not beheld spiritual outpourings of which the world at large is today ignorant. You do not have to sneak up behind this spiritually experienced youth and whisper religion in his ears; you can come right out, face-to-face, and talk with him. You do not need to disguise religious truths with a cloak of worldly things; you can bring these truths to him openly in their natural guise. Youth may prove to be not more fearful of them than you are. There is no need for gradual approaches, for "bedtime" stories, for coddling, for patronizing, or for any of the other childish devices used in efforts to reach those spiritually inexperienced and all but spiritually dead.

* * *

You teachers have a great mission. As teachers you stand upon the highest peak in education, for what teaching can compare in priceless value and in far-reaching effect with that which deals with man as he was in the eternity of yesterday, as he is in the mortality of today, and as he will be in the forever of tomorrow? Not only time but eternity is your field. Salvation of yourself not only but of those who come within the purlieus of your temple is the blessing you seek and which, doing your duty, you will gain. How brilliant will be your crown of glory, with each soul saved an encrusted jewel thereon.

But to get this blessing and to be so crowned, you must, I say once more, teach the gospel. You have no other function and no other reason for your presence in a Church school system.

You do have an interest in matters purely cultural and in matters of purely secular knowledge, but, I repeat again for emphasis, your chief interest, your essential and all but sole duty, is to teach the gospel of the Lord Jesus Christ as that has been revealed in these latter days. You are to teach this gospel, using as your sources and authorities the standard works of the Church and the words of those whom God has called to lead His people in these last days. You are not, whether high or low, to intrude into your work your own peculiar philosophy, no matter what its source or how pleasing or rational it seems to you to be. To do so would be to have as many different churches as we have seminaries—and that is chaos.

You are not, whether high or low, to change the doctrines of the Church or to modify them as they are declared by and in the standard works of the Church and by those whose authority it is to declare the mind and will of the Lord to the Church. The Lord has declared that He is "the same yesterday, today, and forever."[16]

I urge you not to fall into that childish error, so common now, of believing that merely because man has gone so far in harnessing the forces of nature and turning them to his own use that therefore the truths of the Spirit have been changed or transformed. It is a vital and significant fact that man's conquest of the things of the Spirit has not marched side by side with his conquest of things material. The opposite sometimes seems to be true. Man's power to reason has not matched his power to figure. Remember always and cherish the great truth of the Intercessory Prayer:

> *And this is life eternal, that they might know thee the only true God, and Jesus Christ, whom thou hast sent.*[17]

This is an ultimate truth; so are all spiritual truths. They are not changed by the discovery of a new element, a new ethereal wave, nor by clipping off a few seconds, minutes, or hours of a speed record.

You are not to teach the philosophies of the world, ancient or modern, pagan or Christian, for this is the field of the public schools. Your sole field is the gospel, and that is boundless in its own sphere.

We pay taxes to support those state institutions whose function and work it is to teach the arts, the sciences, literature, history, the languages, and so on through the whole secular curriculum. These institutions are to do this work. But we use the tithes of the Church to carry on the Church school system, and these are impressed with a holy trust. The Church seminaries and institutes are to teach the gospel.

In thus stating this function time and time again, and with such continued insistence as I have done, it is fully appreciated that carrying out the function may involve the matter of "released time" for our seminaries and institutes. But our course is clear. If we cannot teach the gospel, the doctrines of the Church, and the standard works of the Church—all of them—on "released time" in our seminaries and institutes, then we must face giving up "released time" and try to work out some other plan of carrying on the gospel work in those institutions. If to work out some other plan be impossible, we shall face the abandonment of the seminaries and institutes and the return to Church colleges and academies. We are not now sure, in the light of developments, that these should ever have been given up.

We are clear upon this point, namely, that we shall not feel justified in appropriating one further tithing dollar to the upkeep of our seminaries and institutes of religion unless they can be used to teach the gospel in the manner prescribed. The tithing represents too much toil, too much self-denial, too much sacrifice, and too much faith to be used for the colorless instruction of the youth of the Church in elementary ethics. This decision and situation must be faced when the next budget is considered. In saying this, I am speaking for the First Presidency.

◆ ◆ ◆

All that has been said regarding the character of religious teaching, and the results which in the very nature of things must follow a failure properly to teach the gospel, applies with full and equal force to seminaries, to institutes, and to any and every other educational institution belonging to the Church school system.

The First Presidency earnestly solicit the wholehearted help and cooperation of all you men and women who, from your work on the firing line, know so well the greatness of the problem that faces us and that so vitally and intimately affects the spiritual health and the salvation of our youth and also the future welfare of the whole Church. We need you; the Church needs you; the Lord needs you. Restrain not yourselves, nor withhold your helping hand.

In closing, I wish to pay a humble but sincere tribute to teachers. Having worked my own way through school—high school, college, and professional school—I know something of the hardship and sacrifice this demands, but I know also the growth and satisfaction that come as we reach the end. So I stand here with a knowledge of how many, perhaps most of you, have come to your present place. Furthermore, for a time I tried, without much success, to teach school, so I know also the feelings of those of us teachers who do not make the first grade and must rest in the lower ones.

I know the present amount of actual compensation you get and how very sparse it is—far, far too sparse. I wish from the bottom of my heart we could make it greater, but the drain on the Church income is already so great for education that I must in honesty say there is no immediate prospect for betterment. Our budget for this school year is $860,000, or almost 17 percent of the estimated total cost of running the whole Church, including general administration and stake, ward, branch, and mission expenses for all purposes, including welfare and charities. Indeed, I wish I felt sure that the prosperity of the people would be so ample that they could and would certainly pay tithes enough to keep us going as we are.

So I pay my tribute to your industry, your loyalty, your sacrifice, your willing eagerness for service in the cause of truth, your faith in God and in His work, and your earnest desire to do the things that our ordained leader and prophet would have you do. And I entreat you not to make the mistake of thrusting aside your leader's counsel or of failing to carry out his wish or of refusing to follow his direction. David of old, privily cutting off only the skirt of Saul's robe, uttered the cry of a smitten heart:

> *The Lord forbid that I should do this thing unto my master, the Lord's anointed, to stretch forth mine hand against him, seeing he is the anointed of the Lord.*[18]

May God bless you always in all your righteous endeavors. May He quicken your understanding, increase your wisdom, enlighten you by experience, bestow upon you patience and charity, and, as among your most precious gifts, endow you with the discernment of spirits that you may certainly know the spirit of righteousness and its opposite as they come to you. May He give you entrance to the hearts of those you teach and then make you know that as you enter there, you stand in holy places that must be neither polluted nor defiled, either by false or corrupting doctrine or by sinful misdeed. May He enrich your knowledge with the skill and power to teach righteousness. May your faith and your testimonies increase and your ability to encourage and foster them in others grow greater every day—all that the youth of Zion may be taught, built up, encouraged, and heartened; that they may not fall by the wayside but go on to eternal life; and that by these blessings coming to them, you through them may be blessed also. And I pray all this in the name of Him who died that we might live, the Son of God, the Redeemer of the world, Jesus Christ, amen.

NOTES

1. Daniel Webster, "Second Reply to Hayne," speech delivered in the U.S. Senate, 26–27 January 1830; also Webster, "The Reply to Hayne," in Edwin P. Whipple, *The Great Speeches and Orations of Daniel Webster* (Boston: Little, Brown, and Company, 1891), 227.

2. Matthew 5:48.

3. Mosiah 27:31.

4. Job 19:26–27.

5. Galatians 1:8.

6. 1 Corinthians 2:11–12.

7. Romans 8:5.
8. Galatians 5:16–18.
9. Doctrine and Covenants 58:3.
10. Doctrine and Covenants 76:12, 19–24, 28.
11. Moses 1:11.
12. Articles of Faith 1:13.
13. Matthew 7:9–10.
14. 1 Corinthians 3:2.
15. 1 Corinthians 13:11.
16. 2 Nephi 27:23.
17. John 17:3.
18. 1 Samuel 24:6.

The Second Century of Brigham Young University

Spencer W. Kimball

+ *BYU Founders Day Address, October 10, 1975*

INTRODUCTION

Spencer W. Kimball was president of The Church of Jesus Christ of Latter-day Saints when he gave this seminal address at the Founders Day commemoration on October 10, 1975—almost a hundred years to the day after the university's founding. Speaking prophetically, President Kimball envisioned a remarkable destiny for BYU in its second century. His talk drew upon his visionary 1967 speech "Education for Eternity"; it also became the basis for his inaugural charge to Jeffrey R. Holland in 1980. This speech was unique as a major address by a president of the Church in that it was entirely focused on BYU's mission. Its soaring expectations and sobering admonitions have guided the pursuit of excellence at BYU for nearly half a century. It has become a foundational discourse for the university, much as "The Charted Course of the Church in Education" (pages 23–41) has for the Church Educational System.

This talk has been excerpted; for the full text, visit speeches.byu.edu/envisioning-BYU.

*As previous First Presidencies
have said, and we say again
to you, we expect (we do not
simply hope) that Brigham
Young University will "become
a leader among the great
universities of the world."
To that expectation I would
add, "Become a unique
university in all of the world."*

— SPENCER W. KIMBALL

: 🌿 :

MY BELOVED brothers and sisters: It was almost eight years ago that I had the privilege of addressing an audience at the Brigham Young University about "Education for Eternity."[1] Some things were said then that I believe, then and now, about the destiny of this unique university. I shall refer to several of those ideas again, combining them with some fresh thoughts and impressions I have concerning Brigham Young University as it enters its second century.

I am grateful to all who made possible the Centennial Celebration for the Brigham Young University, including those who have developed the history of this university in depth. A centennial observance is appropriate, not only to renew our ties with the past but also to review and reaffirm our goals for the future. My task is to talk about BYU's second century. Though my comments will focus on Brigham Young University, it is obvious to all of us here that the university is, in many ways, the center of the Church Educational System. President David O. McKay described the university as "the hub of the Church educational wheel."[2] Karl G. Maeser described Brigham Young Academy as "the parent trunk of a great educational banyan tree,"[3] and recently it has been designated "the flagship."[4] However it is stated, the centrality of this university to the entire system is a very real fact of life. What I say to you, therefore, must take note of things beyond the borders of this campus but not beyond its influence. We must ever keep firmly in mind the needs of those ever-increasing numbers of Latter-day Saint youth in other places in North America and in other lands who cannot attend this university, whose needs are real, and who represent, in fact, the majority of Latter-day Saint college and university students.

In a speech I gave to many of the devoted alumni of this university in the Arizona area, I employed a phrase to describe the Brigham Young University as becoming an "educational Everest." There are many ways in which BYU can tower above other universities—not simply because of the size of its student body or its beautiful campus but because of the unique light BYU can send forth into the educational world. Your light must have a special glow, for while you will do many things in the programs of this university that are done elsewhere, these same things can and must be done better here than others do them. You will also do some special things here that are left undone by other institutions.

EDUCATION FOR ETERNITY

First among these unique features is the fact that education on this campus deliberately and persistently concerns itself with "education for eternity," not just for time. The faculty has a double heritage that they must pass along: the secular knowledge that history has washed to the feet of mankind along with the new knowledge brought by scholarly research, and also the vital and revealed truths that have been sent to us from heaven.

This university shares with other universities the hope and the labor involved in rolling back the frontiers of knowledge even further, but we also know that through the process of revelation there are yet "many great and important things"[5] to be given to mankind that will have an intellectual and spiritual impact far beyond what mere men can imagine. Thus, at this university, among faculty, students, and administration, there is and must be an excitement and an expectation about the very nature and future of knowledge that underwrites the uniqueness of BYU.

Your double heritage and dual concerns with the secular and the spiritual require you to be "bilingual." As scholars you must speak with authority and excellence to your professional colleagues in the language of scholarship, and you must also be literate in the language of spiritual things. We must be more bilingual, in that sense, to fulfill our promise in the second century of BYU.

BYU is being made even more unique, not because what we are doing is changing but because of the general abandonment by other universities of their efforts to lift the daily behavior and morality of their students.

From the administration of BYU in 1967 came this thought:

[Brigham Young] *University has been established by the prophets of God and can be operated only on the highest standards of Christian morality. . . . Students who instigate or participate in riots or open rebellion against the policies of the university cannot expect to remain at the university.*

. . . The standards of the Church are understood by students who have been taught these standards in the home and at church throughout their lives.

First and foremost, we expect BYU students to maintain a single standard of Christian morality. . . .

. . . Attendance at BYU is a privilege and not a right[,] and . . . students who attend must expect to live its standards or forfeit the privilege.[6]

We have no choice at BYU except to "hold the line" regarding gospel standards and values and to draw men and women from other campuses also—all we can—into this same posture, for people entangled in sin are not free. At this university (that may to some of our critics seem unfree) there will be real individual freedom. Freedom from worldly ideologies and concepts unshackles man far more than he knows. It is the truth that sets men free. BYU, in its second century, must become the last remaining bastion of resistance to the invading ideologies that seek control of curriculum as well as classroom. We do not resist such ideas because we fear them but because they are false. BYU, in its second century, must continue to resist false fashions in education, staying with those basic principles that have proved right and have guided good men and women and good universities over the centuries. This concept is not new, but in the second hundred years we must do it even better.

When the pressures mount for us to follow the false ways of the world, we hope in the years yet future that those who are part of this university and the Church Educational System will not attempt to counsel the board of trustees to follow false ways. We want, through your administration, to receive all your suggestions for making BYU even better. I hope none will presume on the prerogatives of the prophets of God to set the basic direction for this university. No man comes to the demanding position of the presidency of the Church except his heart and mind are constantly open to the impressions, insights, and revelations of God. No one is more anxious than the Brethren who stand at the head of this Church to receive such guidance as the Lord would give them for the benefit of mankind and for the people of the Church. Thus, it is important to remember what we have in the revelations of the Lord: "And thou shalt not command him who is at thy head, and at the head of the church."[7] If the governing board has as much loyalty from faculty and students, from administration and staff as we have had in the past, I do not fear for the future!

The Church Board of Education and the Brigham Young University Board of Trustees involve individuals who are committed to truth as well as to the order of the kingdom. I observed while I was here in 1967 that this institution and its leaders should be like the Twelve as they were left in a very difficult world by the Savior:

> *The world hath hated them, because they are not of the world, even as I am not of the world.*
>
> *I pray not that thou shouldest take them out of the world, but that thou shouldest keep them from the evil.*
>
> *They are not of the world, even as I am not of the world.*[8]

This university is not of the world any more than the Church is of the world, and it must not be made over in the image of the world.

We hope that our friends, and even our critics, will understand why we must resist anything that would rob BYU of its basic uniqueness in its second century. As the Church's commissioner of education said on the occasion of the inaugural of President Dallin H. Oaks:

*Brigham Young University seeks to improve and "sanctify" itself for
the sake of others—not for the praise of the world, but to serve the
world better.*[9]

That task will be persisted in. Members of the Church are willing
to doubly tax themselves to support the Church Educational System,
including this university, and we must not merely "ape the world." We
must do special things that would justify the special financial out-
pouring that supports this university.

As the late President Stephen L Richards once said, "Brigham
Young University will never surrender its spiritual character to sole
concern for scholarship." BYU will be true to its charter and to such
addenda to that charter as are made by living prophets.

PURSUIT OF ACADEMIC EXCELLENCE

I am both hopeful and expectant that out of this university and the
Church Educational System there will rise brilliant stars in drama,
literature, music, sculpture, painting, science, and in all the scholarly
graces. This university can be the refining host for many such individuals who will touch men and women the world over long after they
have left this campus.

We must be patient, however, in this effort, because just as the
city of Enoch took decades to reach its pinnacle of performance in
what the Lord described as occurring "in process of time,"[10] so the
quest for excellence at BYU must also occur "in process of time."

*Ideals are like stars; you will not succeed in touching them
with your hands. But like the seafaring man on the desert of waters,
you choose them as your guides, and following them you will reach
your destiny.*[11]

I see even more than was the case nearly a decade ago a widening
gap between this university and other universities, both in terms of
purposes and in terms of directions. Much has happened in the inter-
vening eight years to make that statement justifiable. More and more

is being done, as I hoped it would, to have here "the greatest collection of artifacts, records, writings . . . in the world."[12] BYU is moving toward preeminence in many fields, thanks to the generous support of the tithe payers of the Church and the excellent efforts of its faculty and students under the direction of a wise administration.

These changes do not happen free of pain, challenge, and adjustment. Again, harking back, I expressed the hope that the BYU vessel would be kept seaworthy by taking "out all old planks as they decay and put[ting] in new and stronger timber in their place," because the *Flagship BYU* "must sail on and on and on."[13] The creative changes in your academic calendar, your willingness to manage your curriculum more wisely, your efforts to improve general education, your interaction of disciplines across traditional departmental lines, and the creation of new research institutes here on this campus—all are evidences that the captain and crew are doing much to keep the BYU vessel seaworthy and sailing. I refer to the centers of research that have been established on this campus, ranging from family and language research on through to research on food, agriculture, and ancient studies. Much more needs to be done, but you must "not run faster or labor more than you have strength and means provided."[14] While the discovery of new knowledge must increase, there must always be a heavy and primary emphasis on transmitting knowledge—on the quality of teaching at BYU. Quality teaching is a tradition never to be abandoned. It includes a quality relationship between faculty and students. Carry these over into BYU's second century!

Brigham Young undoubtedly meant both teaching and learning when he said:

> Learn everything that the children of men know, and be prepared for the most refined society upon the face of the earth, then improve upon this until we are prepared and permitted to enter the society of the blessed—the holy angels that dwell in the presence of God.[15]

We must be certain that the lessons are not only taught but are also absorbed and learned. We remember the directive that Karl G.

Maeser made to President John Taylor "that no infidels will go from my school."[16]

[To the founders of what is today known as Snow College, President Taylor said:] *Whatever you do, be choice in your selection of teachers. We do not want infidels to mould the minds of our children. They are a precious charge bestowed upon us by the Lord, and we cannot be too careful in rearing and training them. I would rather have my children taught the simple rudiments of a common education by men of God, and have them under their influence, than have them taught in the most abstruse sciences by men who have not the fear of God in their hearts. . . . We need to pay more attention to educational matters, and do all we can to procure the services of competent teachers. Some people say, we cannot afford to pay them. You cannot afford not to pay them; you cannot afford not to employ them. We want our children to grow up intelligent, and to walk abreast with the peoples of any nation. God expects us to do it; and therefore I call attention to this matter. I have heard intelligent practical men say, it is quite as cheap to keep a good horse as a poor one, or to raise good stock as inferior animals. And is it not quite as cheap to raise good intelligent children as to rear children in ignorance.*[17]

Thus, we can continue to do as the Prophet Joseph Smith implied that we should when he said, "Man was created to dress the earth, and to cultivate his mind, and glorify God."[18]

CULTIVATION OF SPIRITUAL VALUES

We cannot do these things except we continue, in the second century, to be concerned about the spiritual qualities and abilities of those who teach here. In the book of Mosiah we read, "Trust no one to be your teacher nor your minister, except he be a man of God, walking in his ways and keeping his commandments."[19] William R. Inge said, "I have no fear that the candle lighted in Palestine . . . years ago will ever be put out."[20]

We must be concerned with the spiritual worthiness, as well as the academic and professional competency, of all those who come here to teach. William Lyon Phelps said:

> *I thoroughly believe in a university education for both men and women; but I believe a knowledge of the Bible without a college course is more valuable than a college course without the Bible.*[21]

Students in the second century must continue to come here to learn. We do not apologize for the importance of students searching for eternal companions at the same time that they search the scriptures and search the shelves of libraries for knowledge. President McKay observed on one occasion that

> *a university is not a dictionary, a dispensary, nor is it a department store. It is more than a storehouse of knowledge and more than a community of scholars. University life is essentially an exercise in thinking, preparing, and living.*[22]

We do not want BYU ever to become an educational factory. It must concern itself with not only the dispensing of facts but with the preparation of its students to take their place in society as thinking, thoughtful, and sensitive individuals who, in paraphrasing the motto of your centennial, come here dedicated to love of God, pursuit of truth, and service to mankind.

There are yet other reasons why we must not lose either our moorings or our sense of direction in the second century. We still have before us the remarkable prophecy of John Taylor when he observed:

> *You will see the day that Zion will be as far ahead of the outside world in everything pertaining to learning of every kind as we are today in regard to religious matters. You mark my words, and write them down, and see if they do not come to pass.*[23]

Surely we cannot refuse that rendezvous with history because so much of what is desperately needed by mankind is bound up in our being willing to contribute to the fulfillment of that prophecy. Others, at times, also seem to have a sensing of what might happen. Charles H. Malik, former president of the United Nations General Assembly, voiced a fervent hope when he said that

> *one day a great university will arise somewhere . . . I hope in America . . . to which Christ will return in His full glory and power, a university which will, in the promotion of scientific, intellectual, and artistic excellence, surpass by far even the best secular universities of the present, but which will at the same time enable Christ to bless it and act and feel perfectly at home in it.*[24]

Surely BYU can help to respond to that call!

By dealing with basic issues and basic problems, we can be effective educationally. Otherwise, we will simply join the multitude who have so often lost their way in dark, sunless forests even while working hard. It was Thoreau who said, "There are a thousand hacking at the branches of evil to one who is striking at the root."[25] We should deal statistically and spiritually with root problems, root issues, and root causes in BYU's second century. We seek to do so, not in arrogance or pride but in the spirit of service. We must do so with a sense of trembling and urgency because what Edmund Burke said is true: "The only thing necessary for the triumph of evil is for good men to do nothing."[26]

Learning that includes familiarization with facts must not occur in isolation from concern over our fellowmen. It must occur in the context of a commitment to serve them and to reach out to them.

In many ways the dreams that were once generalized as American dreams have diminished and faded. Some of these dreams have now passed so far as institutional thrust is concerned to The Church of Jesus Christ of Latter-day Saints and its people for their fulfillment. It was Lord Acton who said on one occasion:

It was from America that the plain ideas that men ought to mind their own business, and that the nation is responsible to Heaven for the acts of the State—ideas long locked in the breast of solitary thinkers, and hidden among Latin folios—burst forth like a conqueror upon the world they were destined to transform, under the title of the Rights of Man. . . .

. . . And the principle gained ground, that a nation can never abandon its fate to an authority it cannot control.[27]

Too many universities have given themselves over to such massive federal funding that they should not wonder why they have submitted to an authority they can no longer control. Far too many no longer assume that nations are responsible to heaven for the acts of the state. Far too many now see the Rights of Man as merely access rights to the property and money of others, and not as the rights traditionally thought of as being crucial to our freedom.

It will take just as much sacrifice and dedication to preserve these principles in the second century of BYU—even more than that required to begin this institution in the first place, when it was once but a grade school and then an academy supported by a stake of the Church. If we were to abandon our ideals, would there be any left to take up the torch of some of the principles I have attempted to describe?

I am grateful, therefore, that, as President Oaks observed, "There is no anarchy of values at Brigham Young University."[28] There never has been. There never will be. But we also know, as President Joseph Fielding Smith observed in speaking on this campus, that "knowledge comes both by reason and by revelation."[29] We expect the natural unfolding of knowledge to occur as a result of scholarship, but there will always be that added dimension that the Lord can provide when we are qualified to receive and He chooses to speak:

A time to come in the which nothing shall be withheld, whether there be one God or many gods, they shall be manifest.

And further,

> *All thrones and dominions, principalities and powers, shall be*
> *revealed and set forth upon all who have endured valiantly for the*
> *gospel of Jesus Christ.*[30]

As the pursuit of excellence continues on this campus and else-where in the Church Educational System, we must remember the great lesson taught to Oliver Cowdery, who desired a special outcome—just as we desire a remarkable blessing and outcome for BYU in the second century. Oliver Cowdery wished to be able to translate with ease and without real effort. He was reminded that he erred, in that he "took no thought save it was to ask."[31] We must do more than ask the Lord for excellence. Perspiration must precede inspiration; there must be effort before there is excellence. We must do more than pray for these outcomes at BYU, though we must surely pray. We must take thought. We must make effort. We must be patient. We must be professional. We must be spiritual. Then, in the process of time, this will become the fully anointed university of the Lord about which so much has been spoken in the past.

We can sometimes make concord with others, including scholars who have parallel purposes. By reaching out to the world of scholars, to thoughtful men and women everywhere who share our concerns and at least some of the items on our agenda of action, we can multi-ply our influence and give hope to others who may assume that they are alone.

In other instances, we must be willing to break with the educa-tional establishment (not foolishly or cavalierly, but thoughtfully and for good reason) in order to find gospel ways to help mankind. Gospel methodology, concepts, and insights can help us to do what the world cannot do in its own frame of reference.

In some ways the Church Educational System, in order to be unique in the years that lie ahead, may have to break with certain pat-terns of the educational establishment. When the world has lost its way on matters of principle, we have an obligation to point the way. We can, as Brigham Young hoped we would, "be a people of profound learning pertaining to the things of the world,"[32] but without being tainted by what he regarded as "the pernicious, atheistic influences"[33] that flood in unless we are watchful. Our scholars, therefore, must be sentries as well as teachers!

We surely cannot give up our concerns with character and conduct without also giving up on mankind. Much misery results from flaws in character, not from failures in technology. We cannot give in to the ways of the world with regard to the realm of art. President Marion G. Romney brought to our attention not long ago a quotation in which Brigham Young said that "there is no music in hell."[34] Our art must be the kind that edifies man, that takes into account his immortal nature, and that prepares us for heaven, not hell.

CHALLENGES FOR BYU'S FUTURE

One peak of educational excellence that is highly relevant to the needs of the Church is the realm of language. BYU should become the acknowledged language capital of the world in terms of our academic competency and through the marvelous "laboratory" that sends young men and women forth to service in the mission field. I refer, of course, to the Language Training Mission. There is no reason why this university could not become the place where, perhaps more than anywhere else, the concern for literacy and the teaching of English as a second language is firmly headquartered in terms of unarguable competency as well as deep concern.

I have mentioned only a few areas. There are many others of special concern, with special challenges and opportunities for accomplishment and service in the second century.

We can do much in excellence and, at the same time, emphasize the large-scale participation of our students, whether it be in athletics or in academic events. We can bless many and give many experience while, at the same time, we are developing the few select souls who can take us to new heights of attainment.

It ought to be obvious to you, as it is to me, that some of the things the Lord would have occur in the second century of BYU are hidden from our immediate view. Until we have climbed the hill just before us, we are not apt to be given a glimpse of what lies beyond. The hills ahead are higher than we think. This means that accomplishments and further direction must occur in proper order, after we have done our part. We will not be transported from point A to point Z without having to pass through the developmental and demanding experiences of all the points of achievement and all the milestone markers that lie between!

This university will go forward. Its students are idealists who have integrity, who love to work in good causes. These students will not only have a secular training but will have come to understand what Jesus meant when He said that the key of knowledge, which had been lost by society centuries before, was "the fulness of [the] scriptures."[35] We understand, as few people do, that education is a part of being about our Father's business and that the scriptures contain the master concepts for mankind.

We know there are those of unrighteous purposes who boast that time is on their side. So it may seem to those of very limited vision. But of those engaged in the Lord's work, it can be truly said, "Eternity is on our side! Those who fight that bright future fight in vain!"

I hasten to add that as the Church grows global and becomes more and more multicultural, a smaller and smaller percentage of all our Latter-day Saint college-age students will attend BYU or the Hawaii Campus or Ricks College or the LDS Business College. It is a privileged group who are able to come here. We do not intend to neglect the needs of the other Church members wherever they are, but those who do come here have an even greater follow-through responsibility to make certain that the Church's investment in them provides dividends through service and dedication to others as they labor in the Church and in the world elsewhere.

To go to BYU is something special. There were Brethren who had dreams regarding the growth and maturity of Brigham Young University, even to the construction of a temple on the hill they had long called Temple Hill, yet "dreams and prophetic utterances are not self-executing. They are fulfilled only by righteous and devoted people making the prophecies come true."[36]

So much of our counsel given to you here today as you begin your second century is the same counsel we give to others in the Church concerning other vital programs—you need to lengthen your stride, quicken your step, and (to use President N. Eldon Tanner's phrase) continue your journey. You are headed in the right direction! Such academic adjustments as need to be made will be made out of the individual and collective wisdom we find when a dedicated faculty interacts with a wise administration, an inspired governing board, and an appreciative body of students.

I am grateful that the Church can draw upon the expertise that exists here. The pockets of competency that are here will be used by the Church increasingly and in various ways.

We want you to keep free as a university—free of government control, not only for the sake of the university and the Church but also for the sake of our government. Our government, state and federal, and our people are best served by free colleges and universities, not by institutions that are compliant out of fears over funding.

We appreciate the effectiveness of the programs here. But we must do better in order to be better, and we must be better for the sake of the world!

As previous First Presidencies have said, and we say again to you, we expect (we do not simply hope) that Brigham Young University will "become a leader among the great universities of the world."[37] To that expectation I would add, "Become a unique university in all of the world!"

May I thank now all those who have made this Centennial Celebration possible and express appreciation to the alumni, students, and friends of the university for the Centennial Carillon Tower that is being given to the university on its one hundredth birthday. Through these lovely bells will sound the great melodies that have motivated the people of the Lord's church in the past and will lift our hearts and inspire us in the second century—with joy and even greater determination. This I pray in the name of Jesus Christ, amen.

DEDICATION OF THE CARILLON TOWER AND BELLS

Our Father in Heaven, we are grateful for this, the gift of thy people, the alumni, the faculty, the staff, and the friends of Brigham Young University, for this collection of fifty-two bells in this carillon tower on the campus of this, Thy great university.

We are grateful for the faithfulness and craftsmanship of those who constructed the bells, those who have transported them, and those who have placed them into the tower.

Father, we are grateful for the diversity of the bells in their size, versatility, and music-giving tones, for the clavier and the clappers and the magnetic tape and the keyboard, and we ask Thee, O Father, to protect this tower, these bells, and all pertaining to them, and we pray that the carillonneur will have the preciseness and the ability to create beautiful music from the bells in this tower.

Father, we thank Thee for this institution and what it has meant in the lives of hundreds of thousands of people and their posterity, for the truths they have learned here, for the characters that have been built, for the families that have been strengthened here. Let Thy Spirit continue to be with the president of this institution and his associates, the faculty, the students, alumni, staff, and friends of this university and their successors that Thy Spirit may always abide here and that stalwarts may emerge from this institution to bring glory to Thee and blessings to the people of this world.

Just as these bells will lift the hearts of the hearers when they hear the hymns and anthems played to Thy glory, let the morality of the graduates of this university provide the music of hope for the inhabitants of this planet. We ask that all those everywhere who open their ears to hear the sounds of good music will also be more inclined to open their ears to hear the good tidings brought to us by Thy Son.

Now, dear Father, let these bells ring sweet music unto Thee. Let the everlasting hills take up the sound, let the mountains shout for joy and the valleys cry aloud, and let the seas and dry lands tell the wonders of the Eternal King.

Let the rivers and the brooks flow down with gladness; let the sun, the moon, and the stars sing together and let the whole creation sing the glory of our Redeemer forevermore.

Now, our Father, we dedicate this carillon tower, the bells, the mechanical effects and equipment, and all pertaining to this compound and ask Thee that Thou wouldst bless it and protect it against all destructive elements. Bless it that it may give us sweet music and that because of it we may love and serve Thee even more.

In the name of Jesus Christ, amen.

NOTES

1. See Spencer W. Kimball, "Education for Eternity," pre-school address to BYU faculty and staff, 12 September 1967.

2. See also Ernest L. Wilkinson, ed., *Brigham Young University: The First One Hundred Years,* 4 vols. (Provo: BYU Press, 1975–76), 2:573.

3. Karl G. Maeser, in Alma P. Burton, *Karl G. Maeser: Mormon Educator* (Salt Lake City: Deseret Book, 1953), 73.

4. Marion G. Romney, "Why the J. Reuben Clark Law School?" dedicatory address and prayer of the J. Reuben Clark Law School Building, 5 September 1975.

5. Articles of Faith 1:9.

6. Ernest L. Wilkinson, "A Letter to Parents," BYU, July 1967, 2, 8; see also excerpt of letter in Wilkinson, "Welcome Address," BYU devotional address, 21 September 1967.

7. Doctrine and Covenants 28:6.

8. John 17:14–16.

9. Neal A. Maxwell, "Greetings to the President," *Addresses Delivered at the Inauguration of Dallin Harris Oaks,* 12 November 1971 (Provo: BYU Press, 1971), 1.

10. Moses 7:21.

11. Carl Schurz, address in Faneuil Hall, Boston, 18 April 1859.

12. Kimball, "Education for Eternity."

13. Kimball, "Education for Eternity."

14. Doctrine and Covenants 10:4.

15. Brigham Young, *Journal of Discourses,* 26 vols. (London: Latter-day Saints' Book Depot, 1854–86), 16:77 (25 May 1873).

16. Karl G. Maeser, quoted in John Taylor, *Journal of Discourses* 20:48 (4 August 1878).

17. John Taylor, *Journal of Discourses* 24:168–69 (19 May 1883).

18. Joseph Smith, "Selections: Cultivate the Mind," *Evening and Morning Star* 1, no. 1 (June 1832): 8.

19. Mosiah 23:14.

20. William R. Inge, *Christian Ethics and Modern Problems* (London: Hodder and Stoughton, 1930), 394.

21. William Lyon Phelps, *Human Nature in the Bible* (New York: Charles Scribner's Sons, 1922), ix.

22. David O. McKay, "A Message for LDS College Youth," BYU address, 8 October 1952; also excerpted in McKay, *Gospel Ideals* (Salt Lake City: Improvement Era, 1953), 436.

23. John Taylor, *Journal of Discourses* 21:100 (13 April 1879).

24. Charles H. Malik, "Education in Upheaval: The Christian's Responsibility," *Creative Help for Daily Living* 21, no. 18 (September 1970): 10.

25. Henry David Thoreau, *Walden* (1854), I, "Economy."

26. Attributed to Edmund Burke.

27. Lord Acton, *The History of Freedom and Other Essays* (1907), chapter 2.

28. Dallin H. Oaks, "Response," *Addresses Delivered at Inauguration,* 12 November 1971, 21.

29. Joseph Fielding Smith, "Educating for a Golden Era of Continuing Righteousness," BYU campus education week address, 8 June 1971, 2.

30. Doctrine and Covenants 121:28–29.

31. Doctrine and Covenants 9:7.

32. Brigham Young, "Remarks," *Deseret News Weekly,* 6 June 1860, 97.

33. Brigham Young, in letter to his son Alfales Young, 20 October 1875.

34. Brigham Young, *Journal of Discourses* 9:244 (6 March 1862).

35. Doctrine and Covenants 42:15.

36. Ernest L. Wilkinson and W. Cleon Skousen, *Brigham Young University: A School of Destiny* (Provo: BYU Press, 1976), 876.

37. Harold B. Lee, "Be Loyal to the Royal Within You," BYU devotional address, 11 September 1973.

The Mission of Brigham Young University

• *November 4, 1981*

INTRODUCTION

When President Jeffrey R. Holland began his administration, the university did not have a formal mission statement. It was felt that BYU needed to set forth its mission publicly, clearly, succinctly, and boldly. President Holland briefly discussed writing that statement in a BYU devotional in 1981. He said that he "tried to read almost everything that had been said about BYU and then attempted to reduce that down to a single statement . . . as to why BYU exists" ("Virtus et Veritas," BYU devotional address, 8 September 1981). He then drafted a lofty, eloquent mission statement that, with very little modification, was endorsed by the board and adopted by the university. It has guided and inspired BYU for more than four decades.

The mission of Brigham Young University… is to assist individuals in their quest for perfection and eternal life.

— THE MISSION OF BYU

THE MISSION OF Brigham Young University—founded, supported, and guided by The Church of Jesus Christ of Latter-day Saints—is to assist individuals in their quest for perfection and eternal life. That assistance should provide a period of intensive learning in a stimulating setting where a commitment to excellence is expected and the full realization of human potential is pursued.

All instruction, programs, and services at BYU, including a wide variety of extracurricular experiences, should make their own contribution toward the balanced development of the total person. Such a broadly prepared individual will not only be capable of meeting personal challenge and change but will also bring strength to others in the tasks of home and family life, social relationships, civic duty, and service to mankind.

To succeed in this mission the university must provide an environment enlightened by living prophets and sustained by those moral virtues which characterize the life and teachings of the Son of God. In that environment these four major educational goals should prevail:

- All students at BYU should be taught the truths of the gospel of Jesus Christ. Any education is inadequate which does not emphasize that His is the only name given under heaven whereby mankind can be saved. Certainly all relationships within the BYU community should reflect devout love of God and a loving, genuine concern for the welfare of our neighbor.
- Because the gospel encourages the pursuit of all truth, students at BYU should receive a broad university education. The arts, letters, and sciences provide the core of such an education, which will help students think clearly, communicate effectively, understand important ideas in their own

cultural tradition as well as that of others, and establish clear standards of intellectual integrity.

* In addition to a strong general education, students should also receive instruction in the special fields of their choice. The university cannot provide programs in all possible areas of professional or vocational work, but in those it does provide the preparation must be excellent. Students who graduate from BYU should be capable of competing with the best in their fields.

* Scholarly research and creative endeavor among both faculty and students, including those in selected graduate programs of real consequence, are essential and will be encouraged.

In meeting these objectives BYU's faculty, staff, students, and administrators should also be anxious to make their service and scholarship available to The Church of Jesus Christ of Latter-day Saints in furthering its work worldwide. In an era of limited enrollments, BYU can continue to expand its influence both by encouraging programs that are central to the Church's purposes and by making its resources available to the Church when called upon to do so.

We believe the earnest pursuit of this institutional mission can have a strong effect on the course of higher education and will greatly enlarge Brigham Young University's influence in a world we wish to improve.

Approved by the BYU Board of Trustees
November 4, 1981

The Aims of a
BYU Education

• *March 1, 1995*

INTRODUCTION

The Aims of a BYU Education builds upon the Mission of Brigham Young University. Focusing on student outcomes, it attempts to articulate the desired effect of a BYU education in the lives of students. The document appeared just as higher education was undergoing a fundamental paradigm shift from a "teaching paradigm" to a "learning paradigm" (Robert B. Barr and John Tagg, "From Teaching to Learning—New Paradigm for Undergraduate Education," *Change: The Magazine of Higher Learning* 27, no. 6 [November–December 1995]: 12–26). The aims prepared the university to translate its educational aspirations into learning outcomes, as would soon be required by its accrediting bodies. The sections were purposefully ordered "to envelop BYU's intellectual aims within a more complete, even eternal, perspective that begins with spiritual knowledge and ends with knowledge applied to the practical tasks of living and serving" (page 71).

BYU seeks to develop
students of faith, intellect,
and character who have
the skills and the desire
to continue learning and
to serve others throughout
their lives.

— THE AIMS OF A
BYU EDUCATION

: ⚜ :

*Education is the power to think clearly, the power to act well in the
world's work, and the power to appreciate life.* —Brigham Young[1]

THE MISSION OF Brigham Young University is "to assist individuals in their quest for perfection and eternal life."[2] To this end,
BYU seeks to develop students of faith, intellect, and character who
have the skills and the desire to continue learning and to serve others
throughout their lives. These are the common aims of all education
at BYU. Both those who teach in the classroom and those who direct
activities outside the classroom are responsible for contributing to
this complete educational vision.

The statement that follows reaffirms and expands on the earlier
and more general Mission Statement adopted in 1981. As the quotations under each heading suggest, this document also draws on
the religious and educational teachings of the university's founding
prophet, Brigham Young. Quotations within the text come from the
scriptures and from the counsel of modern prophets, whose teachings
about BYU lay the foundation of the university's mission.

The following four sections discuss the expected outcomes of the
BYU experience. A BYU education should be (1) spiritually strengthening, (2) intellectually enlarging, and (3) character building, leading
to (4) lifelong learning and service. Because BYU is a large university with a complex curriculum, the intellectual aims are presented
here in somewhat greater detail than the other aims. Yet they are
deliberately placed within a larger context. The sequence flows from
a conscious intent to envelop BYU's intellectual aims within a more
complete, even eternal, perspective that begins with spiritual knowledge and ends with knowledge applied to the practical tasks of living
and serving.

SPIRITUALLY STRENGTHENING

Brother Maeser, I want you to remember that you ought not to teach even the alphabet or the multiplication tables without the Spirit of God. —Brigham Young[3]

The founding charge of BYU is to teach every subject with the Spirit. It is not intended "that all of the faculty should be categorically teaching religion constantly in their classes, but . . . that every . . . teacher in this institution would keep his subject matter bathed in the light and color of the restored gospel."[4]

This ideal arises from the common purpose of all education at BYU—to build testimonies of the restored gospel of Jesus Christ. A shared desire to "seek learning, even by study and also by faith"[5] knits BYU into a unique educational community. The students, faculty, and staff in this community possess a remarkable diversity of gifts, but they all think of themselves as brothers and sisters seeking together to master the academic disciplines while remaining mastered by the higher claims of discipleship to the Savior.

A spiritually strengthening education warms and enlightens students by the bright fire of their teachers' faith while enlarging their minds with knowledge. It also makes students responsible for developing their own testimonies by strenuous effort. Joseph Smith's words apply equally to faculty and students at BYU: "Thy mind, O man! if thou wilt lead a soul unto salvation, must stretch as high as the utmost heavens, and search into and contemplate the darkest abyss, and the broad expanse of eternity—thou must commune with God."[6] Students need not ignore difficult and important questions. Rather, they should frame their questions in prayerful, faithful ways, leading them to answers that equip them to give "a reason of the hope that is in" them[7] and to articulate honestly and thoughtfully their commitments to Christ and to His Church.

INTELLECTUALLY ENLARGING

Every accomplishment, every polished grace, every useful attainment in mathematics, music, and in all science and art belong to the Saints, and they should avail themselves as expeditiously as possible of the wealth of knowledge the sciences offer to every diligent and persevering scholar. —Brigham Young[8]

The intellectual range of a BYU education is the result of an ambitious commitment to pursue truth. Members of the BYU community rigorously study academic subjects in the light of divine truth. An eternal perspective shapes not only how students are taught but what they are taught. In preparing for the bachelor's degree, students should enlarge their intellects by developing skills, breadth, and depth: (1) skills in the basic tools of learning, (2) an understanding of the broad areas of human knowledge, and (3) real competence in at least one area of concentration. Further graduate studies build on this foundation.

Undergraduate

1. **Skills.** BYU undergraduates should acquire the basic tools needed to learn. The essential academic learning skills are the abilities to think soundly, to communicate effectively, and to reason proficiently in quantitative terms. To these ends, a BYU bachelor's degree should lead to:

- Sound thinking—reasoning abilities that prepare students to understand and solve a wide variety of problems, both theoretical and practical. Such skills include the ability to keep a proper perspective when comparing the things that matter most with things of lesser import. They also include the ability to engage successfully in logical reasoning, critical analysis, moral discrimination, creative imagination, and independent thought.
- Effective communication—language abilities that enable students to listen, speak, read, and write well; to communicate effectively with a wide range of audiences in one's area of

expertise as well as on general subjects. For many students this includes communicating in a second language.

* Quantitative reasoning—numerical abilities that equip students with the capacity to understand and explain the world in quantitative terms; to interpret numerical data; and to evaluate arguments that rely on quantitative information and approaches.

2. Breadth. BYU undergraduates should also understand the most important developments in human thought as represented by the broad domains of knowledge. The gospel provides the chief source of such breadth because it encompasses the most comprehensive explanation of life and the cosmos, supplying the perspective from which all other knowledge is best understood and measured. The Lord has asked His children to "become acquainted with all good books, and with languages, tongues, and people";[9] to understand "things both in heaven and in the earth, and under the earth; things which have been, things which are, things which must shortly come to pass; things which are at home, things which are abroad; the wars and the perplexities of the nations . . . ; and a knowledge also of countries and of kingdoms."[10]

"Because the gospel encourages the pursuit of all truth, students at BYU should receive a broad university education [that will help them] understand important ideas in their own cultural tradition as well as that of others."[11] Specifically, BYU undergraduate students should be educated in the following broad areas of human knowledge:

* Religion—the doctrines, the covenants, the ordinances, the standard works, and the history of the restored gospel, as well as an awareness of other religious traditions.
* Historical perspective—the development of human civilization, appreciation for the unique contributions of America to modern civilization, and a general historical perspective, including perspective on one's own discipline.
* Science—the basic concepts of the physical, biological, and social sciences, and a recognition of the power and limitations

of the scientific method—preferably through laboratory or field experience.

* Arts and letters—lively appreciation of the artistic, literary, and intellectual achievements of human cultures—including Western culture and, ideally, non-Western as well.
* Global awareness—informed awareness of the peoples, cultures, languages, and nations of the world.

3. Depth. BYU undergraduates should develop competence in at least one area of concentration. Competence generally demands study in depth. Such in-depth study helps prepare students for their life's work; it also teaches them that genuine understanding of any subject requires exploring it fully. Students normally acquire such depth from their major and minor fields. BYU's religion requirement also asks all students to develop depth in scriptural studies and religion.

Depth does not result merely from taking many courses in a field. Indeed, excessive course coverage requirements may discourage rather than enhance depth. Depth comes when students realize "the effect of rigorous, coherent, and progressively more sophisticated study." Depth helps students distinguish between what is fundamental and what is only peripheral; it requires focus, provides intense concentration, and encourages a "lean and taut" degree that has a "meaningful core" and a purposefully designed structure.[12] In addition to describing carefully structured academic majors, this description applies to well-designed BYU courses of all kinds.

The chief result of depth is competence. BYU's students should be "capable of competing with the best students in their field."[13] Even so, undergraduate study should be targeted at entrance-level, not expert-level, abilities. The desire for depth should not lead to bachelor's degrees that try to teach students everything they will need to know after graduation. Students should be able to complete their degrees within about four years. Undergraduate programs should prepare students to enter the world of work or to pursue further study. Often this requires educational activities that help upperclassmen culminate their studies by integrating them in a capstone project, honors thesis, senior seminar, or internship. By the time they graduate, students should grasp their discipline's essential knowledge and skills (such as mathematical reasoning, statistical analysis, computer literacy, foreign language fluency, laboratory techniques, library research, and teaching methods), and many should have participated in scholarly or creative activities that let them demonstrate their mastery.

Graduate

Building on the foundation of a strong bachelor's degree, graduate education at BYU asks for even greater competency. Graduate studies may be either academic or professional and at either the master's or doctoral level. In all cases, BYU graduate programs, like undergraduate programs, should be spiritually strengthening as well as intellectually enlarging.

Graduate programs should help students achieve excellence in the discipline by engaging its primary sources; mastering its literature, techniques, and methodologies; and undertaking advanced systematic study—all at a depth that clearly exceeds the undergraduate level. In addition, graduate programs should prepare students to contribute to their disciplines through their own original insights, designs, applications, expressions, and discoveries. Graduate study should thereby enable a variety of contributions—such as teaching complex knowledge and skills, conducting original research, producing creative work that applies advanced learning in the everyday world, and extending professional service to the discipline and to society.

These intellectual aims of a BYU education are intended to give students understanding, perspective, motivation, and interpersonal abilities—not just information and academic skills. BYU should furnish students with the practical advantage of an education that integrates academic skills with abstract theories, real-world applications, and gospel perspectives. Such an education prepares students who can make a difference in the world, who can draw on their academic preparation to participate more effectively in the arenas of daily life. They are parents, Church leaders, citizens, and compassionate human beings who are able to improve the moral, social, and ecological environment in which they and their families live. They are scientists and engineers who can work effectively in teams and whose work reflects intellectual and moral integrity; historians who write well and whose profound understanding of human nature and of divine influences informs their interpretation of human events; teachers whose love for their students as children of God is enriched by global awareness and foreign language skill; artists whose performances seek to be flawless in both technique and inspiration; business leaders whose economic judgments and management styles see financial reward not as an end but as a means to higher ends. BYU graduates thus draw on an educated intellect to enhance not only what they *know* but also what they *do* and, ultimately, what they *are*.

CHARACTER BUILDING

A firm, unchangeable course of righteousness through life is what secures to a person true intelligence. —Brigham Young[14]

Because it seeks to educate students who are renowned for what they are as well as for what they know, Brigham Young University has always cared as much about strong moral character as about great mental capability. Consequently, a BYU education should reinforce such moral virtues as integrity, reverence, modesty, self-control, courage, compassion, and industry. Beyond this, BYU aims not merely to teach students a code of ethics but to help them become partakers of the divine nature. It aspires to develop in its students character traits that flow from the long-term application of gospel teachings to their lives. This process begins with understanding humankind's eternal nature and ends with the blessing of eternal life, when human character reflects in fully flowered form the attributes of godliness. Along the way, the fruits of a well-disciplined life are augmented and fulfilled by the fruits of the spirit of Jesus Christ—such as charity, a Christlike love for others, which God "hath bestowed upon all who are true followers of his Son, Jesus Christ."[15] Students thus perfect their quest for character development by coming unto Christ through faith, repentance, and righteous living. Then their character begins to resemble His, not just because they think it should but because that is the way they are.

President David O. McKay taught that character is the highest aim of education: above knowledge is wisdom, and above wisdom is character. "True education," he explained, "seeks to make men and women not only good mathematicians, proficient linguists, profound scientists, or brilliant literary lights, but also honest men with virtue, temperance, and brotherly love."[16] Consequently, a BYU education should bring together the intellectual integrity of fine academic discipline with the spiritual integrity of personal righteousness. The result is competence that reflects the highest professional and academic standards—strengthened and ennobled by Christlike attributes.

Thus understood, the development of character is so important that BYU "has no justification for its existence unless it builds character, creates and develops faith, and makes men and women of strength and courage, fortitude, and service—men and women who will become stalwarts in the Kingdom and bear witness of the . . . divinity of the gospel of Jesus Christ. It is not justified on an academic basis only."[17] Rather, it fulfills its promise when "the morality of the graduates of this University provide[s] the music of hope for the inhabitants of this planet."[18]

Every part of the BYU experience should therefore strengthen character—academic integrity in taking a test or writing a research paper; sportsmanship on the playing field; the honest reporting of research findings in a laboratory; careful use of university funds derived from the tithes of Church members; treating all other people with dignity and fairness; and wholehearted acceptance of commitments made to bishops and parents. Character is constructed by small decisions. At this personal level of detail, BYU will realize its hope of teaching "those moral virtues which characterize the life and teachings of the Son of God."[19]

LIFELONG LEARNING AND SERVICE

We might ask, when shall we cease to learn? I will give you my opinion about it; never, never. . . . We shall never cease to learn, unless we apostatize from the religion of Jesus Christ. —Brigham Young[20]

Our education should be such as to improve our minds and fit us for increased usefulness; to make us of greater service to the human family. —Brigham Young[21]

Well-developed faith, intellect, and character prepare students for a lifetime of learning and service. By "entering to learn" and continuing to learn as they "go forth to serve," BYU students strengthen not only themselves—they "also bring strength to others in the tasks of home and family life, social relationships, civic duty, and service to mankind."[22]

1. **Continual Learning.** BYU should inspire students to keep alive their curiosity and prepare them to continue learning throughout their lives. BYU should produce careful readers, prayerful thinkers, and active participants in solving family, professional, religious, and social problems. They will then be like Abraham of old, who had been "a follower of righteousness, desiring also to be one who possessed great knowledge, and to be a greater follower of righteousness, and to possess a greater knowledge, . . . desiring to receive instructions, and to keep the commandments of God." In this lifelong quest, they, like Abraham, will find "greater happiness and peace and rest."[23] Thus a BYU diploma is a beginning, not an end, pointing the way to a habit of constant learning. In an era of rapid changes in technology and information, the knowledge and skills learned this year may require renewal the next. Therefore, a BYU degree should educate students in how to learn, teach them that there is much still to learn, and implant in them a love of learning "by study and also by faith."[24]

2. **Service.** Since a decreasing fraction of the Church membership can be admitted to study at BYU, it is ever more important that those who are admitted use their talents to build the kingdom of God on the earth. Hence, BYU should nurture in its students the desire

to use their knowledge and skills not only to enrich their own lives but also to bless their families, their communities, the Church, and the larger society. Students should learn, then demonstrate, that their ultimate allegiance is to higher values, principles, and human commitments rather than to mere self-interest. By doing this, BYU graduates can counter the destructive and often materialistic self-centeredness and worldliness that afflict modern society. A service ethic should permeate every part of BYU's activities—from the admissions process through the curriculum and extracurricular experiences to the moment of graduation. This ethic should also permeate each student's heart, leading him or her to the ultimate wellspring of charity—the love for others that Christ bestows on His followers.

CONCLUSION

Education is a good thing, and blessed is the man who has it, and can use it for the dissemination of the Gospel without being puffed up with pride. —Brigham Young[25]

These are the aims of a BYU education. Taken together, they should lead students toward wholeness: "the balanced development of the total person."[26] These aims aspire to promote an education that helps students integrate all parts of their university experience into a fundamentally sacred way of life—their faith and reasoning, their knowledge and conduct, their public lives and private convictions. Ultimately, complete wholeness comes only through the Atonement of Him who said, "I am come that they might have life, and that they might have it more abundantly."[27] Yet a university education, guided by eternal principles, can greatly "assist individuals in their quest for" that abundant "eternal life."[28]

A commitment to this kind of education has inspired the prophets of the past to found Church schools, like BYU, on the principle that "to be learned is good if they hearken unto the counsels of God."[29] These prophets have known the risks of such an enterprise, for "that happiness which is prepared for the saints" shall be hid forever from those "who are puffed up because of their learning, and their wisdom."[30] Yet they have also known that education plays a vital role in realizing the promises of the Restoration; that a broad vision of education for self-reliance and personal growth is at the very heart of the gospel when the gospel is at the heart of education. To the degree that BYU achieves its aims, the lives of its students will confirm Brigham Young's confidence that education is indeed "a good thing," blessing all those who humbly and faithfully use it to bless others.

NOTES

1. Brigham Young, quoted by George H. Brimhall in "The Brigham Young University," *Improvement Era* 23, no. 9 (July 1920), 831.

2. The Mission of Brigham Young University (4 November 1981).

3. Brigham Young, in Reinhard Maeser, *Karl G. Maeser: A Biography by His Son* (Provo: Brigham Young University, 1928), 79.

4. Spencer W. Kimball, "Education for Eternity," pre-school address to BYU faculty and staff, 12 September 1967.

5. Doctrine and Covenants 88:118.

6. Joseph Smith, *Teachings of the Prophet Joseph Smith*, sel. Joseph Fielding Smith (Salt Lake City: Deseret Book Company, 1972), 137.

7. 1 Peter 3:15.

8. Brigham Young, *Journal of Discourses*, 26 vols. (London: Latter-day Saints' Book Depot, 1854–86), 10:224 (April and May 1863).

9. Doctrine and Covenants 90:15.

10. Doctrine and Covenants 88:79.

11. Mission of BYU.

12. Memorandum to the Faculty No. 13.

13. Mission of BYU.

14. Brigham Young, *Journal of Discourses* 8:32 (5 April 1860).

15. Moroni 7:48.

16. David O. McKay, "Why Education?" *Improvement Era* 70, no. 9 (September 1967), 3.

17. Spencer W. Kimball, "On My Honor," BYU devotional address, 12 September 1978.

18. Spencer W. Kimball, "The Second Century of Brigham Young University," BYU devotional address, 10 October 1975.

19. Mission of BYU.

20. Brigham Young, *Journal of Discourses* 3:203 (17 February 1856).

21. Brigham Young, *Journal of Discourses* 14:83 (9 April 1871).

22. Mission of BYU.

23. Abraham 1:2.

24. Doctrine and Covenants 88:118.
25. Brigham Young, *Journal of Discourses* 11:214 (29 April 1866).
26. Mission of BYU.
27. John 10:10.
28. Mission of BYU.
29. 2 Nephi 9:29.
30. 2 Nephi 9:42–43.

Inspiring
Learning

Kevin J Worthen

◆ *BYU University Conference Address,*
August 22, 2016

INTRODUCTION

In this university conference address, President Kevin J Worthen captured the essence of BYU's mission and aims in a memorable two-word phrase: "inspiring learning." The idea of inspiring learning quickly spread across campus, guiding educational initiatives and enabling student learning in new and expansive ways.

This talk has been excerpted; for the full text, visit speeches.byu.edu/envisioning-BYU.

Inspiring learning requires faith both by the students and by the faculty member. It is not an easy task, but it is an inspiring one.

— Kevin J Worthen

IT IS A JOY to be with you this morning. There is something about the beginning of a new school year that brings hope and optimism.

LEARNING AT BRIGHAM YOUNG UNIVERSITY

I think by now you know me well enough to correctly predict that my message today will somehow focus on the mission statement. I continue to be impressed with how the language in this three-decade-old document sheds clarifying light on many of the new situations, new challenges, and new opportunities we encounter. I believe there was inspiration in the creation of that document and that inspiration will come from continued reflection on its principles.

So, as we reflect on this year's conference theme, which reminds us that "the Lord requireth the heart and a willing mind,"[1] I hope that what occupies a good portion of our hearts and minds is the role we are to play in assisting our students "in their quest for perfection and eternal life."[2] The mission statement makes it clear that our primary role in that process is to help our students learn. We are to provide them "a period of intensive learning."[3] That phrase describes the rigor of the learning experience our students should have. Other portions of the mission statement describe the content and outcomes of that learning.

In terms I hope are now familiar to all of you, the mission statement indicates that, above all else, our students should learn "the truths of the gospel of Jesus Christ."[4] In addition, they should experience learning that is "broad"—learning that enables them to

think clearly, communicate effectively, understand important ideas in their own cultural tradition as well as that of others, and establish clear standards of intellectual integrity.[5]

Our students should also experience learning "in the special fields of their choice"—learning that will enable them to compete "with the best in their fields."[6] In addition, they should experience learning that renders them

> *not only . . . capable of meeting personal challenge and change but . . . also* [of bringing] *strength to others in the tasks of home and family life, social relationships, civic duty, and service to mankind.*[7]

The aims document effectively boils all these down to four main points: we are to provide learning that is "(1) spiritually strengthening, (2) intellectually enlarging, and (3) character building, leading to (4) lifelong learning and service."[8]

Notice how each aim is directly connected to specific portions of the mission statement. The spiritually strengthening aim links to specific portions of the mission statement. The intellectually enlarging aim links to other portions, as does the character building aim. Other sections of the mission statement explain the lifelong learning and service aim. And there are even more links.

These convey the truth that one cannot fully understand the aims unless one fully understands the mission statement. While the aims may be easier to remember—I venture to guess that more people can recite the aims than can provide a word-for-word rendition of the mission statement—they are not independent and freestanding ideas that supplement the mission statement. They derive directly from the mission statement and provide a shorthand description of its key learning principles.

THE TERM "INSPIRING LEARNING"

Perhaps out of a desire to simplify things as much as possible—and perhaps as a result of a diminishing capacity to remember even four things—but largely in an effort to succinctly explain what we are about in a way that allows people to easily remember, I have tried to simplify the core learning goals even more while still emphasizing that a full understanding requires a return to the mission statement.

After discussions with many of you in many settings, I have concluded that one two-word description that achieves that end is "inspiring learning." Note again that one cannot understand the full meaning of the term "inspiring learning" without a full understanding of the mission statement. Just as the aims document is a summary and not a replacement for the mission statement, the two-word description "inspiring learning" is a summary and not a replacement.

Inspiring is an interesting word. It derives from the Latin term *inspirare*, which means "to breathe into" and, more specifically, "to breathe life into."[9] *Inspiring* is both a noun and an adjective. The noun can be defined as the act of inspiring or motivating. In this sense, the term "inspiring learning" describes actions that inspire or motivate students to learn. As an adjective, *inspiring* is a modifier. In this context it describes a kind of learning: learning that inspires—or, more precisely, in our setting, learning that leads to inspiration or revelation.

When I use the term "inspiring learning," I have in mind both meanings of the word *inspiring*. I hope we inspire our students to learn. And I hope that learning leads to inspiration. When both things happen, inspiring learning occurs, and we can then know we are on the right track to achieve the core goals set forth in our mission statement.

While the term "inspiring learning" may not be familiar to you, my guess is that many of you are familiar with the phenomenon. Inspiring learning occurs in many of our classrooms for many of our students on a regular basis. Indeed, it may happen so often that we fail to appreciate how exhilarating it can be. We grow used to it. Sometimes it takes someone from outside the university to point it out to us. Here is one example.

This past January, New York University professor of journalism Jay Rosen came to campus as a guest lecturer. Let me share with you what he posted shortly after his visit:

> *This was the scene a few days ago when I gave a guest lecture at Brigham Young University, which of course is a Mormon school. . . .*
> *A most unusual thing happened before I was introduced. Unusual for me, normal at Brigham Young. Dale Cressman, who organized the event and guided me around campus, asked a student*

to begin the event with a prayer. The student stood and prayed for help in "feeling grateful for the opportunity to learn." I wish more college students felt that way and expressed it as well as she did.

I found the BYU students a joy to teach. They were extremely engaged. With good humor they tolerated me asking and reasking them the same question ten times, answering in a slightly different way each time, which allowed me to make a new point in response. After the talk, at least a dozen of them thanked me, and each one shook my hand, looked me in the eye, and made a personal connection. "Grateful for the opportunity to learn" . . . that wasn't just words to them.

It was one of the best experiences I have had in 30 years as a professor.[10]

That is an example of inspiring learning. And classrooms are the central places in which that kind of learning occurs. I hope we can make each of our classrooms a place of inspiring learning, a place in which students become excited about learning and in which that learning leads to revelation.

LEARNING BY EXPERIENCE

While it is essential that our formal classrooms be sites of inspiring learning, that by itself will not completely fulfill our mission. Let me return to the mission statement, this time to the second paragraph:

All instruction, programs, and services at BYU, including a wide variety of extracurricular experiences, should make their own contribution toward the balanced development of the total person.[11]

Note "all instruction," including "a wide variety of extracurricular experiences." Some of the most important inspiring learning opportunities occur outside the formal classroom setting through experiences that are, in that sense, extracurricular. And, without implying either that we have fully perfected classroom instruction or that we are going to emphasize classroom instruction less, let me suggest that one way we can enhance the quality of inspiring learning at BYU is to expand both the quantity and quality of the kind of learning that occurs outside the formal classroom—the kind of instruction that many call "experiential learning." Just like classroom learning, experiential learning can produce the kind of inspiring learning that our mission statement challenges us to provide.

Experiential learning has become somewhat of a buzzword in academia in recent years. However, for us there is a deeper, even doctrinal reason for pursuing learning by experience in a systematic way. We are all quite familiar with the scriptural injunction that we "seek learning, even by study and also by faith."[12] That describes two key ways by which we learn important truths: by study and by faith. But those are not the only ways by which we learn essential knowledge and skills. Gospel teaching instructs us that we learn by study, we learn by faith, and we learn by experience.

Learning by experience is a central purpose of our mortal journey. As Elder David A. Bednar once observed, "Learning by faith and from experience are two of the central features of the Father's plan of happiness."[13] We could not have simply memorized celestial laws in our premortal life and declared ourselves fit for the celestial kingdom. We needed to come to this mortal existence to experience certain things we could not experience in our premortal life and to learn from those experiences. Experience is a key part of our mortal learning process.

Similarly, students cannot learn all they need to learn by memorizing or even discussing principles in a classroom, as exhilarating as that may be. Experience connects theory with application and deepens our understanding of the principles and truths we learn.

And, in my view, experiential learning can be inspiring learning in both senses of that term. It can both inspire students to deeper learning and be the type of learning that leads to inspiration.

There is ample evidence that experiential learning can inspire and excite students to learn in ways that have a deep and long-lasting impact. Describing the results of his study about student learning at Harvard, Professor Richard J. Light observed:

> *I assumed that most important and memorable academic learning goes on inside the classroom, while outside activities provide a*

useful but modest supplement. The evidence shows that the oppo-
site is true. . . . When we asked students to think of a specific, critical
incident or moment that had changed them profoundly, four-fifths
of them chose a situation or event outside of the classroom.[14]

Likewise, in a 2008 study, George D. Kuh, the founding director
of the widely used National Survey of Student Engagement (NSSE),
identified ten teaching and learning practices that have especially high
impact on students. Five of those—including such things as internships, service learning, and undergraduate research—involved activities that would easily fit into the category of experiential learning.[15]

Other studies underscore the point. A 2014 survey of approxi-
mately 30,000 college students conducted by Purdue University and
the Gallup Poll evaluated the relationship between various college
experiences and subsequent success at work and overall life well-
being. The survey sought to correlate high measures of work engagement and well-being with various college experiences.

The results were telling. Workplace success did not correlate with
the size of the university attended, large or small, or with whether the
university was private or public. But other factors did seem to matter.
Specifically, the study found that the chances that individuals would
thrive at work—the highest measure of work engagement—doubled
if during college they "had an internship or job where they were
able to apply what they were learning in the classroom, were actively
involved in extracurricular activities and organizations, and worked
on projects that took a semester or more to complete."[16] The first two
clearly involve experiential learning; the third may as well.

Evidence from our own campus also illustrates the ways in which
experiences outside the classroom can inspire students to learn. Let
me cite as one example the Phage Hunters program in the College of
Life Sciences. This program enlists students early on—sometimes as
freshmen on their very first day of class—to begin original research.
The students collect soil samples and for the next two semesters work
to isolate and identify a bacteriophage that has never been seen before.

One project involved students working under the direction of
Professor Sandra Hope, who was searching for a viable way to treat a

disease that affects honeybee hives. Notice in this video the involvement of the students. [A video presentation was shown.]

As noted, the student most prominently featured in the video, Bryan Merrill, signed up for the Phage Hunters class as a sophomore. After completing the class, Bryan was hired as a TA and worked as a research assistant and mentor to other students in the class. By the time he graduated from BYU with his master's degree in molecular biology, Bryan had already published (or copublished) eight research articles and had worked on twenty-three genome sequences. He is currently pursuing a doctoral degree in microbiology and immunology at Stanford University. Bryan's initial experience with phages clearly inspired lifelong and career-enhancing learning.

I believe such experiential learning activities can also help students learn to be inspired. Given the nature of the phenomenon being measured, there are no academic studies—at least none that I could find—that address the impact that experiential learning may have on a person's ability to receive inspiration or revelation. But there is other evidence that, at this unique institution, is at least as persuasive.

We are all familiar with the Book of Mormon account of Lehi's sons going back to Jerusalem to obtain the plates of brass. In a sometimes overlooked portion of that account, Lehi noted three times that the Lord commanded him that he should send his sons back to get the plates,[17] thereby making it clear that Lehi was not supposed to do this himself.

Having been the father of sons who were the ages of Nephi and his brethren at the time, I have some sense that had Lehi been given the simple direction just to go get the plates, he would have attended to the task himself. It would have been simpler and easier. That is how it is with teenage boys sometimes. However, the Lord made it clear that Lehi was to send his sons.

Why? I suggest that at least part of the reason is that the Lord wanted Nephi and his brethren to have an experiential learning opportunity. It may have been easier and faster for Lehi to get the plates himself, but God was not interested just in getting the plates. He was also interested—more interested—in helping Lehi's sons in their quest for perfection and eternal life. And He furthered that process by providing those sons with a learning experience that caused at least one of them, Nephi, to receive inspiration.

When Nephi returned to the camp after that learning experience, he came back not only with the plates but with a greater faith in God and a greater understanding of how inspiration comes. He had experienced inspiring learning.

Nephi's experience in obtaining the plates—or, more precisely, Lehi's experience in facilitating that experience—demonstrates an important truth about the kind of inspiring learning that comes from experience. It requires that the teacher have great patience and a clear understanding of the larger purpose involved. Perhaps as a result of God's commanding him multiple times that he should send his sons, Lehi came to realize that, as important as the plates were—and they were of great importance, as demonstrated by the fact that Nephi took Laban's life to obtain them—securing their possession was not the main object of the experience. The main purpose was to refine Lehi's children, who were also God's children.

Similarly, as important as our research may be—and some of it is of enormous importance, some of it life-changing, even lifesaving—it is, in the long run, not as important as the eternal development of our students. I applaud and admire the way so many of you pursue both of these ends with full purpose of heart and mind, without sacrificing either. But it is hard work.

Again, one illustration will stand as proxy for numerous others that might be provided. [A video presentation was shown.]

Taking students, especially undergraduate students, into such projects as the Antarctica study of nematodes requires a great amount of perspective and faith. In an email, Professor Byron J. Adams explained:

> *Supporting a single human being in Antarctica is the most expensive, most difficult, and most precious part of doing research down there. If something happens and a single slot opens up . . . , we have* [to select] *a person best suited to help with the project. . . . Most of the time that means bringing down other famous scientists, or postdoctoral fellows* [who] *are highly skilled in a single*

area. However, on several occasions I've been able to justify bring-ing students down because I can train them very well . . . on exactly what they need to do. And because my students have always been exceptionally awesome (hard working, skilled, fun to be around), my colleagues are happy to have them on the team.

So far, six different students have accompanied Professor Adams to Antarctica, three of them undergraduates. This coming year he will take two other graduate students. And while there are risks, there are also enormous rewards. Professor Adams reported:

The first undergrad I brought to Antarctica is now a faculty member in another department in my college. The second one is a faculty member at the University of California, Riverside. The third is just beginning his medical residency in OB/GYN. The first grad student I brought down is now a geneticist at a USDA research center; the rest are still in my program working toward graduation.

ENHANCING INSPIRING LEARNING AT BYU

Inspiring learning requires faith both by the students and by the faculty member. It is not an easy task, but it is an inspiring one.

So we might ask ourselves: What can we do to enhance the impact of these kinds of inspiring learning experiences at BYU in the coming year and in the coming years? Let me make three simple suggestions.

First, we can expand the number of students who have a mean-ingful experiential learning opportunity. We can, for example, look for ways to provide more faculty mentoring opportunities for them. The impact of faculty mentoring can be enormous. In a report summariz-ing a large number of academic studies, clinical psychologist and pro-fessor of psychology W. Brad Johnson said:

Compared to nonmentored individuals, those with mentors tend to be more satisfied with their careers, enjoy more promotions and higher income, report greater commitment to the organization or profession, and are more likely to mentor others in turn.[18]

The impact is even greater at a place like BYU, where we are interested in more than academic or temporal success. Because we challenge faculty members to be leaders in their fields of research and because we also ask them to be faithful in the gospel, BYU faculty members provide living examples of the power of learning by study and by faith. Students can first see, then work with, and eventually emulate role models who have demonstrated that they can excel in both their fields and their faithfulness. Experience of that kind is truly inspiring in both senses of the word.

However, there is a limit to the number of faculty mentorship opportunities we can provide. As good as they are, our faculty have only twenty-four hours in a day, and they are already stretched almost to the limit. Fortunately, other experiential learning opportunities can also promote inspiring learning. Internships, study abroad programs, fieldwork, service learning opportunities, and even on-campus work are all experiences that, when properly structured, can provide opportunities to both inspire students to learn and help students learn to be inspired.

To increase the number of students who can have such experiences, this year the university provided substantial additional funding to each college, with the central stipulation that the funds be directed to students to facilitate a structured experiential learning opportunity. Because the calendar year is not yet complete, it is too early to measure the overall impact of this increased funding in terms of the number of students having such opportunities. However, anecdotal reports from every college indicate that the funds have allowed numerous students to have an experiential learning opportunity that they otherwise would have had to forego for economic reasons.

The results have been encouraging—enough that we are working to provide additional funding again in 2017 and to make securing even more funds one of the top fundraising priorities for the university.

Second, in addition to increasing the number of opportunities for inspiring learning experiences, we can work to make the opportunities have even more impact by being more purposeful and intentional about what happens in those activities. While traveling in a foreign country can be a life-changing experience, through careful and thoughtful planning, the impact of the experience can be magnified severalfold. Similarly, internships provide insights into the skills required to succeed in an occupation, but increased planning and foresight can make the experience considerably more meaningful by ensuring that certain kinds of activities occur and that there is adequate opportunity for reflection. I challenge all involved in such activities to make sure we are maximizing the amount of good that can result from them.

Finally, we can increase the number of inspiring learning moments for our students if we recognize that both experiential learning and classroom learning are enhanced by the quality of the relationships we develop with our students. Research has shown that "high impact [learning] practices are powerful in part because they are relationship rich."[19] The 2014 Gallup-Purdue survey I mentioned earlier found that one of the key factors that correlated with success in *both* work engagement *and* overall well-being was a high-quality relationship with a faculty member. According to that data, a graduate's chances of thriving at work *and* in life *doubled* if the student "had a professor who cared about them as a person, made them excited about learning, and encouraged them to pursue their dreams."[20]

BYU should be a leader in this regard. Our mission statement provides that

> *all relationships within the BYU community should reflect devout love of God and a loving, genuine concern for the welfare of our neighbor.*[21]

If our students feel this, they will be inspired to learn, and they will learn to be inspired in profound ways.

Let me share one example. Four years ago one of our graduate engineering students, Shannon Zirbel, received a $100,000 fellowship from NASA to work on a project with laminate-compliant mechanisms in space. She received a lot of attention, and we used her success in our fundraising efforts for the new Engineering Building. People resonated with the idea that their donations might help bright students like Shannon be involved in cutting-edge work. She was very articulate and very gracious to share her time in informing people about her work as part of our fundraising effort.

It was only some time later that I learned the more complete story of her BYU experience that led to the fellowship. I share portions of her account with her permission:

> When I graduated from high school, I went to [Georgetown] University. . . . I had a misconception about BYU—I thought girls just came here to get married, . . . so I didn't even apply to BYU. . . . Two years later I went on a mission. During my mission I served with several companions who were students at BYU, and my opinion of BYU changed entirely. When I came home from my mission, I applied to and was accepted at BYU. . . .
>
> I'm not brilliant. But I work hard, so I know I can accomplish good things, and hard things. But I need ready reassurance. Maybe it's because I'm a [woman]. A [woman] in a male-dominated field, surrounded by men who, by nature, think differently than I do. Do you know how hard that is sometimes?
>
> One of my biggest concerns about staying for a PhD was the qualifying exams. Just prior to my taking them . . . , Dr. [Larry] Howell gave me a blessing. Being able to receive a priesthood blessing from my advisor was one of the highlight experiences of attending BYU. Every morning of the exam week I went in to get "words of encouragement" from Dr. Howell.
>
> On Wednesday morning (before the dynamics exam), as I was leaving his office, I said, "I'll try to make you proud."
>
> He replied, "You already have."
>
> Can I tell you how much of a difference that made for me? I went into the exam feeling blissful, feeling like I didn't have anything I needed to prove. I just had to do my best, and that was going to be enough. He couldn't have said anything more perfect. I've had many experiences like that with professors at BYU, where they have shown such genuine concern for me.

Inspiring learning will be greatly enhanced if those with whom we interact feel Christ's love for them through us.

Our efforts to enhance inspiring learning—the kind of education for eternity described in our mission statement—can have an enormous impact on all of our students. But it need not and should not end there. This initiative is inspiring and will give us the opportunity to magnify the impact of what we do here. However, I believe we can best accomplish that by focusing on our principal and board-directed role, which is to enhance the learning experience of our students in all the ways described in the mission statement. We need not alter or change our focus; we simply need to do well—to do better—what we are already doing and then look for new ways to share.

The mission statement succinctly sums up how we can best help in words that, though written nearly thirty-five years ago, seem somehow to have this initiative specifically in mind:

> *In meeting these objectives BYU's faculty, staff, students, and administrators should also be anxious to make their service and scholarship available to The Church of Jesus Christ of Latter-day Saints in furthering its work worldwide.*[22]

We should be anxious to make our service and scholarship available to the Church in this exciting worldwide endeavor, but we can best do so by meeting the objectives set forth in the mission statement.

Our mission is clear and simple. It can, in one sense, be captured in the phrase "inspiring learning." But it is more accurately and more fully described in our inspiring and inspired mission statement. As we face the opportunities and challenges of the coming year, I urge you to return to that mission statement often and to contemplate what your role is in carrying out that mission. I promise that as you do so, inspiration will come. It will come to you and it will come to your students.

You are not here by accident and they are not here by accident. Our coming together will allow God's work to go forward, both in our own individual lives and in the lives of others on this campus and throughout the world. I so testify, in the name of Jesus Christ, amen.

NOTES

1. Doctrine and Covenants 64:34.
2. The Mission of Brigham Young University (4 November 1981).
3. Mission of BYU.
4. Mission of BYU.
5. Mission of BYU.
6. Mission of BYU.
7. Mission of BYU.
8. The Aims of a BYU Education (1 March 1995).
9. *Oxford English Dictionary Online*, s.v. "inspire," etymology, oed.com /view/Entry/96990?redirectedFrom=inspire.
10. Jay Rosen, Facebook, 16 January 2016, facebook.com/photo.php?fbid =10153157675541548.
11. Mission of BYU.
12. Doctrine and Covenants 88:118.
13. David A. Bednar, "Seek Learning by Faith," *Ensign*, September 2007.
14. Richard J. Light, *Making the Most of College: Students Speak Their Minds* (Cambridge, Massachusetts: Harvard University Press, 2001), 8; quoted in Peter Felten, John N. Gardner, Charles C. Schroeder, Leo M. Lambert, and Betsy O. Barefoot, *The Undergraduate Experience: Focusing Institutions on What Matters Most* (San Francisco: Jossey-Bass, 2016), 26.
15. See George D. Kuh, *High-Impact Educational Practices: What They Are, Who Has Access to Them, and Why They Matter* (Washington, DC: Association of American Colleges and Universities, 2008); cited in Felten, *Undergraduate Experience*, 20–21.
16. Gallup and Purdue University, Executive Summary, in *Great Jobs, Great Lives: The 2014 Gallup-Purdue Index Report*, 6, luminafoundation.org/files /resources/galluppurdueindex-report-2014.pdf.
17. See 1 Nephi 3:2, 4–5.
18. W. Brad Johnson, *On Being a Mentor: A Guide for Higher Education Faculty* (Mahwah, New Jersey: Lawrence Erlbaum Associates, 2007), 4; quoted in Felten, *Undergraduate Experience*, 53.
19. Felten, *Undergraduate Experience*, 48; citing Jayne E. Brownell and Lynn E. Swaner, *Five High-Impact Practices: Research on Learning Outcomes, Completion, and Quality* (Washington, DC: Association of American Colleges and Universities, 2010).
20. Gallup, *Great Jobs, Great Lives*, 6.
21. Mission of BYU.
22. Mission of BYU.

Religious Education in BYU's Prophetic Historical Context

Bruce C. Hafen

♦ Address to BYU Religious Education Faculty and Staff, August 28, 2019

INTRODUCTION

Though Elder Hafen was particularly addressing religious educators when he gave this speech, he chose to focus on the broader history and mission of BYU. Elder Hafen traced the history of why prophets have chosen to preserve a few Latter-day Saint colleges and universities—such as BYU and its sister institutions—in which religion can be integrated across the entire campus, rather than opt exclusively for the much less expensive and simpler model of Latter-day Saint institutes, where the faith is taught next door to secular universities. The history Elder Hafen recounted illustrates both the problems and promises of teaching and learning at a fully integrated Latter-day Saint university such as BYU.

This talk has been excerpted; for the full text, visit speeches.byu.edu/envisioning-BYU.

*The best way for a
Latter-day Saint student
to reconcile the competing
values of faith and intellect
is to be mentored by teachers
and leaders whose daily
lives, attitudes, and teaching
authentically demonstrate
how deep religious faith and
demanding intellectual rigor
are mutually reinforcing.*

— Bruce C. Hafen

: ⚘ :

I BEGIN WITH a question of perspective about BYU. For Latter-day Saint students, is education on the three BYU campuses qualitatively different from education at a state school with a nearby Latter-day Saint institute? Many key variables are hard to measure—comparative educational quality, social opportunities (especially a temple marriage), and the likelihood of real religious growth, in both understanding Church doctrine and learning to live it. Moreover, how can one quantify the unique, multilayered effects of simply living for a few years in a Zion-like village (such as Laie, Rexburg, or Provo)—experiencing daily the spirit of "the gathering" as the Saints knew it in Nauvoo or in the early pioneer settlements? Obviously, some students will benefit more than others in such a place, depending on what a given student brings to the campus. Yet clearly many thousands of Latter-day Saint students and their families believe passionately that these qualitative differences—"the BYU experience," whatever that is and however it is measured—are worth years of preparation and sacrifice.

How have the most influential founders of the three modern BYU campuses seen these differences? By substantially enlarging all three student bodies in the last seven decades, what were they trying to create, and why? They didn't need to invest vast tithing resources in the Church universities just because state schools didn't have space. On the contrary, in recent years, access to higher education has become almost universally available in the United States. To explore what may have motivated the key founders, let's consider some historical context.

105

THE HISTORY OF CHURCH EDUCATION

The Church's commitment to educating Latter-day Saint youth came as a doctrinal mandate of the Restoration. For example, "I, the Lord, am well pleased that there should be a school in Zion."[1] The applications of this premise are further displayed in the impressive historical exhibit *Educating the Soul: Our Zion Tradition of Learning and Faith* in the Joseph F. Smith Building on the Provo campus. On this foundation, Church efforts to find the right balance between the religious and the secular in its approach to higher education have a long history.

By 1900—due primarily to inadequate public education in Utah, an influx of settlers of other faiths, and the creation of new pioneer colonies beyond the Great Basin—the Church had created more than thirty stake academies for secondary education in locations stretching from Canada to Mexico. And even though the Utah Territory began establishing public schools in 1890, most of the academies continued to function as private Church schools and colleges until well into the twentieth century.[2] Brigham Young University in Provo was the only school designated as a university, a decision the Church Board of Education made in 1903.

By 1920 the commissioner of Church education was a young apostle named David O. McKay. Before his call to the Twelve in 1906, he had been a faculty member and then the principal of Weber Stake Academy (now Weber State University). He recommended to the board that the Church divest itself of all but a handful of its postsecondary schools because the Church simply could not afford to provide a college education for all its members.

Then in 1926, also citing costs, Adam S. Bennion went even further as commissioner. He recommended that the Church *entirely* "withdraw from the academic field [in higher education] and center upon religious education" by creating new institutes of religion near selected state colleges.[3] The first institute began that same year at the University of Idaho in Moscow. Elder Bennion told the board that he believed the people teaching in the state universities were "in the main . . . seeking the truth."[4]

However, Elder McKay felt that the Church had not established Church schools "merely . . . because the state did not do it"; rather, the Church established these schools, he said, *"to make Latter-day Saints."*[5] He continued, saying, *"We ought to consider these Church schools from the standpoint of their value to the Church more than from the standpoint of duplicating public school work."*[6]

Elder McKay later said he had therefore "voted against . . . [giving] the church's junior colleges to the states of Utah, Arizona, and Idaho."[7] However, the First Presidency decided in 1930 that the Church should (1) divest itself of all its colleges except BYU and LDS College in Salt Lake City (later LDS Business College) and (2) expand institutes of religion on selected other campuses. For example, the Church transferred Snow, Dixie, and Weber Colleges to the state of Utah. The Church also offered Ricks College (now BYU–Idaho) to Idaho beginning in 1931, but the state legislature repeatedly declined it, even though the Church had offered to donate all of the college's assets if Idaho would agree to operate the school. With encouragement from President McKay as a new member of the First Presidency, the Church finally decided to keep Ricks College in 1937.[8]

The institutes of religion grew during the 1930s and 1940s. Then in 1951, David O. McKay became president of the Church and Ernest L. Wilkinson was appointed as both president of BYU and Church commissioner of education. During the next twenty years, President McKay actively established a new vision of Church higher education. Both BYU and Ricks College grew rapidly, and the Church College of Hawaii (now BYU–Hawaii) was founded in 1955.

In 1957 the Church announced plans to create eight additional junior colleges as potential feeder schools for BYU. Then, for financial reasons, in 1963 the First Presidency dropped the junior college plan and reaffirmed its commitment to the institutes of religion.[9]

Nonetheless, the Church's support for BYU, Ricks, and Hawaii remained strong. For example, during the McKay presidency, BYU's enrollment expanded from 5,500 in 1950 to 25,000 in 1971.

BYU AS A RELIGIOUS INSTITUTION

So the three BYU campuses are significant exceptions to a general policy of not providing higher education on a Church campus. The spiritual architect who most magnified the window of exceptions was President McKay, acting in his prophetic role. These three campuses are thus living monuments to his educational vision and inspiration.

And what was his vision? President McKay answered that question with his entire life's work and teachings. As he told a BYU audience in 1937:

> **Brigham Young University is primarily a religious institution.** *It was established for the **sole purpose** of associating with facts of science, art, literature, and philosophy the truths of the gospel of Jesus Christ. . . .*
>
> *In making religion its paramount objective, the university touches the very heart of all true progress. . . .*
>
> *I emphasize **religion** because the Church university offers more than mere theological instruction. Theology as a science "treats of the existence, character, and attributes of God," and theological training may consist merely of intellectual study. Religion is subjective and denotes the influences and motives to human conduct and duty which are found in the character and will of God. One may study theology without being religious.*[10]

This is an expanded version of what President McKay had told the board in 1926: "We establish[ed] the schools to make Latter-day Saints."[11] He also taught repeatedly his conviction that "character is the aim of true education," and he believed that "modern education" gave inadequate emphasis to helping students develop "true character."[12] He was also disturbed as early as 1926 by "the growing tendency all over the world to sneer at religion" in secular state education.[13]

I sense in President McKay's attitudes an implicit belief that providing religious education in an institute next to a secular university would not do as much "to make Latter-day Saints" as might be possible on a BYU campus. His concept was to create a conscious integration of fine academic departments, extracurricular programs, and the teaching of the religious life—all on the same campus, pursuing a unified vision about becoming educated followers of Jesus Christ and blessing the Church by blessing the youth of Zion. So when he said, "We ought to consider these Church schools from the standpoint of their value to the Church," he was describing a religious mission, not simply an educational mission—but it is a religious mission in which higher education plays a central role.

Inspired by this vision, other Church leaders have often encouraged BYU faculty to integrate religious perspectives into their teaching. For example, when the J. Reuben Clark Law School was founded at BYU in 1973, President Marion G. Romney said the school's purpose was to study the laws of man "in the light of the 'laws of God.'"[14] And the Aims of a BYU Education, a formal part of the university's official purpose since the 1990s, states that "the founding charge of BYU is to teach every subject with the Spirit."[15] In the words of President Spencer W. Kimball, this does not mean "that all of the faculty should be categorically teaching religion constantly in their classes," but it does expect "that every . . . teacher . . . would keep [their] subject matter bathed in the light and color of the restored gospel."[16]

The aims document goes on to say that "a BYU education should be . . . intellectually enlarging" with regard to intellectual skills, depth, and breadth.[17] In describing the desired breadth of an intellectual education, the aims document states:

> *The gospel provides the chief source of such breadth because it encompasses the most comprehensive explanation of life and the cosmos, supplying the perspective from which all other knowledge is best understood and measured.*[18]

This approach doesn't simply balance the sacred and the secular, or faith and reason, as if the two realms were of equal importance. Rather, President McKay's vision consciously avoids allowing the academic disciplines to judge or stand superior to the gospel or the Church. As one Latter-day Saint scholar observed:

There is the danger that [the] *use of scholarly tools—which requires the privileging of those tools—will breed habits of mind that reflexively privilege secular scholarship over the gospel.*[19]

This is a risk in some approaches to Mormon studies, which may look at the gospel primarily through the lenses of the academic disciplines.

Because of that risk, Elder Neal A. Maxwell "was always dismayed by Latter-day Saint [scholars and] professionals who" allowed the premises and perspectives of "their disciplines [to] take priority over their understanding of the gospel."[20] And he was disappointed by teachers who, as he put it, "'fondle their doubts' . . . in the presence of Latter-day Saint students who [are] looking for spiritual mentoring."[21] Thus Elder Maxwell, like President McKay or President Romney, "looked at all knowledge through the gospel's lens."[22] They knew they

could integrate a secular map of reality into the broader religious map, but the smaller secular map, with its more limited tools and framework, often wasn't large enough to include religious insights. Thus the gospel's larger perspective influenced [their] *view of the academic disciplines more than the disciplines influenced* [their] *view of the gospel.*[23]

Similarly, President Boyd K. Packer once urged Church Educational System (CES) faculty to avoid judging "the Church, its doctrine, organization, and leadership, present and past, by the principles of their own profession"; rather, he said, we should "judge the professions of man against the revealed word of the Lord."[24]

All BYU faculty enjoy full academic freedom to teach and model this expansive view of education. At most other universities, faculty are constrained by understandable academic conventions from mixing their personal religious views freely with their teaching and scholarly work. Indeed, on most campuses these days, they would probably be expected to bracket their faith to avoid such mixing.[25] The institutional academic freedom allowed by BYU's explicit, written religious mission consciously removes those brackets, like taking the mute out of a trumpet. And that unmuting allows the talented trumpets of BYU faculty to give an especially certain sound while integrating their faith with their academic teaching—a fortunate quality both for BYU students and for Latter-day Saints generally.

The best way for a Latter-day Saint student to reconcile the competing values of faith and intellect is to be mentored by teachers and leaders whose daily lives, attitudes, and teaching authentically demonstrate how deep religious faith and demanding intellectual rigor are mutually reinforcing.

In addition, faculty whose lives reflect a completeness of heart, soul, and mind can fulfill much of President McKay's vision by the way they mentor their students—in how they share themselves both in class and in personal interactions. Recent research among BYU students tells us that a great deal of "spiritually strengthening" and "intellectually enlarging"[26] teaching on the campus comes from personal examples and mentoring by professors in all disciplines.

When faculty feel responsible for students' personal development as well as for their cognitive education, they will find ways to let their students see how gifted Latter-day Saint teachers and scholars integrate their professional competence into their overarching religious faith—"complete person" role modeling that those students are much less likely to find elsewhere. As BYU's academic stature keeps growing, its faculty will feel increased pressures to be more concerned with published scholarship and national reputation than with their students. Yet at the same time, as the new CES guidelines[27] recognize, the current moment seems to pose greater challenges to students' religious faith, which heightens each student's need for informed and faith-filled mentoring.

Alan L. Wilkins, former BYU academic vice president, recently described the sobering implications of these competing pressures:

> *Some will argue that we just have to be more scholarly in today's context to have much influence in the larger academic community. How and whether that can be done and still strengthen our students spiritually in ways that build faith and character . . . is the* **most important question before us at BYU currently.**[28]

EXPECTATIONS OF BYU RELIGIOUS
EDUCATION FACULTY

President Kevin J Worthen has distributed to you a document titled "Strengthening Religious Education in Institutions of Higher Education," approved by the Church Board of Education on June 12, 2019. These guidelines state that "the purpose of religious education is to teach the restored gospel of Jesus Christ from the scriptures and modern prophets in a way that helps each student develop faith in" the Father, the Son, His Atonement, and the restored gospel; to help students "become lifelong disciples of Jesus Christ"; and to "strengthen their ability to find answers, resolve doubts, [and] respond with faith."[29] The statement then describes the conditions that guide religion faculty hiring, work, and promotion—providing, for example, that faculty must "be sound doctrinally."[30]

This document reaffirms principles that the board (which has always included the First Presidency) has needed to reemphasize every generation or so since BYU's founding in 1875, primarily due to the recurring tendency of some BYU faculty to teach and write about religion from a more secular perspective.

An important early example of this tendency unfolded in the early 1900s. The board had designated Brigham Young Academy as a university in 1903. Then, starting in 1907, President George H. Brimhall hired two sets of brothers—Ralph and William Chamberlin and Henry and Joseph Peterson—who had the academic credentials to help "transform the . . . college into a full-fledged university, comparable to the country's recognized universities."[31] The men taught biology, philosophy, education, and psychology. Three of the four held graduate degrees from the University of Chicago, Harvard, and Cornell; the other had studied at Harvard, Chicago, and the University of California.

The new faculty members all believed they had successfully reconciled the modernist ideas they had encountered in graduate school with their religious faith; indeed, they were convinced that their enlarged intellectual perspectives would enrich the "ideal of education which had [always] been cherished in the Church" by harmonizing all knowledge "within an institution devoted primarily to religious education."[32] Thus they embarked on a well-intentioned "campaign to enliven [BYU] students academically by introducing the latest developments" in the major disciplines.[33] As it turned out, however, their views essentially "discounted the historical reality of any scripture."[34]

By the end of 1910, reports from disturbed local Church leaders and parents led Horace H. Cummings, superintendent of Church education, to investigate. After finding that most of the students and many of the faculty were accepting the new theories, Cummings reported to the board that the new professors were teaching BYU faculty to apply secular theories to Church teachings "in such a way as to disturb, if not destroy, the faith of the pupils."[35]

President Brimhall, who was originally sympathetic toward the new faculty, was troubled when he heard some students say they had stopped praying. Then he had a dream that convinced him Cummings was right. In the dream that he reported to Cummings, President Brimhall saw a group of BYU professors casting, as if fishing, some kind of bait into the sky, where a flock of snow-white birds was happily circling. When the birds took the bait, they fell to the earth and turned out to be BYU students, who said to President Brimhall:

> *"Alas, we can never fly again!"* . . .
> *Their Greek philosophy had tied them to the earth. They could believe only what they could demonstrate in the laboratory. Their prayers could go no higher than the ceiling. They could see no heaven—no hereafter.*[36]

A special committee that included several members of the Twelve verified the findings in the Cummings report. The board accepted these conclusions, resolving that teachers appointed "in Church schools must be in accord with Church doctrine. [Three of the] professors were given the choice of conforming or resigning."[37] All three left BYU, along with a few other professors.[38]

Some who disagreed with this outcome were distressed, believing that the board's approach meant that BYU would never be able to teach essential academic subjects with the depth and rigor required of a legitimate university—let alone a superior one—and that students would not be allowed to explore the ambiguities sometimes found in biblical and Church history and doctrine. However, experience since then on both counts resoundingly shows otherwise.

Then, in the years after the first institute of religion was founded in 1926 at the University of Idaho, a number of institute teachers and BYU religion teachers left Utah to seek advanced degrees in religion at noted universities in an effort to "set an academic standard in theology."[39] Some of them, such as Sidney B. Sperry, returned with superb graduate school training guided by bedrock faith that enabled a lifelong contribution of teaching and scholarship to BYU's mission in religious education.

Indeed, Professor Sperry's experience at the University of Chicago Divinity School had been so successful that apostle and commissioner of Church education Joseph F. Merrill invited several professors from the Chicago Divinity School to teach at BYU's summer school in the 1930s—echoing a pattern from the 1920s, when other prominent non-Latter-day Saint Bible scholars had been invited to lecture at BYU's summer school on religious education and how to teach the Bible.[40]

Building on this Chicago connection, the Church encouraged a number of Latter-day Saint graduate students to seek divinity school training there and elsewhere, as Elder Merrill and the Brethren wanted to bolster the ranks of qualified teachers of religion for both BYU and the emerging institutes of religion.

A number of these teachers returned fortified with Sperry-like attitudes and training. Several others, however, were overly influenced by their graduate school religion professors who, like those three BYU faculty members in 1910, reflected the growing academic secularism of their time. As later described by Elder Boyd K. Packer, himself a career religion teacher before his call as a General Authority, "A number of them went [to graduate programs in religion in the 1920s and 1930s]. Some who went never returned. And some of them who returned never came back."[41] A few of these actually left the Church, "and with each [of these] went a following of [their] students—a terrible price to pay."[42]

Elder John A. Widtsoe agreed: "Heaven forbid that we shall send our men away again to Divinity schools for training. The experiment, well intentioned, did not work out."[43]

These unfortunate developments became the catalyst for what may be the most influential discourse on Church education in the last century: "The Charted Course of the Church in Education," delivered by President J. Reuben Clark Jr. to Church religion teachers at Aspen Grove in 1938. (For example, I saw President Marion G. Romney put aside his own notes and quote this entire talk as his message to the BYU faculty in the early 1970s.) In this address, President Clark paid tribute to the teachers' loyalty, sacrifice, faith, and righteous desires. He asked God to bless them with "entrance to the hearts of those you teach and then make you know that as you enter there, you stand in holy places."[44] He praised the youth of the Church, saying, "They want to gain testimonies of [the gospel's] truth," and added soberly that these youth are

> *not now doubters but . . . seekers after truth. Doubt must not be planted in their hearts. Great is the burden and the condemnation of any teacher who sows doubt in a trusting soul. . . .*
> *These students fully sense the hollowness of teachings that would make the gospel plan a mere system of ethics.*[45]

A generation later, when Boyd K. Packer was the supervisor of seminaries and institutes, he heard some local Church leaders report that, "while studying religion at Church schools," members of their stakes "had lost their testimonies" because some faculty were teaching "the unusual things that they had discovered in their academic wandering."[46] As had happened in 1911 and in 1938, these concerns led the First Presidency in 1954 to send Elder Harold B. Lee, assisted by other General Authorities, to instruct and correct all of the Church's religion teachers during five weeks of summer school at BYU.

In 1958 the faculty in BYU's Division of Religion successfully petitioned the board to be designated the College of Religious Instruction as part of their effort "to *elevate* religion . . . to [a] high level of academic respectability."[47]

However, in 1972, during his first year as BYU president, President Dallin H. Oaks felt a need to review a broad range of issues in religious education. So he asked me (I was then his assistant) to help research and evaluate those issues. In addition to extensive historical research and selected in-depth interviews, we invited written comments from all religion faculty.

After the board considered President Oaks's findings and recommendations, they made some important changes that sent messages reaffirming familiar historic principles. For example, graduate degrees in religion were eliminated. As Elder Packer later explained, the Brethren hoped the nonreligion faculty at BYU would lead the world as authorities in their disciplines. But in the field of religion, "it is not to a university . . . that the world must turn for ultimate authority."[48] Rather, the First Presidency and the Twelve are those who have ultimate religious authority in the Church.

Moreover, the title College of Religious Instruction was replaced by Religious Education. One of the messages here was that religious education shouldn't be limited to one college; rather, all BYU academic colleges should contribute to and draw from religious education. Aligning with this direction, President Oaks initiated a process to select carefully a number of faculty from the other colleges whom he then invited to teach a Book of Mormon class on a continuing basis. To underscore his commitment, he assigned himself to teach one of those classes. In addition, the board wanted to signal that the faculty from *all* disciplines should feel responsible "for the spiritual development of their students."[49] Another implicit message was that the typical assumptions behind "publish or perish" shouldn't apply in the same way to religion faculty as they might in other academic colleges.

In a meeting held two years after these changes were announced, Elder Packer delivered a key discourse—some of which I have quoted—on the history of Church religious education.[50] The occasion for that meeting was the retirement of Dean Roy W. Doxey and the introduction of Jeffrey R. Holland, then thirty-three years old, as the new dean of Religious Education at BYU. It was an appropriate time for reflection and recalibration. I recommend President Packer's talk for frequent rereading.

PROGRESS IN RELIGION AND SCHOLARSHIP

During the 1970s and 1980s, BYU took an astonishing leap forward in the quality of its teaching, learning, and scholarship. The higher education community began to see the university in an increasingly favorable light. A national *U.S. News and World Report* poll in the mid-1990s ranked BYU among the country's top twenty-five undergraduate teaching universities.

These decades ran parallel with a general cultural revolution that had been ignited on college campuses by student free-speech protests at Berkeley in 1964—a movement with vague but multiple causes that spread and eventually shook the very foundations of American education, challenging traditions and institutional authority at every hand. The momentum of the student movement was accelerated by perceived overlaps with such broader public causes as the campaign for racial equality and opposition to the war in Vietnam. It also fueled and was fueled by growing secularization and a passionate emphasis on individual rights.

In this environment, BYU's increased academic quality attracted many able new faculty whose graduate school training often reflected the new individualistic, anti-institutional assumptions. Still, most of these new professors felt downright liberated by BYU's religious atmosphere because nearly all of them were devoted Latter-day Saints who welcomed the freedom—not allowed elsewhere—to include their religious beliefs in their teaching. As the number of new faculty grew, so did the number of gifted students. Their presence and their curiosity enriched both the intellectual and spiritual quality of campus-wide conversations. They wanted to know how to articulate and how to exemplify BYU's educational vision in ways that would enliven its spiritual foundations while helping the university contribute seriously to a society riven with intellectual confusion and growing moral decay.

However, as had happened in prior generations, a few of the faculty attracted by BYU's increased stature felt more allegiance to the secular and sometimes politicized values of their graduate school disciplines than to the traditional religious values of the

campus. As the university's provost from 1989 to 1996, I saw repeatedly what happened when the values of these few faculty clashed
with the expectations of the board, other faculty, students, and the
larger BYU community. In some ways those days felt like a sequel to
the Brimhall era of 1911. Yet the 1990s version was more subtle and
complex because faculty and student attitudes ranged across a broad
spectrum of mostly desirable values and attitudes rather than fitting
into neat black-and-white compartments that asked for a simple
choice between intellectual and spiritual values.

These circumstances required the board and BYU to clarify—
once more—some key concepts and relationships among faculty, students, administration, and the board about the very idea of BYU. We
needed a meeting of the minds; we needed to become of one heart.
And our resolution needed full participation by the faculty and the
board, with a written set of principles that would bless both us and
those who came after us with clarity, harmony, and shared purpose.

In a story too long to recount here, the administration appointed
a faculty committee on academic freedom chaired by John S. Tanner
of the English Department and assisted by James D. Gordon of the
Law School. Over the course of many demanding months, the committee drafted and redrafted a twenty-five-page policy statement that
defined and integrated the roles of both individual faculty academic
freedom and the university's institutional academic freedom as a
Church-sponsored university.

As eventually approved by both the faculty and the board, this
statement, which is still official BYU policy, represents an informed
consensus that blends individual and institutional academic freedom
into a harmonious reaffirmation of BYU's character and mission—in
President McKay's familiar words, "a religious institution . . . established for the sole purpose of associating with facts of science, art,
literature, and philosophy the truths of the gospel of Jesus Christ."

A key portion of the policy is based on past board guidelines,
applying them in more specific terms:

> *The exercise of individual and institutional academic freedom must
> be a matter of reasonable limitations* [on individual freedom]. *In*

*general, at BYU a limitation is reasonable when the faculty behavior or expression **seriously and adversely** affects the university mission or the Church. . . . Examples would include expression with students or in public that:*

- *contradicts or opposes, rather than analyzes or discusses, fundamental Church doctrine or policy;*
- *deliberately attacks or derides the Church or its general leaders; or*
- *violates the Honor Code because the expression is dishonest, illegal, unchaste, profane, or unduly disrespectful of others.*

Reasonable limits are based on careful consideration of what lies at the heart of the interests of the Church and the mission of the university.[51]

RELIGIOUS EDUCATION IN THE DIGITAL AGE

The decades from the early 1990s until today then ushered in the digital age, which has introduced totally unforeseen and massive challenges and opportunities for religious education everywhere. As President M. Russell Ballard said to all CES religious educators in 2016:

It was only a generation ago that our young people's access to information about our history, doctrine, and practices was basically limited to materials printed by the Church. Few students came in contact with alternative interpretations. Mostly, our young people lived a sheltered life.

Our curriculum at that time, though well-meaning, did not prepare students for today—a day when students have instant access to virtually everything about the Church from every possible point of view. Today, what they see on their mobile devices is likely to be faith-challenging as much as faith-promoting. Many of our young people are more familiar with Google than they are with the gospel, more attuned to the Internet than to inspiration, and more involved with Facebook than with faith.[52]

President Ballard also said:

> *Gone are the days when a student asked an honest question and a teacher responded, "Don't worry about it!" Gone are the days when a student raised a sincere concern and a teacher bore his or her testimony as a response intended to avoid the issue. Gone are the days when students were protected from people who attacked the Church. . . .*
>
> *You can help students by teaching them what it means to combine study and faith as they learn. Teach them by modeling this skill and approach in class.*[53]

As part of its response to this need, the Church posted eleven new Gospel Topics essays on churchofjesuschrist.org in 2015, providing thorough, well-documented articles on many of the topics that had attracted the most interest and visibility by anti-Church websites, podcasts, and blogs—topics such as plural marriage, race and the priesthood, gender, the Mountain Meadows Massacre, Heavenly Mother, and Joseph Smith's translations of the Book of Mormon and the book of Abraham.

All of these and similarly controversial topics had been described in detail for years by Latter-day Saint scholars—as reflected, for example, in the impressive four volumes of the *Encyclopedia of Mormonism*, jointly published by the Macmillan Company and BYU in 1992. But until the advent of the internet, encyclopedias, like typical anti-Church literature, had remained buried in accessible but little-used libraries.

In 2016, however, President Ballard counseled Church religion teachers to

> *know the content in these* [Gospel Topics] *essays like you know the back of your hand. If you have questions about them, then please ask someone who has studied them and understands them. . . .*
>
> *You should also become familiar with the Joseph Smith Papers website and the Church history section on* [churchofjesuschrist .org] *and other resources by faithful Latter-day Saint scholars.*[54]

This general context helps to explain why the new 2019 guidelines for strengthening religious education include among the purposes of religious education "strengthen[ing] [students'] ability to find answers, resolv[ing] doubts, respond[ing] with faith, and giv[ing] reason for the hope within them in whatever challenges they may face."⁵⁵ It may also help explain why *Saints*, the new official history of the Church, is written not as a scholarly treatise but in narrative language and personal stories that are accessible to younger readers while providing the natural historical context for previously less understood issues.

Another development that has been hastened by the digital age is the emergence of academic Mormon studies programs at several leading universities, headed by either Latter-day Saint or other scholars. "Mormon studies is the interdisciplinary academic study of the beliefs, practices, history and culture of those known by the term *Mormon*."⁵⁶

The Mormon studies movement is in many ways beneficial for the Church, having considerably increased awareness of the Church's doctrines, history, and culture among many secular university students and faculty—both a cause and an effect of the Church's having come increasingly "out of obscurity"⁵⁷ in recent decades.

At the same time, writing and teaching from a Mormon studies perspective poses special challenges for Latter-day Saint teachers, especially faculty at Church-sponsored campuses, because the general conventions of academic study typically expect participants to bracket their faith and to reason from secular, not religious, premises. In other words, Mormon studies scholars are expected to look at Church doctrine and history through the lenses of their academic disciplines—as opposed to looking at their disciplines through the lens of the gospel, as contemplated in President McKay's vision of BYU.

Elder Jeffrey R. Holland addressed these risks in a significant discourse to the faculty and staff at BYU's Neal A. Maxwell Institute for Religious Scholarship in 2018. Speaking on behalf of the BYU Board of Trustees, Elder Holland said that, for one thing, the term *Mormon studies* was no longer appropriate for use by the Maxwell Institute, given President Russell M. Nelson's recent counsel about the use of *Mormon* by Church members.⁵⁸

Regarding secular premises, Elder Holland acknowledged that Mormon studies programs elsewhere are normally "oriented toward an audience *not* of our faith and *not* for faith-building purposes."[59] And while these programs may "provide a 'thoughtful consideration of the Restoration's distinctive culture and convictions,'"[60] such secular premises for teaching and writing by Latter-day Saints for Church audiences or those on the BYU campus would be "certainly . . . troubling" to the BYU trustees.[61]

As for BYU faculty who bracket their faith for the sake of Mormon studies expectations, Elder Holland said that "any scholarly endeavor at BYU . . . must never be *principally* characterized by stowing one's faith in a locker while we have a great exchange with those not of our faith."[62] He then quoted Elder Maxwell's comment: "Some hold back by not appearing overly committed to the Kingdom, lest they incur the disapproval of . . . peers who might disdain such consecration."[63] Elder Holland added that one who "studiously pursues strict *neutrality* by 'bracketing' will miss the chance for genuine, even profound, dialogue on matters of *common* interest"[64]—an approach that "has cost scholars credibility with readers because . . . no one knows" where the authors stand.[65]

So, to come full circle on the matter of the board's expectations of BYU religion faculty, the history of BYU makes it pretty clear that the new guidelines President Worthen has given us are indeed a restatement of principles and values the board has upheld since 1911—consistently applying those principles as needed to the changing circumstances of the times.

NOTES

1. Doctrine and Covenants 97:3.

2. See Harold R. Laycock, s.v. "academies," in Daniel H. Ludlow, ed., *Encyclopedia of Mormonism,* 5 vols. (New York: Macmillan, 1992), 1:11.

3. Adam S. Bennion, quoted in minutes of the meeting of the General Church Board of Education, 23 March 1926, 160, in Manuscript Collections, UA 1376 box 1, L. Tom Perry Special Collections, Harold B. Lee Library, Brigham Young University, Provo, Utah; quoted in Ernest L. Wilkinson, ed., *Brigham Young University: The First One Hundred Years,* 4 vols. (Provo: BYU Press, 1975–76), 2:76.

4. Adam S. Bennion, quoted in board minutes, 23 March 1926, 160; quoted in Wilkinson, *Years,* 2:76.

5. David O. McKay, quoted in minutes of the meeting of the General Church Board of Education, 3 March 1926, 148, in Manuscript Collections, UA 1376 box 1, L. Tom Perry Special Collections, Harold B. Lee Library, BYU; emphasis added.

6. David O. McKay, quoted in board minutes, 3 March 1926, 150; emphasis added.

7. Gregory A. Prince and William Robert Wright, *David O. McKay and the Rise of Modern Mormonism* (Salt Lake City: University of Utah Press, 2005), 196.

8. Negotiations between the Idaho legislature, local college leaders, and the Church continued throughout the difficult Great Depression years of 1931 to 1937. In 1934, David O. McKay was called into the First Presidency and he became "'the dominant educational advisor in the church.' His influence was evident when" the college finally "received the welcome news that Ricks was to be maintained as a Church school" (David L. Crowder, *The Spirit of Ricks: A History of Ricks College* [Rexburg, Idaho: Ricks College, 1997], 142; for a complete account, see pages 109–51).

9. See Prince and Wright, *David O. McKay,* 196–97.

10. David O. McKay, "The Church University," *Messenger* 11, no. 10 (October 1937): 3–4; emphasis added and emphasis in original; quoting *Webster's International Dictionary of the English Language,* ed. Noah Porter (Springfield, Massachusetts: G. & C. Merriam Company, 1907), s.v. "theology," 1495.

11. David O. McKay, quoted in board minutes, 3 March 1926, 148.

12. David O. McKay, "True Education," remarks at the dedication of the Church College of New Zealand, Temple View, New Zealand, 24 April 1958; quoted in Prince and Wright, *David O. McKay,* 160–61. See also McKay, "True Education," *Instructor,* August 1961, 253.

13. David O. McKay, quoted in board minutes, 23 March 1926, 159; also quoted in Wilkinson, *Years,* 2:75.

14. Marion G. Romney, quoting Doctrine and Covenants 93:53, in "Becoming J. Reuben Clark's Law School," address delivered at the opening ceremonies of the first day of classes for the BYU J. Reuben Clark Law School, 27 August 1973.

15. The Aims of a BYU Education (1 March 1995).

16. Spencer W. Kimball, "Education for Eternity," pre-school address to BYU faculty and staff, 12 September 1967.

17. Aims of BYU.

18. Aims of BYU.

19. Nathan Oman, "'Out of Zion Shall Go Forth the Law' (Isaiah 2:3)," *FARMS Review of Books* 12, no. 1 (2000): 132.

20. Bruce C. Hafen, *A Disciple's Life: The Biography of Neal A. Maxwell* (Salt Lake City: Deseret Book, 2002), 166.

21. Hafen, quoting Neal A. Maxwell, in *A Disciple's Life*, 166.

22. Hafen, *A Disciple's Life*, 166.

23. Hafen, *A Disciple's Life*, 166–67.

24. Boyd K. Packer, "The Mantle Is Far, Far Greater Than the Intellect," *BYU Studies* 21, no. 3 (Summer 1981): 259.

25. See Jeffrey R. Holland, "The Maxwell Legacy in the 21st Century," *2018 Annual Report*, Neal A. Maxwell Institute for Religious Scholarship, 16; J. Spencer Fluhman, "Friendship: An Editor's Introduction," *Mormon Studies Review* 1, no. 1 (2014): 3–5; Jon D. Levenson, *The Hebrew Bible, the Old Testament, and Historical Criticism: Jews and Christians in Biblical Studies* (Louisville, Kentucky: Westminster/John Knox Press, 1993), 105; and Stephen Prothero, "Belief Unbracketed: A Case for the Religion Scholar to Reveal More of Where He or She Is Coming From," *Harvard Divinity Bulletin* 32, no. 2 (Winter/Spring 2004): 10–11.

26. Aims of BYU.

27. See Church Educational System (CES), "Strengthening Religious Education in Institutions of Higher Education" (12 June 2019).

28. Alan L. Wilkins to Bruce C. Hafen, email correspondence, 23 December 2016; emphasis added.

29. CES, "Strengthening Religious Education."

30. CES, "Strengthening Religious Education."

31. Wilkinson, *Years*, 1:409.

32. Ralph V. Chamberlin, *Life and Philosophy of W. H. Chamberlin* (Salt Lake City: Deseret News Press, 1925), 137.

33. Richard Sherlock, "Campus in Crisis: BYU's Earliest Conflict Between Secular Knowledge and Religious Belief," *Sunstone* 10, no. 5 (May 1985): 30.

34. Noel B. Reynolds, "The Coming Forth of the Book of Mormon in the Twentieth Century," *BYU Studies* 38, no. 2 (1999): 20.

35. Horace H. Cummings, letter quoted in minutes of the meeting of the General Church Board of Education, 2 December 1910, 176, in Manuscript Collections, UA 1376 box 1, L. Tom Perry Special Collections, Harold B. Lee Library, BYU; quoted in Wilkinson, *Years*, 1:419.

36. George H. Brimhall, as told to Horace H. Cummings and recorded in "Lesson XLI: False Doctrines in Church Schools," in *Autobiography of Horace Cummings*, unpublished, page 41-6, in MSS 1575, L. Tom Perry Special Collections, Harold B. Lee Library, BYU; spelling modernized. Quoted in Wilkinson, *Years*, 1:422; see also page 421.

37. Sherlock, "Campus in Crisis: BYU's Earliest Conflict," 32. See Wilkinson, *Years*, 1:425–26, 428, note 63.

38. See Reynolds, "Coming Forth," 22.

39. Boyd K. Packer, "Seek Learning Even by Study and Also by Faith," address to BYU instructors of religion, April 1974; in *"That All May Be Edified": Talks, Sermons, and Commentary by Boyd K. Packer* (Salt Lake City: Bookcraft, 1982), 43.

40. See Packer, "Seek Learning," 43.

41. Packer, "Seek Learning," 43.

42. Packer, "Seek Learning," 43–44.

43. John A. Widtsoe, letter to Howard S. McDonald, 19 November 1948, in Office of the President's Correspondence, UA 1087 box 13 folder 6, L. Tom Perry Special Collections, BYU; quoted in Wilkinson, *Years,* 2:455.

44. J. Reuben Clark Jr., "The Charted Course of the Church in Education," address given during BYU summer school at BYU Aspen Grove, 8 August 1938.

45. Clark, "Charted Course."

46. Packer, "Seek Learning," 45.

47. Richard O. Cowan, "A History of the College of Religious Instruction," unpublished manuscript, October 1972, 27–28; quoted in Packer, "Seek Learning," 47; emphasis in Packer.

48. Packer, "Seek Learning," 48.

49. Packer, "Seek Learning," 49.

50. See Packer, "Seek Learning," 41–55.

51. BYU Academic Freedom Policy (1 April 1993), policy.byu.edu/view/academic-freedom-policy; emphasis in original.

52. M. Russell Ballard, "The Opportunities and Responsibilities of CES Teachers in the 21st Century," address to CES religious educators, 26 February 2016, churchofjesuschrist.org/broadcasts/article/evening-with-a-general-authority/2016/02/the-opportunities-and-responsibilities-of-ces-teachers-in-the-21st-century.

53. Ballard, "Opportunities and Responsibilities."

54. Ballard, "Opportunities and Responsibilities."

55. CES, "Strengthening Religious Education."

56. Wikipedia, s.v. "Mormon studies."

57. Doctrine and Covenants 1:30.

58. See Holland, "Maxwell Legacy," 14; see also Russell M. Nelson, "The Correct Name of the Church," *Ensign,* November 2018.

59. Holland, "Maxwell Legacy," 15; emphasis in original.

60. Holland, "Maxwell Legacy," 15; quoting Terryl Givens, David Holland, and Reid Neilson, External Review of the Neal A. Maxwell Institute for Religious Scholarship, December 2014, 6.

61. Holland, "Maxwell Legacy," 15.

62. Holland, "Maxwell Legacy," 16; emphasis in original.

63. Neal A. Maxwell, "Discipleship and Scholarship," *BYU Studies* 32, no. 3 (Summer 1992): 8; quoted in Holland, "Maxwell Legacy," 16.

64. Holland, "Maxwell Legacy," 16; emphasis in original. Paraphrasing Levenson, *The Hebrew Bible*, 84; see also page 105.

65. Holland, "Maxwell Legacy," 16, summing up Stephen Prothero's thoughts; see Prothero, "Belief Unbracketed," 10–11.

The Second Half of the Second Century of Brigham Young University

Jeffrey R. Holland

• *BYU University Conference Address,*
August 23, 2021

INTRODUCTION

When Elder Holland gave this talk, it was one of three addresses during university conference that spoke to the need for BYU to remain faithful to its unique mission, as President Kimball had admonished in his centennial address. Elder Holland emphasized what must happen during the second half of BYU's second century. Having loved BYU for nearly three-fourths of a century, Elder Holland spoke with great feeling, reminding the audience that "BYU will become an 'educational Mt. Everest' only to the degree it embraces its uniqueness, its singularity" (page 139).

This talk has been excerpted; for the full text, visit speeches.byu.edu/envisioning-BYU.

My beloved brothers and sisters, "a house…divided against itself…cannot stand," and I will go to my grave pleading that this institution not only stands but stands unquestionably committed to its unique academic mission and to the Church that sponsors it.

—Jeffrey R. Holland

: ❧ :

Someone once told me that the young speak of the future because they have no past, while the elderly speak of the past because they have no future. Although it damages that little aphorism, I who have no future have come to you as the veritable Ancient of Days to speak of the future of BYU, but a future anchored in our distinctive past. If I have worded that just right, it means I can talk about anything I want.

I am grateful that the full university family is gathered today—faculty, staff, and administration. Regardless of your job description, I am going to speak to all of you as teachers, because at BYU that is what all of us are. Thank you for being faithful role models in that regard. We teach at BYU.

I can't be certain, but I think that it was in the summer of 1948 when I had my first BYU experience. I would have been seven years old. We were driving back to St. George in a 1941 Plymouth from one of our rare trips to Salt Lake City. As we came down old highway 91, I saw high on the side of one of the hills a huge block Y—white and bold and beautiful.

I don't know how to explain that moment, but it was a true epiphany for a seven-year-old, if a seven-year-old can have an epiphany. If I had already seen that Y on the drive up or at any other time, I couldn't remember it. That day I probably was seeing it for the first time. I believe I was receiving a revelation from God. I somehow knew that bold letter meant something special—something special to me—and that it would one day play a significant role in my life. When I asked my mother what it meant, she said it was the emblem of a university. I thought about that for a moment, still watching that letter on the side of the hill, and then said quietly to her, "Well, it must be the greatest university in the world."

My chance to actually get on campus came in June 1952, four years after that first sighting. That summer I accompanied my parents to one of the early leadership weeks—a precursor to what is now the immensely popular BYU Education Week held on campus. That means I came here for my first BYU experience sixty-nine years ago, with a preview of that four years earlier. If anyone in this audience has been coming to this campus longer than that, please come forward and give this talk. Otherwise, sit still and be patient.

My point, dear friends, is simply this: I have loved BYU for nearly three-fourths of a century. Only my service in and testimony of The Church of Jesus Christ of Latter-day Saints—which includes and features foremost my marriage and the beautiful children it has given us—have affected me as profoundly as has my decision to attend Brigham Young University. No one in my family had. In so testifying, I represent literally hundreds of thousands of other students who made that decision and say that same thing.

So, for the legions of us over the years, I say: Thank you. Thank you for what you do. Thank you for classes taught and meals served and grounds so well kept. Thank you for office hours and lab experiments and testimonies shared—gifts given to little people like me so we could grow up to be big people like you. Thank you for choosing to be at BYU, because your choice affected our choice, and, like Mr. Frost's poetic path, "that has made all the difference."[1]

"A TROWEL IN ONE HAND AND A MUSKET IN THE OTHER"

I asked President Kevin J Worthen for a sample of the good things that have been happening of late, and I was delighted at the sheaf of items he gave me—small type, single-spaced lines, reams, it looked like—everything from academic recognitions and scholarly rankings to athletic successes and the reach of BYUtv. Karl G. Maeser would be as proud as I was.

But President Worthen and I both know those aren't the real success stories of BYU. These are rather, as some say of ordinances in the Church, "outward signs of an inward grace."[2] The real successes at BYU are the personal experiences that thousands here have had—personal experiences difficult to document or categorize or list. Nevertheless, these are so powerful in their impact on the heart and mind that they have changed us forever.

I run a risk in citing any examples beyond my own, but let me mention just one or two.

One of our colleagues seated here this morning wrote of his first-semester, pre-mission enrollment in my friend C. Wilfred Griggs's History of Civilization class. But this was going to be civilization seen through a BYU lens. So, as preambles to the course, Wilf had the students read President Spencer W. Kimball's talk "The Second Century of Brigham Young University"[3] and the first chapter of Hugh Nibley's book *Approaching Zion*.[4]

Taken together, our very literate friend said these two readings "forged an indestructible union in my mind and heart between two soaring ideals—that of a consecrated university with that of a holy city. Zion, I came to believe, would be a city with a school [and, I would add, a temple, creating] something of a celestial college town, or perhaps a college kingdom."

After his mission, our faculty friend returned to Provo, where he fell under the soul-expanding spell of John S. Tanner, "the platonic ideal of a BYU professor—superbly qualified in every secular sense, totally committed to the kingdom, and absolutely effervescing with love for the Savior, his students, and his subject. He moved seamlessly from careful teacher analysis to powerful personal testimony. He knew scores of passages from Milton and other poets by heart, [yet] verses of scripture flowed, if anything, even more freely from the abundance of his consecrated heart: I was unfailingly edified by the passion of his teaching and the eloquence of his example."[5]

Why would such a one come back to teach at BYU after a truly distinguished postgraduate experience that might well have taken him to virtually any university in America? Because, our colleague said, "in a coming day the citizens of Zion 'shall come forth with songs of everlasting joy' [Moses 7:53]. I hope," he wrote, "to help my students hear that chorus in the distance and to lend their own voices, in time, to its swelling refrain."[6]

Such are the experiences we hope to provide our students at BYU, though probably not always so poetically expressed. But imagine then the pain that comes with a memo like this one I recently received. These are just a half-dozen lines from a two-page document:

"You should know," the writer said, "that some people in the extended community are feeling abandoned and betrayed by BYU. It seems that some professors (at least the vocal ones in the media) are supporting ideas that many of us feel are contradictory to gospel principles, making it appear to be about like any other university our sons and daughters could have attended. Several parents have said they no longer want to send their children here or donate to the school.

"Please don't think I'm opposed to people thinking differently about policies and ideas," the writer continued. "I'm not. But I would hope that BYU professors would be bridging those gaps between faith and intellect and would be sending out students who are ready to do the same in loving, intelligent, and articulate ways. Yet I fear that some faculty are not supportive of the Church's doctrines and policies and choose to criticize them publicly. There *are* consequences to this. After having served a full-time mission and marrying her husband in the temple, a friend of mine recently left the Church. In her graduation statement on a social media post, she credited [such and such a BYU program and its faculty] with the radicalizing of her attitudes and the destruction of her faith."[7]

Fortunately we don't get too many of those letters, but this one isn't unique. Several of my colleagues get the same kind, with almost all of them ultimately being forwarded to poor President Worthen. Now, most of what happens on this campus is absolutely wonderful. That is why I began as I did, with my own undying love of this place. But every so often we need a reminder of the challenge we constantly face here. Maybe it is in this meeting. I certainly remember my own experiences in these wonderful beginning-of-the-school-year meetings and how much it meant to me to be with you then. Well, it means that again today.

Here is something I said on this subject forty-one years ago, almost to the day. I was young. I was unprepared. I had been president for all of three weeks.

I said then and I say now that if we are an extension of The Church of Jesus Christ of Latter-day Saints, taking a significant amount of sacred tithes and other precious human resources, all of which might well be expended in other worthy causes, surely our integrity demands that our lives "be absolutely consistent with and characteristic of the restored gospel of Jesus Christ."[8] At a university there will always be healthy debate regarding a whole syllabus full of issues. But until "we all come [to] the unity of the faith, and . . . [have grown to] the measure of the stature of the fulness of Christ,"[9] our next best achievement will be to stay in harmony with the Lord's anointed, those whom He has designated to declare Church doctrine and to guide Brigham Young University as its trustees.[10]

In 2014, seven years ago, then Elder Russell M. Nelson came to campus for a BYU leadership meeting. His remarks were relatively brief, but, tellingly, he said:

> *With the Church growing more rapidly in the less prosperous countries, we . . . must conserve sacred funds more carefully than ever before.*
>
> *At BYU we must ally ourselves even more closely with the work of our Heavenly Father. . . .*
>
> *A college education for our people is a sacred responsibility, [but] it is not essential for eternal life.*[11]

A statement like that gets my attention, particularly because just a short time later President Nelson started to chair our board of trustees. Russell M. Nelson is very, very good at listening to us. We who sit with him every day have learned the value of listening carefully to him.

Three years later, in 2017, Elder Dallin H. Oaks, not then but soon to be in the First Presidency, where he would sit only one chair—one heartbeat—away from the same position President Nelson now has, quoted our colleague Elder Neal A. Maxwell, who had said:

> *In a way [Latter-day Saint] scholars at BYU and elsewhere are a little bit like the builders of the temple in Nauvoo, who worked with a trowel in one hand and a musket in the other. Today*

scholars building the temple of learning must also pause on occasion to defend the kingdom. I personally think this is one of the reasons the Lord established and maintains this university. The dual role of builder and defender is unique and ongoing. I am grateful we have scholars today who can handle, as it were, both trowels and muskets.[12]

To this, Elder Oaks then challengingly responded, "I would like to hear a little more musket fire from this temple of learning."[13] He said this in a way that could have applied to a host of topics in various departments, but the one he specifically mentioned was the doctrine of the family and defending marriage as the union of a man and a woman.[14] Little did he know that while many would hear his appeal, especially the School of Family Life, which moved quickly and visibly to assist, some others fired their muskets all right, but unfortunately they didn't always aim at those hostile to the Church. We thought a couple of stray rounds even went north of the Point of the Mountain!

My beloved brothers and sisters, "a house . . . divided against itself . . . cannot stand,"[15] and I will go to my grave pleading that this institution not only stands but stands unquestionably committed to its unique academic mission and to the Church that sponsors it. We hope it isn't a surprise to you that your trustees are *not* deaf or blind to the feelings that swirl around marriage and the whole same-sex topic on campus—and a lot of other topics. I and many of my Brethren have spent more time and shed more tears on this subject than we could ever adequately convey to you this morning or any morning. We have spent hours discussing what the doctrine of the Church can and cannot provide the individuals and families struggling over this difficult issue. So it is with a little scar tissue of our own that we are trying to avoid—and hope *all* will try to avoid—language, symbols, and situations that are more divisive than unifying at the very time we want to show love for *all* of God's children.

In that spirit, let me go no farther before declaring unequivocally my love and that of my Brethren for those who live with this same-sex challenge and so much complexity that goes with it. Too often the world has been unkind—in many instances crushingly cruel—to these, our brothers and sisters. Like many of you, *we* have spent hours with them, and we have wept and prayed and wept again in an effort to offer love and hope while keeping the gospel strong and the obedience to commandments evident in every individual life.

But it will assist all of us—it will assist everyone—trying to provide help in this matter if things can be kept in some proportion and balance in the process. For example, we have to be careful that love and empathy do not get interpreted as condoning and advocacy or that orthodoxy and loyalty to principle not be interpreted as unkindness or disloyalty to people. As near as I can tell, Christ never *once* withheld His love from anyone, but He also never once said to anyone, "Because I love you, you are exempt from keeping my commandments." We are tasked with trying to strike that same sensitive, demanding balance in our lives.

Musket fire? Yes, we will always need defenders of the faith, but "friendly fire" is a tragedy—and from time to time the Church, its leaders, and some of our colleagues within the university community have taken such fire on this campus. And sometimes it isn't friendly, wounding students and the parents of students. My beloved friends, this kind of confusion and conflict ought not to be. Not here. There are better ways to move toward crucially important goals in these very difficult matters—ways that show empathy and understanding for everyone while maintaining loyalty to prophetic leadership and devotion to revealed doctrine.

My Brethren have made the case for the metaphor of musket fire. There will continue to be those who oppose our teachings—and with that will continue the need to define, document, and defend the faith. But we all look forward to the day when we can "beat [our] swords into plowshares, and [our] spears into pruninghooks" and, at least on this subject, "learn war [no] more."[16] And while I have focused on this same-sex topic this morning more than I would have liked, I pray you will see it as emblematic of a lot of issues our students, our communities, and our Church face in this complex, contemporary world of ours.

THE UNFOLDING DREAM OF BYU

But I digress! Back to the blessings of a school in Zion! Do you see the beautiful parallel between the unfolding of the Restoration and the prophetic development of BYU, notwithstanding that both will have their critics along the way? Just as has the Church itself, BYU has grown in spiritual strength, in the number of people it reaches and serves, and in its unique place among other institutions of higher education. It has grown in national and international reputation. More and more of its faculty are distinguishing themselves, and, even more important, so are more and more of its students.

Reinforcing the fact that so many do understand exactly what that unfolding dream of BYU is that President Worthen spoke about, not long ago one of your number wrote to me this marvelous description of what he thought was the "call" to those who serve at BYU: "The Lord's call [to those of us who serve at BYU] is a . . . call to create learning experiences of unprecedented depth, quality, and impact. . . . As good as BYU is and has been, this is a call to do [better]. It is . . . a call to educate many more students, to more . . . effectively help them become true disciples of Jesus Christ, [and] to prepare them to . . . lead in their families, in the Church, [and] in their [professions] in a world filled with commotion. . . . But [answering this call] . . . cannot be [done successfully] without His . . . help." The writer, one of you, concluded, "I believe that help will come according to the faith and obedience of the tremendously good people of BYU."[17]

I agree wholeheartedly and enthusiastically with such a sense of calling here and with that reference to and confidence in "the tremendously good people of BYU." Let me underscore that idea of such a call by returning to President Kimball's second-century address focused on by President Worthen.

Noting that we are just a few years short of halfway through those second hundred years of which President Kimball spoke, I think it would be fascinating to know if we are, in fact, making any headway on the challenges he laid before us and of which Elder David A. Bednar reminded the BYU leadership team just a few weeks ago.[18]

When you look at President Kimball's talk again, may I ask you to pay particular attention to that sweet prophet's effort to ask that we be unique? In his discourse, President Kimball used the word *unique* eight times and the word *special* eight times. It seems clear to me in my seventy-three years of loving it that *BYU will become an "educational Mt. Everest"*[19] *only to the degree it embraces its uniqueness, its singularity.* We could mimic every other university in the world until we got a bloody nose in the effort, and the world would still say, "BYU who?" No, we must have the will to be different and to stand alone, if necessary, being a university second to none in its role primarily as an undergraduate teaching institution that is unequivocally true to the gospel of the Lord Jesus Christ. If at a future time that mission means foregoing some professional affiliations and certifications, then so be it. There may come a day when the price we are asked to pay for such association is simply too high and too inconsistent with who we are. No one wants it to come to that, least of all me, but if it does, we will pursue our own destiny, a "destiny [that] is not a matter of chance; [but largely] . . . a matter of choice; . . . not a thing to be waited for, [but] . . . a thing to be [envisioned and] achieved."[20]

"Mom, what is that big Y on that mountain?"

"Jeff, it stands for the university here in Provo: Brigham Young University."

"Well, it must be the greatest university in the world."

And so, for me, it is. To help you pursue that destiny in the only real way I know how to help, I leave an apostolic blessing on every one of you this morning as you start another school year. In the name of the Lord Jesus Christ, and with gratitude for His holy priesthood and as if hands were on your head—had we time to do that, we surely would—I bless you personally, each one of you personally. I bless the students who will come under your influence, and I bless the university, including its marvelous president, in its campus-wide endeavor. I bless you that profound personal faith will be your watchword and that unending blessings of personal rectitude will be your eternal reward. I bless your professional work that it will be admired by your peers, and I bless your devotion to gospel truths that it will be the saving grace in some student's life. I bless your families that those you hope will be faithful in keeping their covenants will be saved at least in part because you have been faithful in keeping yours. Light conquers darkness. Truth triumphs over error. Goodness is victorious over evil in the end, every time.

I bless each one of you with every righteous desire of your heart, and I thank you for giving your love and loyalty to BYU, to students like me and my beloved wife. Please, from one who owes so much to this school and who has loved her so deeply for so long, keep her not only standing but standing for what she uniquely and prophetically was meant to be. And may the rest of higher education "see your good works, and glorify [our] Father which is in heaven,"[21] I pray, in the name of Jesus Christ, amen.

NOTES

1. Robert Frost, "The Road Not Taken," *Mountain Interval* (New York: Henry Holt and Company, 1916), 9.

2. See John Wesley, Sermon 16, "The Means of Grace" (1772).

3. See Spencer W. Kimball, "The Second Century of Brigham Young University," BYU devotional address, 10 October 1975.

4. See Hugh W. Nibley, chapter 1, "Our Glory or Our Condemnation," *Approaching Zion,* ed. Don E. Norton, vol. 9, *The Collected Works of Hugh Nibley* (Salt Lake City and Provo: Deseret Book Company and Foundation for Ancient Research and Mormon Studies, 1989), 26–55.

5. Personal correspondence, 1 August 2021.

6. Personal correspondence, 1 August 2021.

7. Personal correspondence, 10 June 2021; emphasis in original.

8. Jeffrey R. Holland, "The Bond of Charity," BYU annual university conference addresss, 26 August 1980, 7.

9. Ephesians 4:13.

10. See Holland, "Bond of Charity."

11. Russell M. Nelson, "Controlled Growth," BYU leadership meeting address, 25 August 2014.

12. Neal A. Maxwell, "Blending Research and Revelation," remarks at the BYU President's Leadership Council meetings, 19 March 2004; quoted in Dallin H. Oaks, "Challenges to the Mission of Brigham Young University," BYU leadership meeting address, 21 April 2017; also quoted in Oaks, "It Hasn't Been Easy and It Won't Get Easier," BYU leadership meeting address, 25 August 2014.

13. Oaks, "Challenges to the Mission."

14. See Oaks, "Challenges to the Mission."

15. Mark 3:25.

16. Isaiah 2:4.

17. Personal correspondence, 21 June 2021.

18. See David A. Bednar, "Look unto Me in Every Thought; Doubt Not, Fear Not," BYU leadership meeting address, 16 April 2021.

19. Spencer W. Kimball, "Installation of and Charge to the President," *Inaugural Addresses,* 14 November 1980, Brigham Young University, 9; see also Kimball, "Second Century."

20. William Jennings Bryan, "America's Mission" (22 February 1899), in *Speeches of William Jennings Bryan,* vol. 2 (New York: Funk and Wagnalls, 1913), 11.

21. Matthew 5:16; see also 3 Nephi 12:16.

DREAMS, PROPHECIES,
AND PRAYERS

: :

For long years I have had
a vision of the BYU.

— Spencer W. Kimball

Everything Pertaining to Learning

John Taylor

* *Discourse in Ephraim, Utah, April 13, 1879*

INTRODUCTION

This prophecy was given by President John Taylor in a discourse delivered on a Sunday morning at a stake conference in Ephraim, Utah. At the time, President Taylor was not only president of The Church of Jesus Christ of Latter-day Saints but also territorial superintendent of district schools for Utah, a position he held from 1877 to 1881. The text for this prophecy was originally published in the *Deseret News Semi Weekly* (1 June 1880) and in the *Journal of Discourses* 21:100 (13 April 1879).

You will see the day that Zion will be as far ahead of the outside world in everything pertaining to learning of every kind as we are today in regard to religious matters. You mark my words, and write them down, and see if they do not come to pass.

Final Address

Karl G. Maeser

*❖ Address to Brigham Young Academy,
January 4, 1892*

INTRODUCTION

On January 4, 1892, Karl G. Maeser and other digni-
taries led the faculty and students assembled in
the ZCMI warehouse—which had been housing
Brigham Young Academy—in a formal procession
to an impressive new academy building. On this
occasion, Maeser gave an emotional farewell address
as outgoing principal. In it, he reiterated BYA's
two founding principles: first, from Joseph Smith,
to teach students to govern themselves; and second, from Brigham
Young, to teach everything with the Spirit. Then he recounted how
the design for the new academy building had been revealed to him
in a dream some years before by Brigham Young himself. After this,
President Maeser bid fond farewell to the academy, bequeathing
his president's chair to his successor and "maybe others after him"
(page 150). The text for this talk was originally printed in *The Normal* 1,
no. 10 (15 January 1892): 82.

This talk has been excerpted; for the full text, visit speeches.byu.edu/envisioning-BYU.

*I had a dream, but, in
the language of Byron,
it "was not all a dream."*

— Karl G. Maeser

: 🌿 :

THERE ARE TWO periods in a man's labors when circumstances seem to dictate to him the advisability of making as few words as possible: they are at the beginning and at the end of his work. At the former occasion he may outline his work and make promises for its faithful execution, but behold, conditions arise, altering the first entirely or preventing the fulfillment of the second. The latter period is at the close of his work, when in most cases it would be best to let the work speak for itself. In the last of these conditions I find myself on the present occasion, at which, after a period of many changing scenes of light and shade, I am about to surrender my office as the principal of this academy into other hands.

When to the students at the beginning of the experimental term, April 24, 1876, the words of the Prophet Joseph Smith—that he taught his people correct principles and they governed themselves accordingly[1]—were given as the leading principle of discipline, and the words of President Brigham Young—that neither the alphabet nor the multiplication table was to be taught without the Spirit of God—were given as the mainspring of all teaching, the orientation for the course of the educational system inaugurated by the foundation of this academy was made, and any deviation from it would lead inevitably to disastrous results, and, therefore, Brigham Young Academy has nailed her colors to the mast.

I had a dream, but, in the language of Byron, it "was not all a dream."[2] One night, shortly after the death of President Brigham Young, I found myself entering a spacious hallway with open doors leading into many rooms, and I saw President Brigham Young and a stranger, while ascending the stairs, beckoning me to follow them. Thus they led me into the upper story containing similar rooms and a large assembly hall, where I lost sight of my guides and awoke.

Deeply impressed with this dream, I drew up the plan of the localities shown to me and stowed it away without any apparent purpose for its keeping, nor any definite interpretation of its meaning, and it lay there almost forgotten for more than six years, when in January 1884 the old academy building was destroyed by fire. The want of new localities caused by that calamity brought into remembrance that paper, which, on being submitted suggestively to the board, was at once approved of, and our architect, a son of President Young, was instructed to put it into proper architectural shape.

However, another period of eight years had to pass, and the same month of January, consecrated in our hearts by the memory of that conflagration, had to come around eight times again ere we were privileged to witness the materialization of that dream, the fulfillment of that prophecy. When in future days people will ask for the name of the wise designer of the interior of this edifice, let the answer be: Brigham Young!

And now a last word to thee, my dear beloved academy: I leave the chair to which the Prophet Brigham had called me, and in which the Prophets John and Wilford have sustained me, and resign it to my successor and maybe others after him, all of whom will be likely more efficient than I was—but forgive me this one pride of my heart that I may flatter myself in saying, "None can be more faithful." God bless Brigham Young Academy, amen.

NOTES

1. See John Taylor, "The Organization of the Church," *Millennial Star* 13, no. 22 (15 November 1851): 337–40.

2. Lord Byron, "Darkness," in *The Prisoner of Chillon and Other Poems* (London: John Murray, 1816), 27.

Accepted in
the Heavens

Zina P. Young Williams Card

♦ In *"Short Reminiscent Sketches of Karl G.
Maeser," undated*

INTRODUCTION

Zina P. Young Williams Card was the daughter of
Brigham Young, a student of Karl G. Maeser, and the
first Ladies Matron (equivalent of dean of women)
at Brigham Young Academy. In "Short Reminiscent
Sketches of Karl G. Maeser," Card told of visiting
with President John Taylor about her concerns
over the dire financial condition of the academy.
He comforted her by telling her of a dream he had
had of her father, Brigham Young, who visited him and told him that
Brother Maeser's school was "accepted in the heavens" and would play
"a part [in] the great plan of life and salvation" (page 156).

This document, along with another that is a record of a vision by
Zina's mother that "Jesus Himself claimed" Brigham Young Academy
as "His school," are found in the Zina Presendia Young Williams Card
Papers: "Short Reminiscent Sketches of Karl G. Maeser" and "Sketch
of School Life in the B.Y.A. 1878–1884," unpublished typescript,
undated, MSS 1421, box 2, folder 20, L. Tom Perry Special Collections,
Harold B. Lee Library, Brigham Young University, Provo, Utah. Someone wrote "probably an address" on the top of Card's "Short Reminiscent Sketches of Karl G. Maeser," so it is possible that this was given
as a speech. The text has been modernized and excerpted.

*Christ Himself was
directing and had a care
over this school.*

—Zina P. Young Williams Card

IN 1875 AN INSPIRATION for founding Church schools was given to the prophet Brigham Young and found expression in establishing Brigham Young Academy of Provo. This story has been told, and all to the fact that in the endowment of the schools the document plainly states forth this fact, that a woman should always be on the board for Church schools. This was followed out in the Provo school, and when in the year that Brother Maeser was appointed to come here as principal, he asked President Young how he wanted this school taught, and the reply was that "every lesson must be taught by the spirit of the gospel or some such expression." This left full sway for Brother Maeser's matchless genius, wonderful inspiration, and boundless knowledge to establish a new system by which the school should be carried on.

We have heard it well told how the few who attended the first school taught here by him were impressed with the fact that he would carry out the instructions given by the prophet of God.

The early death of President Young left Brother Maeser and the board of trustees on this newly established system of education, whose every phase of activities should be in harmony with the principles of the gospel and in accord with the actual application to the accepted methods of education.

How the wonderful gifts that Brother Maeser possessed began to shine and permeate every phase of the school life. His wonderful humor and keen insight as to the needs of those who were attending the school began to be realized by his assistant teachers and General Authorities of the Church.

The school grew, and the old academy was filled to its capacity. President A. O. Smoot, who so nobly stood by the institution of learning, appealed to President Taylor for assistance. President Taylor visited the school, and the situation was fully explained to him of the needs and financial stress that the school was laboring under.

However, this did not bring the desired results, for the assistance given was meager indeed compared with the necessities.

I went to Salt Lake with a special mission upon my mind. After earnest prayer I decided that something must be done. President Taylor sent for me when he found I was there and invited me to join with his family in the old Gardo House, where he then resided. After a pleasant hour with the family, he took me to his private library and said he had something of importance to tell me. While there, I felt impressed to relieve my mind upon the subject that had so distressed us all with regard to the finances of the school. Being the matron to the girls, I was well acquainted with [the school's] troubles and the dark outlook of the future. I told President Taylor that I could not understand how it was that the Spirit of God had inspired my father to establish these Church schools for the benefit of the youth of Zion and the future of our people; why he [John Taylor], as the president of the Church, could not view it in the same light and had not given to the school the support that it seemed to me was an inspiration of the Lord, that Father had intended it should enjoy; and to me it was a mystery that he [John Taylor] did not feel the same inspiration. I could not understand it and had prayed most earnestly that the inspiration of the Lord would rest upon me to look favorably upon our needs.

He took my hand in a fatherly way and said, "My dear child, I have something of importance to tell you that I know will make you happy. I have been visited by your father. He came to me in the silence of the night clothed in brightness and, with a face beaming with love and confidence, told me many things of great importance and, among others, that the school being taught by Brother Maeser was accepted in the heavens and was a part of the great plan of life and salvation; that Church schools should be fostered for the good of Zion's children; that we rejoice to see the awakening among the teachers and the children of our people, for they would need the support of this knowledge and testimony of the gospel, and there was a bright future in store for the preparing for the children of the covenant for future usefulness in the kingdom of God; and that Christ Himself was directing and had a care over this school."

There were many things that he related besides this, but I do not feel at liberty to tell. But this I know and bear testimony, that on several occasions the manifestations have been given that Christ has visited the Church school that was then under the supervision of Brother Maeser.

Education
for Eternity

SPENCER W. KIMBALL

♦ *Pre-school Address to BYU Faculty and Staff,*
September 12, 1967

INTRODUCTION

This talk was given at the annual faculty workshop
at Brigham Young University when Spencer W.
Kimball was a member of the Quorum of the
Twelve Apostles. Although this speech was not
literally a dream or revelation, Elder Kimball artic-
ulated a breathtaking vision for the future of BYU.
"For long years," he said, "I have had a vision of the
BYU greatly increasing its already strong position of
excellence till the eyes of all the world will be upon us" (page 174).
Few who were there ever forgot what they felt when Elder Kimball
lifted the curtain on his extraordinary vision of the future. The effect
was electric and enduring. "Education for Eternity" has thus enjoyed
a long shelf life among seminal university speeches. It figured prominently in subsequent talks about BYU's future and has stirred the
hearts of many, as John Tanner explains in "A House of Dreams"
(pages 235–252), delivered on the fortieth anniversary of this talk.

*Can we not build dream
castles in the air and
build foundations solidly
under them?*

— Spencer W. Kimball

: ❧ :

MY BELOVED BROTHERS AND SISTERS, what a challenge and what
a delightful experience to be with you here tonight.

I am constantly impressed with this beautiful campus. I am awed
by the power of the administration and faculty, and, as I see the thousands of students, I want to sing, "Behold! a royal army."[1]

In all the world, the Brigham Young University is the greatest
institution of learning. This statement I have made numerous times.
I believe it sincerely. There are many criteria by which a university
can be judged and appraised and evaluated. The special qualities of
Brigham Young University lie not in its bigness; there are a number of
much larger universities.

It should not be judged by its affluence and the amount of money
available for buildings, research, and other facilities. It should not
be judged by prestige, for there are more statusful institutions as the
world measures status.

The uniqueness of Brigham Young University lies in its special
role—education for eternity—which it must carry in addition to
the usual tasks of a university. This means concern—curricular and
behavioral—for not only the "whole man" but for the "eternal man."
Where all universities seek to preserve the heritage of knowledge that
history has washed to their feet, this faculty has a double heritage—
the preserving of the knowledge of men and the revealed truths sent
from heaven.

While all universities seek to push back the frontiers of knowledge further and further, this faculty must do that and also keep new
knowledge in perspective so that the avalanche of facts does not carry
away saving, exalting truths from the value systems of our youth.

In addition, this faculty must aid the youth of the kingdom in
establishing yet another educational expectation—that there are yet
"many great and important things"[2] to be revealed which require an

intellectual and spiritual posture of readiness and openness. Where other institutions of higher education aim, in part, at educating and training students for various careers, this faculty must do that vital job and do it superbly well, but it must do far more. It must train a cadre of committed, educated youth who can serve effectively, not only in the world of work but in the growing kingdom of God in which skilled leadership is such a vital commodity.

This time of intellectual testing must also be a time of equivalent testing and flexing in things spiritual too. "The spirit giveth life"[3] is so true in so many ways. When there is an inner emptiness in the life of man, his surroundings, however affluent, cannot compensate. When there is a crisis of purpose, nothing will really seem worthwhile or meaningful. When man's relationship with God has been breached, we will be, as Isaiah said, restless as the "sea, [which] cannot rest."[4]

A university or an individual can have all the surface signs of security and yet still be empty inside. You must fill the classrooms and halls of this campus with facts, but fill them also with the Spirit of the Master Teacher, who said to the Nephites of the things He had done, "Even so shall ye do unto the world."[5]

"Education for eternity" is not the kind of phrase one would expect to have carved in the stone of a new secular university; it is not the kind of commitment that would be widely shared in the retreat from real religion we see around us in the world. Yet it is a task for which we do not apologize. Those who do not share this purpose, however, will respect this faculty for its genuine achievements in the world of secular scholarship. The extra missions noted previously do not excuse you from reasonable achievement in your chosen field. You can, in fact, often be more effective in the service you render students if students see you as individuals who have blended successfully things secular and things spiritual in a way that has brought to you earned respect in both realms.

As I see you leaders here, knowing you personally and recognizing the depth of your knowledge and your outstanding accomplishments in your chosen fields, I honor you and appreciate you greatly. And then I realize also that in the breast of everyone there is a deep spiritual feeling with the Master. We know there are good men and women elsewhere, but here, here we have the choice group.

When measured with the true measuring rod, the Brigham Young University stands preeminent. Certainly the true measure of an institution of learning would be the impact it makes on the total lives of its students. On high levels in business, industry, professional, and other fields, great men and women of prominence in many areas are BYU alumni.

Orison Swett Marden wrote:

> *It is a sad sight to see thousands of students graduated every year from our grand institutions whose object is to make stalwart, independent, self-supporting men turned out into the world saplings instead of stalwart oaks, "memory glands" instead of brainy men, helpless instead of self-supporting, sickly instead of robust, weak instead of strong, leaning instead of erect. "So many promising youths, and never a finished man!"[6]*

You tell me that these nearly seven thousand returned missionaries render a stabilizing influence with their deep religious convictions and their serious application. You tell me that a high percentage of the twenty thousand students actually hold positions of leadership in Church organizations, that nearly all of them attend sacrament meetings, and that the large majority who have income pay their tithing. These students voluntarily assemble weekly to hear religious messages from the leaders of the Church. What a great institution this is, where professors, staff members, and students work together in glorious harmony in stake presidencies, bishoprics, and quorum and auxiliary leadership.

It is notable that numerous students change their lives on this campus. Many who had never seriously planned missions for themselves now eagerly look forward to that day. Many who had given little thought to a temple marriage are here inspired to chart their course in that direction.

How the world needs a light in the dark, even a refuge—a vault for keeping the jewels and treasures of life and a big wastebasket into which can be dumped the trash and filth and destructive ideologies and eccentric activities. While great universities and colleges seem to have abandoned all attempts to influence the moral lives of their students, this university must hold the line. Apparently such an attitude seems to be growing on the campuses of our nation, and what can we expect of the graduates tomorrow?

There are holes in the fabric of our political system; our social world continues to show corruption. A climate is coming into being which seems not only to permit crimes against society but to actually encourage them indirectly. "Is there a 'sick' society in the U.S.?" *U.S. News and World Report* asked in a recent issue.[7]

In the current issue of the *Instructor*, President David O. McKay, after speaking of our carelessness in keeping our bodies fit and calling attention to the peril of physical decay, reminded us that spiritual decay is more serious. He said:

> But, great as is the peril of physical decay, greater is the peril *of spiritual decay. The peril of this century is spiritual apathy. As the body requires sunlight, good food, proper exercise and rest, so the spirit of man requires the sunlight of the Holy Spirit, proper exercise of the spiritual functions, the avoiding of evils that affect spiritual health that are more ravaging in their effects than the dire diseases that attack the body.*
> *. . . Never before have the forces of evil been arrayed in such deadly formation as they are now. . . . Satan and his forces are attacking the high ideals and sacred standards which protect our spirituality. One cannot help but be alarmed by the ever-increasing crime wave.*[8]

In our sick society, children are not required to work; time hangs heavily on their hands. Their crimes run into theft and beatings, and even murders fill more of their time. Haight-Ashbury in San Francisco; Dupont Circle in Washington, DC; and East Village in New York City may be net results of some of the laxities and looseness in morals with increases in illegitimacy. And numerous evils of our time may look to the deteriorating ethical standards proposed often by professors in what are termed great universities. God's ways and eternal standards are laughed at, and "situation ethics"[9]—making each person his own moral judge and authority—seem to be responsible for the sickness of our society. How can it survive?

When these numerous other things are weighed and considered, we come to realize our responsibility at BYU becomes greater and greater. We must carry the torch and light the way, and this faculty and staff must stand like a concrete wall to prevent these strange, worldly ideologies and concepts from invading this, one of the last bastions of resisting strength.

We should be knowledgeable. When we talk of godhood and creatorship and eternal increase, we have already soared far out beyond the comprehension of most men. To attain those great accomplishments, one would need to know all about astronomy, biology, physiology, psychology, and all of the arts and sciences. The obtaining of all this knowledge will come largely after our earth life. These questions are often asked: "Why a doctrine-teaching and a character-building university?" "Why not let men do, think, and move as they please?"

Robert A. Millikan talked about the idea that "science has gone ahead so fast man can spend 50 years just learning how to use wisely what he already knows."[10] Millikan stated:

The Western world has in the past 100 years seen more changes in the external conditions under which the average man lives, and also in his beliefs and fundamental conceptions, than occurred during all the preceding 4,000 years![11]

Our Brigham Young insisted:

Learn everything that the children of men know, and be prepared for the most refined society upon the face of the earth, then improve upon this until we are prepared and permitted to enter the society of the blessed—the holy angels that dwell in the presence of God.[12]

The Lord seems never to have placed a premium on ignorance, and yet He has, in many cases, found His better-trained people unresponsive to the spiritual and has had to use spiritual giants with less training to carry on His work. Peter was said to be ignorant and unlearned while Nicodemus was, as the Savior said, a master, a trained one, an educated man. And while Nicodemus would in his aging process gradually lose his prestige and his strength and go to the grave a man of letters without eternal knowledge, Peter would go to his reputed crucifixion the greatest man in all the world—perhaps still lacking considerably in secular knowledge, which he would later acquire, but being preeminent in the greater, more important knowledge of the eternities and of God and His creations and their destinies. And Paul gave us the key:

> It is sown a natural body; it is raised a spiritual body. There is a natural body, and there is a spiritual body.[13]

> For what man knoweth the things of a man, save the spirit of man which is in him? even so the things of God knoweth no man, but the Spirit of God.[14]

It is interesting to note that most of us have a tendency to want to ape the ways of our neighbor, in styles or curricula or universities. If New York or Paris speaks, the dresses are lengthened or shortened; if San Francisco's Haight-Ashbury speaks, men's hair grows longer, beards appear, and baths are less frequent. If the Joneses have a Cadillac, all want Cadillacs. If a nation has a king, all want a king. We seem reluctant to establish our own standards, make our own styles, or follow our own patterns which are based on dignity, comfort, and propriety.

Israel did want a king. "Now make us a king," they cried to Samuel, "to judge us like all the nations."[15]

And when Samuel prayed, the Lord said, "They have not rejected thee, but they have rejected me, that I should not reign over them."[16]

And then, with the inspiration of the Lord, Samuel pointed out to the people the hazards of having a king. The king would recruit their sons in battle. Their daughters would serve in confectionaries and kitchens and bakeries. Their sons would have to work the king's ground and reap his harvests and make his spears and swords and rebuild his chariots and train his horses. He would appropriate their vineyards and olive yards to feed his servants, and he would tax them heavily.[17]

In spite of all these dire predictions, the people still said, "Nay; but we will have a king over us; . . . like all the [other] nations."[18]

Though our world reels and trembles, we must stand firm and see that behavior troubles do not invade our campus as they do other campuses and that we are not like other universities.

We have been speaking of mind and spirit and body, of the immortal man and the mortal man. We have been speaking of earthly things and spiritual things, of time and eternity. Of the two, the spiritual development is the greater, for it is permanent and lasting, and it incorporates all other proper secular development.

The Lord inspired Jacob to correlate the secular and the spiritual when he said, "To be learned is good if they hearken unto the counsels of God."[19]

Someone has said, "If the world needs a bomb to destroy the cities and its peoples and the world, the laboratory of the American university can supply it."

And we say, "If the world needs messengers of peace and teachers of righteousness and builders of character and inspirers of faith in God, here is the university that can do all this—here at the Brigham Young University."

Even here we give to the first cause our lesser attention and, though we are far in front of other institutions, still we give less time, less thought, and less effort to the actual teaching of the spiritual as contrasted with the secular. But perhaps this imbalance of time and energy and effort is considerably compensated for if all of you instructors in all classes teach the gospel, especially by example. Most of you teach eloquently in this manner. Most of you will be frequent attenders at the temple and will serve in the stakes and wards and priesthood and auxiliary organizations. Some of you will be leaders in general Church positions. All of you will be living all the commandments of the Lord—paying a full tithing and observing the Word of Wisdom—not because it is expected but because it is right.

In your homes will be an absence of friction and conflict—not because forty thousand eyes are upon you but because you love the Lord, your family, and the program. You will observe the Sabbath day and keep it holy as you live all other commandments—not because the multitudes might see you but because of the Lord who gave them. Your home evenings will be regular and inspirational and your family prayers, both morning and night, will be constant—not because you are under command but because you love your family and our BYU family of twenty thousand who will feel the spirituality emanating from you. You will always keep solvent, always be honest to the nth degree, and always be full of integrity—not because you are required to do so to keep your position but because you believe fully that God gives no commandments which are not for our own good. Your example is better than even your precept, for to teach one thing and to do another is like "sounding brass, [and] tinkling cymbal[s]."[20]

This university is not the place for mercenaries. The Revolutionary War was lost by the British partly because they employed mercenaries to fight for them. But the winning colonists had a real cause. If your salary, which we hope is adequate, should be incidental and your grand and magnificent obsession would be the youth and their growth, their vision, and their development, I would hope that each of you in joy and peace and satisfaction would continue to lift the souls and carry forward the character-building program.

It would be my hope that twenty thousand students might feel the normalcy and beauty of your lives. I hope you will each qualify for the students' admiration and affection. It is my hope that these youth will have abundant lives and beautiful families patterned after the ideal of an eternal family, with you for their example.

This would lead me to expect from you honor, integrity, cleanliness, and faith. I would expect you to appear before these young people well dressed, well groomed, and positive—happy people from homes where peace and love have left their warm, vibrant influence as your day begins. I would want them to have the feeling that you, their instructor, that very morning, had come from a loving home where peace reigns and love is enthroned and to know instinctively by your spirit that you were that morning on your knees with your family and that there were soft words of pleading to your Heavenly Father for guidance—not only for your little family kneeling with you but for your larger family also at that moment scurrying about their apartments to get ready for your class.

Brigham Young said:

> *Let our teachers ask the Father, in the name of Jesus, to bestow upon them and upon their scholars the spirit of wisdom and intelligence from heaven; ask for skill to control and ability to teach on the part of the teacher, and willingness to be controlled and aptability to be taught on the part of the scholars.*[21]

I would like these youth to see their instructors in community life as dignified, happy cooperators; in Church life as devout, dependable, efficient leaders; and in personal life as honorable and full of integrity. As President John Taylor said, "Let us live so that . . . angels can minister to us and the Holy Spirit dwell with us."[22]

Here there should be loyalty at its ultimate best. Loyalty is the stuff of which great souls are made. I would expect that no member of the faculty or staff would continue in the employ of this institution if he or she did not have deep assurance of the divinity of the gospel of Christ, the truth of the Church, the correctness of the doctrines, and the destiny of the school.

The BYU is dedicated to the building of character and faith, for character is higher than intellect, and its teachers must in all propriety so dedicate themselves. That goal is the same as that of our Eternal Father: "To bring to pass the . . . eternal life of man."[23] Every instructor knows before coming to this campus what the aims are and is committed to the furthering of those objectives.

If one cannot conscientiously accept the policies and program of the institution, there is no wrong in his moving to an environment that is compatible and friendly to his concepts. But for a Ford employee to downgrade his company or its products, for a General Electric man to be unappreciative of his company, or for an employee of a bank to discredit that institution would be hypocrisy and disloyalty. There are ways to right wrongs, to improve services, or to bring about proper changes. To set about to counter the established policies or approved interpretations of the doctrines of the Church would be disloyal and unbecoming of anyone.

No one could justifiably accept salary or favors from an institution whose policies he could not in principle accept and defend.

This is an institution peculiar and different from all others. Other schools have been organized by states, countries, churches, groups, and individuals. This great university was organized by the Lord God. President J. Reuben Clark Jr. expressed clearly our concepts:

> *Science and worldly knowledge must question every demonstration, every experiment, every conclusion, every phenomenon that seems a fact, for only by this method may the truths of the natural law become known to us, save by specific revelation.*
>
> *But we shall also expect you to know that, in matters pertaining to our spiritual lives, God's revealed will, his laws, his commandments, declared not only directly by himself, but by and through his servants, must be taken unquestioned, because they are the ultimate truths that shape and control our destinies.*[24]

President Clark also said:

> *Now brethren and sisters, it is your privilege to teach the revealed word of God. You are not expected to advance new theories, to give private interpretations, nor to clarify the mysteries. You do not need to, nor can you or anyone else, answer all the questions that the youth can ask. You need not be embarrassed to tell them that you cannot fully answer certain questions and that the Lord has not seen fit to reveal all His mysteries. Perhaps many would like to know the age of the earth, the exact method of its organization, the method of spirit procreation.*

The doctrines of the Church will be revealed through the prophet, and he will interpret them as needed. To one such member who presumed to dictate to the prophet concerning a matter which had been settled long years ago, I wrote:

I cannot believe you would presume to command your God or to make a demand on the prophet of God! No situation or condition could possibly justify you in any such monumental presumption. To any such, I must quote the Lord: "And thou shalt not command him who is at thy head, and at the head of the church."[25]

When the Lord has set a policy and His leaders have established it, certainly it would be in bad taste and improper for people to keep sniping at it.

I knew a man who received his bank salary yet secretly robbed his bank of its money. I knew a woman who was supported by a business, but she constantly revealed its inner weaknesses to her associates. I knew a man who received the confidences of persons in trouble and revealed them to his associates. I knew a man who belonged to the Church and enjoyed its blessings but secretly was constantly downgrading it.

This institution and its leaders should be like the Twelve as they were left in a very difficult world by the Savior:

The world hath hated them, because they are not of the world, even as I am not of the world.

I pray not that thou shouldest take them out of the world, but that thou shouldest keep them from the evil.

They are not of the world, even as I am not of the world.[26]

I like President Ernest L. Wilkinson's statement in an address:

Fundamentally our roots spring from Palmyra, rather than Cambridge. . . . If most institutions of higher learning aspire to be only communities of scholars, we are privileged to be also a congregation of disciples. . . .

[We are men of God first and men of letters second, men of science third and noted men fourth, and men of rectitude rather than academic competence.] *Our academic training must be as impeccable as our lives. . . . A defection that would pass unnoticed elsewhere is exploited relentlessly when it occurs at BYU.*[27]

There are relative truths and there are absolute truths. The gospel is absolute—its basic functions and teachings do not change. President J. Reuben Clark Jr. said:

> The philosopher, in his worldly way, may speak of relative truth in the field of ethics and worldly knowledge, a concept that today and here may be truth, but that tomorrow and there may be error, a truth based upon man's development, his learning, his ethics, his concepts, his hopes, his aspirations, his [God]. . . .
>
> . . . As our knowledge has widened, we, to Job's incomprehensibles, have added almost a universe of unknown physical phenomena. . . .
>
> But we . . . have at our hands unchanging, ultimate truths which God has vouchsafed to us for our guidance, salvation, and exaltation.
>
> They are our shields against temptation and our redemption from sin.
>
> They give us the light for our feet; they guide us on our way.
>
> They draw aside for us the curtains of heaven that, like Stephen of old, we may see "the glory of God, and Jesus standing on the right hand of God" (Acts 7:55).
>
> They are the rocks upon which we build our house that the winds and storms wash not away.
>
> They are the bridge connecting time with eternity, mortality with immortality; over it we walk from worldliness into salvation.[28]

Whereas in other institutions there seem to be faculties and administration groups and students who are fighting for supremacy as to the policies and conduct of the university, BYU is entirely different. It is financed and operated and sustained by the tithes of the people— poor and rich. It is governed by the board of trustees, the members of which are General Authorities of the Church. The prophet, seer, and revelator is the interpreter of the doctrines. It must be ever thus.

And Paul warned us:

Beware lest any man spoil you through philosophy and vain deceit, after the tradition of men, after the rudiments of the world, and not after Christ.[29]

It would not be expected that all of the faculty should be categorically teaching religion constantly in their classes, but it is proper that every professor and teacher in this institution would keep his subject matter bathed in the light and color of the restored gospel and have all his subject matter perfumed lightly with the spirit of the gospel. Always there would be an essence, and the student would feel the presence.

Every instructor should grasp the opportunity occasionally to bear formal testimony of the truth. Every student is entitled to know the attitude and feeling and spirit of his every teacher. Certainly a science instructor or a physical education teacher or a math or art teacher could find an opportunity sometimes to mention spiritual experiences or comment on the gospel truths. This would be in harmony with the spirit of Brigham Young's charge to Karl G. Maeser, so often quoted:

President [Young] *looked steadily forward for a few moments, as though in deep thought, then said: "Brother Maeser, I want you to remember that you ought not to teach even the alphabet or the multiplication tables without the Spirit of God. That is all. God bless you. Good-bye."*[30]

That statement has been used over and over, but we must never forget it. If we begin to ape the world and forget this injunction, we are lost. We pay our taxes; we support state schools; therefore there is no justification whatever for our spending these millions of dollars on this institution unless we mind the purposeful objective given by the prophet.

Many of us have had dreams and visions of the destiny of this great Church university. Joel said, "Your old men shall dream dreams, your young men shall see visions."[31]

Now that we have reached the maximum in enrollment, much of the energy formerly given to growth and expansion can now be concentrated on making our dreams come true. With these revolving twenty thousand choice, last-dispensation students from all over the world running into hundreds of thousands through the years, can we not build dream castles in the air and build foundations solidly under them to develop students, faculty, a campus, and a university which would eclipse all others within the limitations of our courses?

In our world there have risen brilliant stars in drama, music, literature, sculpture, painting, science, and all the graces. For long years I have had a vision of the BYU greatly increasing its already strong position of excellence till the eyes of all the world will be upon us.

President John Taylor so prophesied, as he emphasized his words with this directive:

You will see the day that Zion will be as far ahead of the outside world in everything pertaining to learning of every kind as we are today in regard to religious matters. You mark my words, and write them down, and see if they do not come to pass.[32]

God expects Zion to become the praise and glory of the whole earth; so that kings, hearing of her fame, will come and gaze upon her glory.[33]

With regard to masters, surely there must be many Wagners (Richard Wagner, 1813–1883) in the BYU, approaching him or yet to come in the tomorrows—young people with love of art, talent supreme, and eagerness to create. I hope we at BYU may produce men greater than this German composer, Wagner, but less eccentric and more spiritual.

Who of us has not sat spellbound with *Aida, Il Trovatore,* or other of the masterpieces of Giuseppe Verdi (1813–1901)? Can there never be another Verdi or his superiors? Could we not find and develop a Johann Sebastian Bach (1685–1750)—to whom music, especially organ and choral music, owes almost as much as a religion does to its founder, say some musicians.

Is there anyone here who has not been stirred by the rich melodic voice of Enrico Caruso (1873–1921), the Italian-born operatic tenor? Surely there have been few voices which have inspired so many. Considered to be the greatest voice of his century by many, year after year he was the chief attraction at the Metropolitan Opera.

Would someone say that they produce singers best in Italy, in Germany, in Poland, or in Sweden? Remember, we draw our students from all these places. BYU should attract many and stir their blood with the messages of the ages. And they will sing songs of accomplishment, eternal marriage, and exaltation, and we at BYU shall encourage and train them.

And then there was Patti—Adelina Patti (1843–1919)—who was scintillating in her accomplishments and her greatness. She is known as an Italian singer, though she was born in Madrid. Not only did Patti have a pure, clear-toned voice but a wide range which was excelled only by her personal grace and charm, her pure style, and her loveliness. Surely at this university we can produce many Pattis in the tomorrows.

Then we remember the celebrated Jenny Lind (1820–1887), the Swedish singer with such tone faculty, such musical memory, such supremacy, and such unprecedented triumphs. Do you think there are no more voices like Jenny Lind's? Our day, our time, our people, our generation, and our BYU should produce such as we catch the total vision of our potential and dream dreams and see visions of the future.

Brigham Young said, "Every accomplishment, every polished grace, every useful attainment in mathematics, music, and in all science and art belong to the Saints."[34]

Many of us can still remember the enchanting Madame Ernestine Schumann-Heink (1861–1936), the Bohemian-Austrian, later American lady (who died in Hollywood), who was by many regarded as the greatest contralto of her time and a noble character also. She had sons in World War I on both sides and lost one in the American army and one in the German army.

And here at BYU, many times I have been entranced with sweet and lovely voices. I believe that deep in the throats of these BYU students of today and tomorrow are qualities superior which, superbly trained, can equal or surpass these known great singers. There was also Nellie Melba (1861–1931), the great Australian prima donna—the Melba who captivated her audiences as she sang.

BYU certainly must continue to be the greatest university, unique and different. In these fields and in many others there should be an ever-widening gap between this school and all other schools. The reason is obvious. Our professors and instructors should be peers or superiors to those at any other school in natural ability, extended training, plus the Holy Spirit, which should bring them light and truth. With hundreds of "men of God" and their associates so blessed and trained, we have the base for an increasingly efficient and worthy school.

What is the future for BYU? It has long had a strong music department, but we have hardly begun the great work that could be done here. I envision that day when the BYU symphony will surpass in popularity and performance the Philadelphia Orchestra or the New York Philharmonic group or the Cleveland Symphony.

One great artist was asked which of all his productions was the greatest. His prompt answer was, "The next."

If we strive for perfection—the best and greatest—and are never satisfied with mediocrity, we can excel. In the field of both composition and performance, why cannot the students from here write a greater oratorio than *Messiah* by George Frideric Handel (1685–1759)? The best has not yet been composed nor produced. The students can use the coming of Christ to the Nephites as the material for a greater masterpiece. Our BYU artists tomorrow may write and sing of Christ's spectacular return to the American earth in power and great glory and of His establishment of the kingdom of God on the earth in our own dispensation. No Handel nor other composer of the past or present or future could ever do justice to this great event. How could one ever portray in words and music the glories of the coming of the Father and the Son and the restoration of the doctrines and the priesthood and the keys unless he were an inspired Latter-day Saint schooled in the history and doctrines and revelations and with rich musical ability and background and training? Why cannot the BYU bring forth this producer?

George Bernard Shaw (1856–1950), the Irish dramatist and critic, summed up an approach to life: "[Other people]," he said, "see things; and . . . say, 'Why?' But I dream things that never were; and I say, 'Why not?'"³⁵ We need people here who can dream of things that never were and ask, "Why not?"

Dom Jae passed on this quotation:

> *Blessed is the man with new worlds to conquer. For him the future gleams with promise. He never attains ultimate success—is never satisfied—is ever on the way to better things. Ahead of him there is always another dream castle glittering in the sun—and what fun it is to build foundations under it!*³⁶

Freed largely from expansion and growing pains, we can now pour many firm foundations under our dreams for the future.

And Niccolò Paganini (1782–1840), the Italian violinist! Why cannot we discover, train, and present many Paganinis and other such great artists? And shall we not here at BYU present before the musical world a pianist to excel in astonishing power of execution, depth of expression, and sublimity of noble feeling the noted Hungarian pianist and composer Franz Liszt (1811–1886)? We have already produced some talented artists at the piano, but I have a secret hope to live long enough to come to the BYU auditorium and hear and see at the piano a greater performer than Ignacy Paderewski (1860–1941), the Polish statesman, composer, and pianist. Surely all Paderewskis were not born in Poland in the last century; all talented people with such outstanding re-creative originality, with such nervous power and such romantic appearance, were not concentrated in this one body and two hands! Certainly this noted pianist with his arduous super-brilliant career was not the last of such to be born!

The Italian painter and sculptor Leonardo da Vinci (1452–1519), with his masterful and wonderful technique, made his portraits, figures, and designs true to life. His *Mona Lisa* is celebrated, and in it he was striving to catch the fleeting manifestations of the secret soul of his attractive and winsome subject. He seems to have given inspiration to Raphael and others of the great.

On our last visit to Copenhagen, we were excited and inspired as we drank in the beauty of *Christ and the Twelve Apostles* by Bertel Thorvaldsen (1770–1844). We wondered if anyone, anytime, could produce a greater masterpiece, and yet time and the BYU may surprise the world. Can you see statues on this campus of the Lord, His prophets, and His disciples? There are many of the martyrs and prophets of the centuries who have never been so honored.

Michelangelo Buonarroti (1475–1564) thought of himself only as a sculptor. He was called upon in 1505 by Pope Julius II to build a great monument which the Pope desired to have finished within his lifetime. This monument was never completed, and the controversies which arose embittered a large part of the great artist's life. His three-thousand-five-hundred-square-foot painting in the Sistine Chapel is said to be the most important piece of mural painting of the modern world.

To be an artist means hard work and patience and long-suffering. This artist, Michelangelo, said, "I am a poor man and of little merit, who plod[s] along in the art which God gave me."[37] He also said, "I am more exhausted than man ever was."[38] And when we see Michelangelo's masterpieces of art, we feel, as did Habakkuk:

> *Behold ye among the heathen, and regard, and wonder marvelously: for I will work a work in your days, which ye will not believe, though it be told you.*[39]

But then we ask, "Can there never be another Michelangelo?" Ah! Yes! His *David* in Florence and his *Moses* in Rome inspire adulation. Did all such talent run out in that early century? Could not we find an embodied talent like this but with a soul that was free from immorality and sensuality and intolerance?

Could there be among us embryo poets and novelists like Johann Wolfgang von Goethe (1749–1832)? Have we explored as much as we should? Of the creator of *Faust,* Ralph Waldo Emerson said, "The old Eternal Genius who built the world has confided himself more to this man than to any other."[40] But Goethe was not the greatest nor the last. There may be many Goethes among us even today waiting to be discovered. Inspired students will write great books and novels and biographies and plays.

Can we not find equal talent to those who gave us *A Man for All Seasons, Doctor Zhivago,* and *Ben Hur?* This latter book I read when I was a small boy, and many times I have returned to it. Critics might not agree with me, but I feel that it is a great story. *My Fair Lady* and *The Sound of Music* and such have pleased their millions, but I believe we can improve on them.

We have the great Rembrandt (1606–1669), whose style is original—founded on the work of no other artist—and whose coloring is somber and reaches its highest achievement in combinations of browns and grays. There are few paintings about which so much has been written as Rembrandt's *The Night Watch* or his self-portraits. His morals also have been subject to criticism.

And we have the Italian painter Raphael (1483–1520), generally accepted in the European world as the greatest of religious painters.

It has been said that many of the great artists were perverts or moral degenerates. In spite of their immorality, they became great and celebrated artists. What could be the result if discovery were made of equal talent in men who were clean and free from the vices and thus entitled to revelations?

We have scientists who can help harness the limitless powers and turn them to good for all humanity. There have been Louis Pasteur (1822–1895) and Marie Curie (1867–1934) and Albert Einstein (1879–1955), and we have now Harvey Fletcher (1884–1981) and Henry Eyring (1901–1981), and there will be greater yet.

Then there is William Shakespeare (1564–1616). Everybody quotes Shakespeare. The English poet and dramatist was prodigious in his productions. His *Hamlet* and *Othello* and *King Lear* and *Macbeth* are only preludes to the great mass of his productions. Has anyone other ever been so versatile, so talented, or so remarkable in his art? And yet could the world produce only one Shakespeare?

The Lamanite-Nephite culture means much to the people of the Church, and properly so. Here at BYU, should we not have the greatest collection of artifacts, records, and writings concerning them in the world? Through revelation we have received much knowledge concerning these peoples. Should not BYU then be preeminent in this field of culture?

Perhaps growing up in a backwoods forest in Indiana or Louisiana or in Oregon or Illinois there may be some little deprived boy doing his elementary math on a wood-fire shovel and borrowing books from neighbors and splitting rails who will find his way tomorrow to the BYU, and here in the proper departments he will get the background, knowledge, and inspiration which will send him skyrocketing to fame and honors, perhaps even to the White House—a man to be ever after heralded for his wisdom, bravery, conscience, humanity, and leadership and to be quoted till eternity. His name might be Abraham, his mother's name might be Nancy, and could this be written concerning him as was written of his nineteenth-century counterpart at his birth (Abraham Lincoln, 1809–1865)?

> *Poor Tom! Poor Nance!*
> *Poor young one! born without a chance!*

>   . . . .

> *And—oh, well! send the women-folks to Nance.*
> *Poor little devil! born without a chance!*[41]

The little Abes could have their chances and their greatest talents improved and perfected and their notoriety spring from humble but influential BYU.

Oh, how our world needs statesmen! And we ask again with George Bernard Shaw, "Why not?" We have the raw material, we have the facilities, and we can excel in training. We have the spiritual climate. We must train statesmen, not demagogues—men of integrity, not weaklings who for a mess of pottage will sell their birthright. We must develop these precious youth to know the art of statesmanship, to know people and conditions, and to know situations and problems but also to be men who will be trained so thoroughly in the arts of their future work and in the basic honesties and integrities and spiritual concepts that there will be no compromise of principle.

For years I have been waiting for someone to do justice in recording in song and story and painting and sculpture the story of the Restoration, the reestablishment of the kingdom of God on earth with its struggles and frustrations and the apostasies and inner revolutions and counterrevolutions of those first decades; of the exodus to the West; of the counterreactions; of the transitions; of the persecution days; of the plural marriage and the underground; of the miracle man Joseph Smith, of whom we sing, "Oh, what rapture filled his bosom, For he saw the living God";[42] and of the giant colonizer and builder Brigham Young, by whom this university was organized and for whom it was named.

The story of Mormonism has never yet been written nor painted nor sculptured nor spoken. It remains for inspired hearts and talented fingers yet to reveal themselves. They must be faithful, inspired, active Church members to give life and feeling and true perspective to a subject so worthy. Such masterpieces should run for months in every movie center and cover every part of the globe in the tongue of the people, written by great artists and purified by the best critics.

Our writers and our moving-picture specialists, with the inspiration of heaven, should tomorrow be able to produce a masterpiece which would live forever. Our own talent, obsessed with dynamism from a *cause,* could put into such a story life and heartbeats and emotions and love and pathos, drama, suffering, fear, and courage such as that of the great leader, the mighty modern Moses, who led a people farther than from Egypt to Jericho, who knew miracles as great as the stream from the rock at Horeb, manna in the desert, giant grapes, rain when needed, and battles won against great odds. And the great miracle prophet, the founder of this university, would never die.

Take a Nicodemus and put Joseph Smith's spirit in him, and what do you have? Take a da Vinci or a Michelangelo or a Shakespeare and give him a total knowledge of the plan of salvation of God and personal revelation and cleanse him, and then take a look at the statues he will carve and the murals he will paint and the masterpieces he will produce. Take a Handel with his purposeful effort, his superb talent, and his earnest desire to properly depict the story and give him inward vision of the whole true story and revelation, and what a master you have!

What a great university the BYU now is! A much greater one it can yet become! One of the rich rewards coming from doing great things is the capacity to do still greater things.

The architect Daniel H. Burnham (1846–1912) said:

> *Make no little plans; they have no magic to stir men's blood and probably themselves will not be realized. Make big plans; aim high in hope and work, remembering that a noble, logical diagram once recorded will never die, but long after we are gone will be a living thing, asserting itself with ever-growing insistency. Remember that our sons and grandsons are going to do things that would stagger us. Let your watchword be order and your beacon beauty.*[43]

The BYU must keep its vessel seaworthy. It must take out all old planks as they decay and put in new and stronger timber in their place. It must sail on and on and on.

And now may we suggest to you:

> *It is no time for loitering. There is no use in waiting for the future in the hope that everything will turn out all right. We must become engaged with it. . . .* [Think] *back to the sands of Dunkirk where three hundred thousand of our troops were hemmed in by enemy tanks. We had to get them off the beach. Hundreds of men who had motor boats and fishing boats and dinghies rushed to help. There was no time for pep talks or pampering; there were no charts. They were told* [by the commanding officer]: *"Now off you go and good luck to you—steer for the sound of the guns."*[44]

May God bless this great university and you and us and its impressive student body, I pray, in the name of Jesus Christ, amen.

NOTES

1. "Behold! A Royal Army," *Hymns* (Salt Lake City: The Church of Jesus Christ of Latter-day Saints, 1948), no. 7.

2. Articles of Faith 1:9.

3. 2 Corinthians 3:6.

4. Isaiah 57:20.

5. 3 Nephi 18:25.

6. Orison Swett Marden, *Pushing to the Front* (Petersburg, New York: Success Company, 1911), 21; quoting Ralph Waldo Emerson, "The Transcendentalist," lecture read at the Masonic Temple, Boston, January 1842.

7. "Is There a 'Sick' Society in the U.S.?: Riots, Crime, Youth Revolt," *U.S. News and World Report*, 28 August 1967, 49.

8. David O. McKay, "The Spiritual Life, the True Life of Man," *Instructor*, September 1967, 338.

9. "'Sick' Society," 51.

10. Heading in Robert A. Millikan, "Knowledge Is Power—Not Wisdom," *Rotarian* 66, no. 1 (January 1945): 7.

11. Millikan, "Knowledge Is Power," 7.

12. Brigham Young, "Remarks," *Deseret News*, 4 June 1873, 276; *Journal of Discourses*, 26 vols. (London: Latter-day Saints' Book Depot, 1854–86), 16:77 (25 May 1873).

13. 1 Corinthians 15:44.

14. 1 Corinthians 2:11.

15. 1 Samuel 8:5.

16. 1 Samuel 8:7.

17. See 1 Samuel 8:11–18.

18. 1 Samuel 8:19–20.

19. 2 Nephi 9:29.

20. 1 Corinthians 13:1.

21. Brigham Young, "Remarks," *Deseret News*, 22 October 1862, 129; *Journal of Discourses* 9:369 (31 August 1862); text modernized.

22. John Taylor, "Discourse," *Deseret News Semi-Weekly*, 1 June 1880, 1; *Journal of Discourses* 21:100 (13 April 1879).

23. Moses 1:39.

24. J. Reuben Clark Jr., "Charge to President Howard S. McDonald," *Improvement Era*, January 1946, 63; from the address given at the inauguration of BYU president Howard S. McDonald, 14 November 1945.

25. Spencer W. Kimball, summarizing his letter to Stewart L. Udall, 25 May 1967; quoting Doctrine and Covenants 28:6.

26. John 17:14–16.

27. Ernest L. Wilkinson, BYU address to faculty and staff, 12 September 1966, 6.

28. Clark, "Charge to President Howard S. McDonald," 60, 62.

29. Colossians 2:8.

30. Reinhard Maeser, quoting Brigham Young, in *Karl G. Maeser: A Biography by His Son* (Provo: Brigham Young University, 1928), 79.

31. Joel 2:28.

32. John Taylor, "Discourse," *Deseret News Semi-Weekly,* 1 June 1880, 1; *Journal of Discourses* 21:100 (13 April 1879).

33. John Taylor, "Discourse," *Deseret News,* 25 September 1878, 531; *Journal of Discourses* 20:47 (4 August 1878).

34. Brigham Young, "Instructions," *Deseret News,* 15 July 1863, 17; *Journal of Discourses* 10:224 (April and May 1863).

35. George Bernard Shaw, "In the Beginning," *Back to Methuselah* (1921), part 1, act 1.

36. "Keep Climbing," *Nogales International,* 12 June 1937, 6; quoted by Dom Jae, in "Words of Wisdom," *Observer* 5, no. 1 (October 1962): 2 (Gorham State Teachers College, Gorham, Maine).

37. Michelangelo Buonarroti, letter to Niccolò Martelli, 20 January 1542; in John Addington Symonds, *The Life of Michelangelo Buonarroti: Based on Studies in the Archives of the Buonarroti Family at Florence,* 2 vols. (New York: Charles Scribner's Sons; London: Macmillan, 1911), 2:68.

38. Michelangelo Buonarroti, letter to his family, 24 July 1512; in Julian Klaczko, *Rome and the Renaissance: The Pontificate of Julius II,* trans. John Dennie (New York: G. P. Putnam's Sons, 1903), 344.

39. Habakkuk 1:5.

40. Ralph Waldo Emerson, "Goethe; or, the Writer," *Representative Men: Seven Lectures* (1850).

41. Edmund Vance Cooke, "Born Without a Chance (February 12, 1809)" (1920).

42. "Oh, How Lovely Was the Morning," *Hymns* (Salt Lake City: The Church of Jesus Christ of Latter-day Saints, 1948), no. 136.

43. Daniel H. Burnham, motto for city planners, 1907; quoted in Charles Moore, *Daniel H. Burnham, Architect, Planner of Cities,* 2 vols. (Boston: Houghton Mifflin, 1921), 2:147.

44. "Prospectus for Youth," *Royal Bank of Canada Monthly Letter* 47, no. 4 (April 1966): 1; quoting Commander Eric Wharton, Small Boats Pool, Royal Navy, in Richard Collier, *The Sands of Dunkirk* (London: Collins, 1961), 155: "Now off you go and good luck to you—and steer for the sound of the guns."

Dedicatory Prayers for the Provo Utah Temple and Provo City Center Temple

In the dedicatory prayer of the Provo Utah Temple, President Joseph Fielding Smith pled for God to bless not only the temple but "that great temple of learning, the Brigham Young University, and all that is associated with it" (page 189). He also prayed for "all other Church schools, institutes, and seminaries" (page 189), as well as for "those who teach and study in all academic fields" (page 190).

With the completion of the Provo Utah Temple in 1972, Brigham Young University, the Missionary Training Center, and the temple formed one contiguous campus on which were located three similar but different kinds of houses of faith and learning. Commenting on this unique conjunction, then BYU president Dallin H. Oaks observed: "From the beginning of this dispensation the Lord has associated the temple, the school, and the ministry, a trio now brought together in this spot." Looking out his office window, he would tell visitors that "these three institutions—university, mission, and temple—are the most powerful combination of institutions on

the face of the earth" ("A House of Faith," BYU annual university conference address, 31 August 1977).

Almost forty years after making these remarks as BYU president, Elder Dallin H. Oaks was invited to dedicate a second temple
in Provo. In his dedicatory prayer for the Provo City Center Temple,
Elder Oaks again linked temple, mission, and university, including
both BYU and Utah Valley University. Brigham Young University has
thus been twice blessed by prophets in conjunction with the dedication of two temples.

The following excerpts are from the dedicatory prayers for these
two Provo temples. The full prayers can be found at churchofjesuschrist
.org/temples.

*Let that great temple
of learning, the Brigham
Young University,...
be prospered to the full.*

—Joseph Fielding Smith

:⚜:

LET BRIGHAM YOUNG UNIVERSITY BE PROSPERED

Joseph Fielding Smith

Excerpt from the dedicatory prayer for the
Provo Utah Temple, February 9, 1972

O UR SOULS ARE troubled and we weep because of the wickedness
of the world and the evils that abound on every hand. Out of
deep concern, therefore, we pray for the youth of Zion, for the young
and rising generation, for those who must now prepare themselves to
bear up the kingdom in their time and season. Keep them from evil;
hedge up the way so they may not fall into sin and be overcome by
the world. O Lord, bless the youth of Zion and us their leaders that
we may guide and direct them aright.

We know that thy kingdom shall roll onward and that hosts of the
young and rising generation shall yet stand forth in power and great
glory as witnesses of thy name and teachers of thy law. Preserve them,
O our God; enlighten their minds and pour out upon them thy Holy
Spirit, as they prepare for the great work that shall rest upon them.

Let that great temple of learning, the Brigham Young University,
and all that is associated with it, and all other Church schools, institutes, and seminaries be prospered to the full. Let thy enlightening
power rest upon those who teach and those who are taught, that they
may "seek learning, even by study and also by faith."[1]

Bless us, O Lord, that we may "teach one another the doctrine of
the kingdom,"[2] as thou hast commanded. May we do so with such diligence that thy holy grace shall attend, so that we may "be instructed
more perfectly in theory, in principle, in doctrine, in the law of the
gospel, in all things that pertain unto the kingdom of God."[3]

May those who teach and study in all academic fields have their souls enlightened with spiritual knowledge so they will turn to thy house for blessings and knowledge and learning that surpass all that may be found elsewhere.

NOTES
1. Doctrine and Covenants 88:118.
2. Doctrine and Covenants 88:77.
3. Doctrine and Covenants 88:78.

BLESS ALL OF THESE

Dallin H. Oaks

Excerpt from the dedicatory prayer for the
Provo City Center Temple, March 20, 2016

WE THANK THEE for all of the righteous activities and occupations Thou hast caused to be established in this blessed valley, including the educational efforts of Brigham Young University, Utah Valley University, and Thy missionary training center. We pray that Thou wilt bless all of these in their efforts to enlighten and motivate Thy children in Thy service.

Nailing
Our Colors
to the Mast

Jeffrey R. Holland

* *BYU Devotional Address, September 10, 1985*

INTRODUCTION

In this address, Jeffrey R. Holland recounted a remarkable dream that came to a discouraged and desperate Karl G. Maeser, who had tentatively decided to forsake Brigham Young Academy for greener pastures. In the dream, President Maeser foresaw the growth of the campus up onto Temple Hill. It moved him to stay and steer the academy according to principles taught by Joseph Smith and Brigham Young. Under President Maeser's helmsmanship, BYA "nailed her colors to the mast" (page 197). President Holland resolved to do the same for BYU during his time at the helm.

This talk has been excerpted; for the full text, visit speeches.byu.edu/envisioning-BYU.

*I have had a dream—I have
seen Temple Hill filled with
buildings—great temples of
learning, and I have decided
to remain and do my part.*

— Karl G. Maeser

: ❦ :

O N FOUNDERS DAY, five weeks from now, we will have a com-
memorative reopening of the Karl G. Maeser Building on this
campus. If you have not had a chance to walk to that lovely corner
of our hilltop acreage and see the spectacular job our own physical
plant and the construction companies have done with this grand old
building, please do so. It was the first building built on what an earlier
generation called Temple Hill, built when the dreams of a real university and all that it might become were *only* dreams and indeed seemed
to some only fantasies those many, many years ago. Where once only
that building alone stood on this hill, now think of nearly five hundred buildings and the absolute splendor of every one of them. Think
of the beauty and capacity and availability and cleanliness of any
one of the buildings in which we meet, including this one, and then
remember this from our struggling first president.

With nothing but makeshift facilities and depleted supplies,
President Maeser wrote:

> *I am **worn out and sick in spirit**, . . . and with all my love for
> this academy, I feel that I owe it to my very life, which is need-
> lessly wearing itself out here in an apparently hopeless task, to
> accept any change that will promise me opportunities for perma-
> nent usefulness. . . .*
>
> *[With that] he told his wife and daughter that because there
> seemed to be no real support for a school here and because he
> couldn't earn enough . . . to provide food and raiment for them and
> pay his debts he was going to accept a position at the University of
> Deseret, where he could get a regular salary and adequately pro-
> vide for his family. Accordingly his wife and daughter got things
> packed—and then sat on their trunks for [several] days, until his
> daughter finally mustered enough courage to ask her father when
> they were moving. His response . . . was, "I have changed my mind.*

[We are not moving.] *I have had a dream—I have seen Temple Hill filled with buildings—great temples of learning, and I have decided to remain and do my part."*[1]

Through the generosity of friends like Abraham O. Smoot, work eventually began for a building on University Avenue and Fifth North. Of this period Karl G. Maeser's son wrote:

While the foundation of the new building had been in course of construction, it had been a custom of [my father], *when at home on a Sabbath morning, to walk up to the grounds and stand and gaze upon the work so far done.*

Once when he took [my sister] *Eva with him they stood upon the unfinished foundation, and the child noticing some portions of the wall crumbling, remarked, "papa, do you think they will ever finish this building?"*

"My child," answered the father, "not only this building but others will stand upon this ground and not only here but also upon that hill yonder," pointing to Temple Hill. "Yes, my child, I have seen it all."[2]

The new academy building was dedicated on the day on which Karl G. Maeser was to sever his connection with the school to become the commissioner of education in Salt Lake City. There was probably never a more impressive sight in the history of the school than the triumphal march of the students up to the new building from the temporary quarters of the old ZCMI warehouse downtown. Before leaving that warehouse, Professor Maeser had called the students around him, prayed with them, and told them that if they would carry the spirit of their alma mater not only into their new school but into all their walks of life as well, the Lord would greatly multiply their joys.

Following the dedicatory prayer that day, Brother Maeser gave a short farewell address which included this simple statement of the educational philosophy at Brigham Young Academy.

When to the students, at the beginning of the experimental term, April 24, 1876, the words of the prophet Joseph Smith—that

*he taught his people correct principles and they governed themselves
accordingly—were given as the leading principles of discipline; and
the words of President Brigham Young—that neither the alphabet
nor the multiplication tables were to be taught without the Spirit
of God—were given as the mainspring of all teaching, the orientation for the course of the educational system inaugurated by the
foundation of the academy was made, **and any deviation from
it would have led to disastrous results,** and therefore, Brigham
Young Academy has nailed her colors to the mast.*[3]

In a month when we pay tribute to Karl G. Maeser, and in a year
when we take on even greater visibility as a university, I say again that
we have "nailed [our] colors to the mast." We have stated our principles of education based on the gospel of Jesus Christ, "and any
deviation from it would [lead] to disastrous results." As we take our
increasingly significant and important place *in* the world, it is absolutely imperative that we not be *of* it. We have begun a space-age
conversation with a national and international audience that earlier
generations of students and faculty would not have believed possible.
In telling that story we must not and will not forget those principles
and traditions and truths that have made Brigham Young University
what it is and that have brought us to this moment.

NOTES

1. Ernest L. Wilkinson and W. Cleon Skousen, *Brigham Young University:
A School of Destiny* (Provo: BYU Press, 1976), 84–85; emphasis in original.

2. Reinhard Maeser, quoted in Wilkinson and Skousen, *A School of
Destiny*, 118.

3. Karl G. Maeser, "Final Address" (4 January 1892), *The Normal* 1, no. 10
(15 January 1892): 82; see also Karl G. Maeser, quoted in Alma P. Burton, *Karl
G. Maeser: Mormon Educator* (Salt Lake City: Deseret Book, 1953), 54–55,
emphasis added.

The Dream Is Ours to Fulfill

Bruce C. Hafen

● *BYU University Conference Address, August 25, 1992*

INTRODUCTION

Bruce C. Hafen was provost of Brigham Young University when he gave this address. He called for "wholesighted teaching, with both eyes open," (page 209). Teachers using this method resolve the "faith-versus-reason dilemmas" not just by abstract answers but by fully integrated lives (page 205). Wholesighted teaching, according to Hafen, moves students "from dogmatism through healthy skepticism toward a balanced maturity that can tolerate ambiguity without losing the capacity for deep commitment" (page 209). He concluded his talk by telling of the desert father Abba Felix, who rebuked his followers for wanting to know the truth from wise elders but for being unwilling to live it. Smitten, they groaned, "Pray for us, abba" (page 212). Similarly, Hafen called on the campus community to heed the teachings of its inspired elders on the board of trustees and prayed that BYU might fulfill the dream of becoming "a truly great university [that is] absolutely . . . faithful to the gospel of Jesus Christ" (page 213).

This talk has been excerpted; for the full text, visit speeches.byu.edu/envisioning-BYU.

The dream…has become a consuming vision….Its name is Brigham Young University. Pray for us, abba, for the dream is ours to fulfill.

— Bruce C. Hafen

: ⚘ :

ALMA ONCE DESCRIBED Zarahemla in a way that also describes Brigham Young University: "We are thus highly favored, for we have these glad tidings [the gospel] declared unto us in all parts of our vineyard."[1] That blessing would not be possible here without the hundreds of BYU personnel who live lives of conscientious devotion to the Lord, to His Church, and to the well-being of this community. We don't begin to have the problems other large institutions have with drugs, violence, sexual harassment, dishonesty, and other threats to the workplace that are often associated with personal value systems. Yet our high expectations make it doubly tragic when one of us does disappoint our community interests.

This semester we will begin some long-term academic planning.

UNDERSTANDING THE PURPOSE OF BYU

Our first step will be a dialogue within each department and college under the direction of chairs and deans about the purpose of the university. As Paul B. Pixton has said, the people who are happiest about being at BYU are those who learn why BYU exists.[2] BYU's central mission begins with Richard L. Bushman's attitude: "I am a believer. I believe in God and Christ and want to know them. My relations with scholarship and scholars have to begin there."[3] And our relations with student activities, support services, and all else we do must also begin there. The first theme flowing from this vision is that we nurture *authentic* religion. I will return to some thoughts on that subject as my primary topic today.

Let us consider the integration of our religious and professional aspirations. When our very able committee on academic long-range planning met last fall, one person suggested that we begin by reading the teachings of the prophets about the university. Another suggested that we come to our next meeting in an attitude of fasting and prayer. In that very personal kind of mood, each group member expressed his or her impressions after reading these foundation documents. To my surprise, every person around that table expressed a variation on a single theme: We have been too reticent about the place of religion in academic life at BYU. In Marilyn Arnold's words:

> *The committee could not help wondering why, given the board's makeup and concerns and the religious devotion of nearly all members of the campus community, this matter had not been widely and vigorously discussed before. Perhaps BYU is just now reaching the maturity that allows it to move, in its quest for academic legitimacy, beyond defensiveness and imitation of established institutions. Of course, we must not relax our efforts at academic excellence, but it is time for us also to become more fully the institution envisioned by the prophets.*[4]

DEALING WITH SACRED AND SECULAR
THOUGHT SYSTEMS

The Jewish author Chaim Potok once distinguished between sacred and secular thought systems.[5] He said, "The scholar in [a] sacred system assumes that there is a design and purpose to nature," because God's spirit "hovers over all creation," giving divine origins to the premises of the sacred system.[6] Thus even the most sophisticated scholar in a sacred system faithfully transmits "inherited old and acceptable new scholarship" while respecting the established "boundaries of the system" according to a "predetermined choreography."[7] By contrast, the scholar in a secular system always probes and challenges the system's boundaries, believing "that all premises [originate] . . . with man," the exclusive focus of secular systems.[8] In secular systems, "it is man who gives, man who takes away."[9]

Today Chaim Potok sees "a boiling cauldron of colliding ideas and worldviews" that makes cultural confrontation between sacred and secular systems unavoidable.[10] He suggests four possible responses for the religious person who faces such confrontation. First, the "lockout" approach: one can simply dodge the conflict by erecting impenetrable barriers between the sacred and the secular and then remaining in just one system. Second, "compartmentalization": one creates separate categories of thought that coexist in a "tenuous peace." Third, take down all walls and allow complete "fusion" in which the sacred and secular cultures freely "feed each other," perhaps leading to a "radically new seminal culture." And fourth, "ambiguity": take down most if not all walls and accept a multitude of questions without intending to resolve them.[11]

BYU's history, purposes, and its very nature reflect from every angle what Chaim Potok calls "a sacred system of thought."[12] How then do we handle the natural confrontations between the sacred and our deep commitment to being a serious university? We reject the lockout approach that would shut our eyes to life's conflicts and realities. We are in—even though not of—the world. Yet we also cannot accept the total fusion model. Although the gospel embraces all truth, we must give priority to the truths that lead us to Christ, and we cannot allow our most sacred premises to be altered or even minimized by secularist assumptions. At the same time, we are too open to be rigid compartmentalists. So how do we view the ambiguity and uncertainty that remain? We don't fear ambiguity's questions, partly because, as John S. Tanner has said, we approach our questions from an attitude of faith.[13]

The Restoration actually provides a fifth alternative for integrating sacred and secular thought systems—the model of eternal perspective. The restored gospel of Jesus Christ is the most comprehensive explanation of life and the cosmos available to humankind. This idea is illustrated in C. Terry Warner's essay on Alma's teachings to Korihor.[14] Terry wrote that the main difference between Alma's map of the universe and Korihor's map is that Alma's map is broader. If Alma's map is represented by a ten-foot-by-ten-foot square, Korihor's map is a four-foot-by-four-foot square within Alma's larger square. Alma doesn't have the answer to every question, but he does see and accept the same scientific evidence that Korihor does. Beyond that, he also recognizes evidence of personal meaning and spiritual reality that Korihor's map by definition excludes. As William James said of this type of evidence, "The agnostic [expression] 'thou shalt not believe without coercive sensible evidence' is simply an expression . . . of private personal appetite for evidence of a certain peculiar kind."[15] Not that these limits are all bad: we really don't want science or the government to tell us the ultimate meaning of our lives—we make those choices personally, based on evidence available outside the limited scientific sphere. Thus we can integrate a secular map into the broader sacred map, but our sacred system cannot be made to fit within the smaller secular map.

BOTH EYES OPEN

Similarly, Parker J. Palmer, who recently conducted a valuable seminar for BYU faculty, believes that Western culture's vision of learning suffers from "one-eyed education,"[16] teaching the mind but not the heart. He said:

> There is an illness in our culture . . . [arising] *from our rigid separation of the visible world from the powers that undergird and animate it. . . . That separation . . .* [diminishes] *life, capping off its sources of healing, hope, and wholeness.*[17]

Parker Palmer urges us to teach with "wholesight,"[18] a complete vision of the world in which mind and heart unite "as my two eyes make one in sight," as Robert Frost put it.[19] And "the mind's vision excludes the heart, but the heart's vision can include the mind."[20] The aim of wholesighted education, anchored in a heart that guides the mind, is wholeness. In Alan F. Keele's words, "Great theology and great scholarship are not only compatible but are mutually and limitlessly illuminating."[21] Yet because Alma's vision is the broader one, the gospel should influence our view of our disciplines more than our disciplines influence our view of the gospel.

Many thoughtful Latter-day Saints have enjoyed Chaim Potok's novels because they identify with the conflicts Potok's characters face between sacred and secular systems. The gospel teaches us to take education seriously, but it also teaches us to put the kingdom of God first in our lives. I am acquainted with the spiritual and intellectual biographies of many in this BYU audience and would like to know them all. Each of us, like characters in a Potok story, could recount our personal confrontations between sacred and secular systems of thought.

My struggles were typical. I yearned to know if religious literalism was compatible with a fully breathing, stretching life of the mind. I found that the best resolutions of the faith-versus-reason dilemmas—better than any books or arguments of abstract reasoning—have come from the examples of faithful and competent teachers in my own discipline (one of whom was Dallin H. Oaks) who have answered my questions with their lives. For a generation of Latter-day Saint scientists, one of those role models was Henry Eyring. For many Latter-day Saint doctors, it is Russell M. Nelson. To know teachers such as these is to be set free from the burden—sometimes the agony—of wondering whether serious religious belief and serious professional or academic commitments can fill the same heart at the same time.

One of BYU's highest purposes is to help its students—and to help Church members everywhere—confront such questions in ways that strengthen both their minds and their hearts so they may be fully engaged as productive citizens of both society and the kingdom of God. President David O. McKay once told the BYU faculty that this "is primarily a religious institution. It was established *for the sole purpose* of associating with facts of science, art, literature, and philosophy the truths of the gospel of Jesus Christ."[22] In this vision of BYU, students of the highest potential in every discipline may model their lives after teachers here who are the Henry Eyrings and Russell Nelsons in their fields. That is far less likely at state institutions, even with an institute of religion, because—obviously with some important exceptions—the teachers there tend to be oriented primarily to *either* a sacred *or* a secular system. Thus the best way to teach young people who are struggling to find the place of a sacred system in a profane world is to offer them not just theories but teachers and classmates who have found their own wholesightedness. This opportunity is BYU's unique gift to the youth of Zion.

Spiritual lives really are at stake in resolving the root questions of faith versus reason. For that reason, the risk of confusing our students on these issues is the ugly mirror image of our unique capacity for good, as searing and destructive as our positive potential is magnificent. A valued BYU colleague who is a gifted teacher and an inspired researcher of impeccable academic achievement recently told me that increasing numbers of his students are "falling into his foxhole" seeking help for their wounded religious faith. I asked why he thought there would be more spiritual casualties now. Is the world more wicked? Do brighter students see more dilemmas? He said some of the deepest wounds are inflicted when a thoughtful student senses, even through subtle hints, that a BYU teacher she respects is cynical about the Church. That kind of wound can cut to the quick because it implies to students that the fundamental integration of faith and reason doesn't work, as if in some objective sense it *can't* work. A BYU student would never draw that conclusion from the cynicism of an agnostic professor in a state university because he knows that teacher has long been seeing with only one eye. But when someone who the student believes has spent years looking through both eyes implies that the view is darker with the sacred eye open, the message can be devastating.

THE DANGERS OF DOGMATISM AND CYNICISM

Especially perverse is the teacher who conveys cynicism about the Church as evidence of his commitment to liberal education. That stance can put out both eyes at once because it may offend believing Church members to the point that they attack liberal education as the cause of cynicism. But liberal education is an essential part of the wholesightedness we seek. Indeed, my own liberal education helps me know that cynicism is as intellectually indefensible as dogmatism. In my own student days, the BYU students who troubled me most were the shallow, religious dogmatists. Now I am just as troubled by the shallow, irreligious cynics who delight in poking fun at "Molly Mormon." The only thing that has changed is the direction of the thoughtless posturing; the superficiality has stayed the same.

Neither group has both eyes open. Why would any of us believe we serve the cause of serious education if our primary goal is nothing more than teaching students to "think otherwise" through simplistic posturing and anti-authoritarianism? As Theodore J. Marchese has said, "Beware the huckster and cynic alike."²³

Still, one faculty member has urged that we encourage students and each other to engage in public criticism of the Church because the "courage" involved in "saying unsettling things" will demonstrate that BYU's commitment to liberal education is "indeed working." This argument mistakenly assumes that secular systems are broader than sacred systems. Moreover, there is no connection at all between a superior education and such criticism. Both the educated and the uneducated may be troubled by some Church issue. But whether one expresses those troubles publicly is a function of personal judgment more than it is an expression of integrity or educational depth. It is also a function of how one understands revealed teachings about publicly challenging those we sustain as prophets. Some defend their public criticism on religious grounds, claiming they must protect the Church from its misguided leaders. The irony in that attitude can't help but convey cynicism about the divine influence in a Church based on prophetic leadership. Conscientious *private* communication may ultimately be of real help to the Church and its leaders, but *public* expression by those professing to have both eyes open may simply spray another burst of spiritual shrapnel through the ranks of trusting and vulnerable students.

Of course the premises of our sacred system—and, obviously, the premises of sound liberal education—make spiritual and intellectual freedom absolutely crucial for the development of wholesighted education. You can lead a child to a book, but you can't make her read it—much less understand it. Satan's plan to save us without agency *could not* have worked. Without free inquiry and voluntary action, no understanding, no real testimony, and no personal growth is possible. For example, after Aaron taught him the gospel, the converted Lamanite king wanted his people to embrace the gospel as he had. But instead of imposing his new convictions on his subjects, as did Constantine in the apostate era of early Christianity, the king simply asked that the missionaries be allowed to preach freely. As a result, the Lamanites who "were converted unto the Lord, never did fall away."[24] This did not mean, however, that freedom among the people of Aaron and Alma was unlimited. Korihor was initially free to preach his anti-Christian views because "there was no law against a man's belief" in Zarahemla.[25] But when his expression moved from pursuing his own beliefs to the point of "destroy[ing] the children of God,"[26] he exceeded the limits of the sacred system.

I know that some BYU students are too trusting or too reliant on authority figures, and they expect the Holy Ghost to do their thinking for them. We must rouse them from their dogmatic slumbers, teaching them to "love the Lord . . . with all [their] heart, . . . might, *mind, and strength.*"[27] They need education that liberates them from ignorance and superstition, developing the tough-minded independence on which self-reliant people and democratic societies utterly depend. Thus Alma counseled his people to "stand fast in this liberty wherewith ye have been made free" and to "trust no man to be a king over you. And also trust no one to be your teacher."[28] In other words, of course Hamlet's Ophelia should not expect someone else to tell her what she should think.[29] And beyond doing her own intellectual homework, Ophelia must also, as did Alma, "[fast] and [pray] many days *that I might know these things of myself.*"[30]

But Alma's more complete thought was "trust no one to be your teacher . . . , *except he be a man of God.*"[31] It is just as important that Ophelia trust the man or woman of God as it is that she not trust authority figures in general. The advantage of having a liberal education in a free society is that no one will tell us what to do. But the *disadvantage* is that no one will tell us what to do. The rich young ruler who approached the Savior wanted desperately to know what he should do to inherit eternal life: "Master, what shall I do?"[32] There are two very different meanings to that word, *master*. One is the master of a slave. Another is a teacher in a master-apprentice relationship. The young man approached Christ as an apprentice who fervently *needed* his master's guidance. As Michael Polanyi wrote:

> To learn by example is to submit to authority. You follow your
> master because you trust his manner of doing things. . . . [The]
> hidden rules [of his art] can be assimilated only [if the appren-
> tice] surrenders himself to that extent uncritically . . . [imitating
> the master].[33]

But how can Ophelia know what teacher—what master, in the
best sense—she should trust? The scriptural standard is "except [the
teacher is] a man [or woman] of God." Alma "consecrated . . . all their
teachers; and none were consecrated except they were just men [who]
did watch over their people, and did nourish them with . . . righteousness."[34] What an aspiration for all the consecrated people who work at
BYU, we who—in and out of the classrooms—teach some of the pur-
est and brightest young men and women in all the world. They fulfill
their dreams by coming to this oasis of learning in a spiritually parched
world, yearning to ask the young ruler's question: "What shall I do?"
And they come believing that the faculty and staff here will tell them
what to do—not only to learn to think for themselves but also what
to do to inherit eternal life: wholesighted teaching, with both eyes
open. We move them from dogmatism through healthy skepticism
toward a balanced maturity that can tolerate ambiguity without losing
the capacity for deep commitment. By example as well as by precept,
we teach how to ask good—even searching—questions, how to trust,
and how to know of ourselves. This university's vitality is a continuing
witness for the proposition that within the broad gospel framework,
robust faith and healthy skepticism are not mutually exclusive. The
chosen, consecrated men and women of God who teach and work
here live lives that make that clear.

The ultimate purpose of our integrated teaching model is to teach
our students how to live. As Parker Palmer put it, truth is "an approach
to living—not . . . [just] an approach to knowing."[35] Or as we have
recently described the purpose of the BYU Jerusalem Center, our purpose is not only to orient our students to the Holy Land but also to
orient them to the holy life. How can we do that? Each teacher, faculty, or staff member must find his or her own way, and some settings

are more natural than others for making connections that help students see how secular interests fit within the larger sacred sphere.

Of course we can't pursue excessive digressions that waste precious time in classrooms, offices, and workplaces. But many students, such as Amy Baird Miner, tell us that BYU students hunger for "life talks" as well as "grade talks" from their teachers. Joseph K. Nicholes used to love "teaching moments," those unexpected openings when a teacher, a head resident, a job supervisor, or a leader in a student ward senses an opportunity to step back from the subject at hand and open up the bigger picture of life. For example, one student will always remember how a BYU teacher talked soberly about life's larger purposes after witnessing a fatal accident on the way to class. I know a BYU professor who concluded a rigorous course on logic by telling his students that now they know the rules of logical analysis, but if they build their testimonies on these rules alone, rather than upon the Spirit of God, they are built upon the sand.

Our university courses are not Sunday School classes, but our fears about that legitimate concern can inhibit some of us more than they should. As President Spencer W. Kimball once said, "It is proper that every [BYU] professor and teacher . . . keep his subject matter bathed in the light and color of the restored gospel."[36] We must be cautious about both sentimental emotionalism at one extreme and stale academic neutrality on the other. And of course we should teach students to respect rigorous standards of evidence, but let us not neglect all "anecdotal" evidence. Every personal testimony is in a sense anecdotal, but testimonies of personal experience are among the most powerful forms of data.

THE VALUE OF SCHOLARSHIP AND RELIGIOUS LOYALTY

Another risk of integrating sacred and secular systems, especially in scholarly work, is that integrationists sometimes devalue in some lopsided way either the religious or the professional dimension. I have learned firsthand about this problem through the process of writing and publishing articles on family law in scholarly journals. In all of that work, my reasoning has implicitly proceeded from the teachings of the scriptures about marriage and family life. But my interaction with skeptical reviewers and demanding editors quickly taught me that I should avoid the ineffective approaches of shrill pro-family writers who have no idea what it means to observe rigorous research methodologies and to master the available literature. I know of no better example of meaningful scholarly integration than the work of BYU's Allen E. Bergin, whose work on the place of religious values in psychotherapy recently earned the distinguished service award from the American Psychological Association. He has learned to let his work proceed on a small, empirically based scale that reveals its own conclusions, rather than trumpeting in advance a "moral framework" that implies a preconceived dogmatism. His research speaks for itself when he uses Alma's large map rather than Korihor's small one.

Following Allen Bergin's example in selected disciplines, we should, as Clayne L. Pope has urged, "work within our disciplines with the additional light of the gospel to inform and direct our work."[37] Our audience for this integrated scholarship is not just BYU or the Church but also the entire scholarly world—if our work is rigorous enough to satisfy the highest professional standards. Adapting a phrase from James T. Burtchaell, we can contribute to society in unique and greatly needed ways when our integration is skillful enough to critique the academy from the standpoint of religion, rather than only critiquing religion from the standpoint of the academy.[38]

It isn't enough just to ask that BYU personnel avoid damaging students' religious faith in the ways described by our new academic freedom statement. When we go beyond that minimal threshold to ask whether someone has contributed enough in citizenship, teaching, and scholarship to warrant continuing faculty status or other special recognition, we look for extensive fulfillment of BYU's aspirations, not merely the absence of serious harm. The university's new policy on advancement and continuing status describes this approach.

It also matters how job applicants see these issues. I remember interviewing two well-trained applicants for the same position one day. When I asked how each one felt about the Church influence here, one said, "Oh, the Church is no problem for me. I have learned not to let it get to me." The other said, "The Church and the gospel are my whole life. That is why coming to work at BYU would fulfill my lifelong dream." The vast attitudinal difference between these people was, and should be, a major factor in deciding whom to hire. We aren't looking for people who merely tolerate our environment or who will try not to harm it; we seek believing, thoughtful people for whom this is the freest intellectual and spiritual environment in the world.

Let us consider, finally, the conditions on which our work at BYU may enjoy full access to the revealed truth and prophetic guidance that are the source of our sacred system's life and breath. One of Parker Palmer's favorite stories is about Abba Felix, one of the early Christian "desert teachers."[39]

> Some brothers . . . went to see Abba Felix, and they begged him to say a word to them. But the old man kept silence. After they had asked for a long time, he said to them, "You wish to hear a word?" They said, "Yes, abba." Then the old man said to them, "There are no more words nowadays. When the brothers used to consult the old men and when they did what was said to them, God showed them how to speak. But now, since they ask without doing that which they hear, God has withdrawn the grace of the word from the old men, and they do not find anything to say, because there are no longer any who carry their words out." Hearing this, the brothers groaned, saying, "Pray for us, abba."[40]

Abba Felix's point, says Palmer, is that "truth is evoked from the teacher by the obedience of those who listen and learn—and when that quality is lacking in students, the teacher's words are taken away."[41] Abba Felix's students had only been curious. They desired not the words of life—they wanted words that created an illusion of life while letting them avoid the responsibility of living according to truth.

This was the same condition on which Ammon taught King Lamoni: "Wilt thou hearken unto my words, if I tell thee by what power I do these things?"[42] Thus at BYU we must "hearken unto [the] words" of our all-comprehending system if we are to learn its truths and see all else in its bright light. The highest liberal arts tradition teaches a similar concept: hubris. For the ancient Greeks, no sin was greater than the intellectual pride by which the learned thought themselves wiser than divine sources.

For us, obedience to divine sources first requires that we live a gospel-worthy lifestyle. Further, because ours is a sacred system premised on divinely ordered leadership, each of us must nourish a humble willingness to follow prophetic counsel. The statement by the First Presidency and the Twelve in 1991 counseling against *any* participation in certain kinds of symposia was most unusual, yet very deliberate.[43] Because the statement is for all Church members, it is not primarily a BYU matter—but it clearly speaks to BYU people. It is written in nondirective, nonpunitive terms, but its expectations are clear to those with both eyes open.

Some Church members and leaders have wondered in recent years if BYU's increasing academic stature would develop at the expense of basic Church loyalties. I don't believe that has happened, and I don't believe it will at today's BYU. I believe with all my heart in Jeffrey R. Holland's "consuming vision . . . that we [can] be . . . a truly great university [that is] absolutely . . . faithful to the gospel of Jesus Christ."[44] But that proposition will constantly be tested, and how we are perceived on an issue as elementary as "follow the Brethren" means more than we might imagine. Tip O'Neill used to say that you find out who your friends are not by seeing who is with you when they agree with you but who is with you when they think you might be wrong. And the religious core of a sacred system just might ask its followers to trust the religious imperative even when it does not square with their own opinions.

The BYU dream will forever elude us if, as Abba Felix said, God withdraws the grace of His words from the elders because the young people no longer carry out the teachings of the elders. And even though I believe our collective religious commitment is stronger now than ever before, if a few among us create enough reason for doubt about the rest of us, that can erode our support among Church members and Church leaders enough to mortally wound our ability to pursue freely the dream of a great university in Zion. Somehow we must sense how much is at stake in how we deal with this issue. Pray for us, abba, because the dream really is ours to fulfill.

Almost exactly one hundred years ago, when the Church already had several stake academies, including Brigham Young Academy in Provo, the First Presidency released James E. Talmage from heading LDS College in Salt Lake City and assigned him to create the plans for what Talmage's biographer called "a genuine Church university."[45] Talmage was stirred to the core at "the prospect of . . . founding . . . an institution . . . that would merit recognition by the established centers of learning throughout the nation and the world. It was a dream he had cherished for many years."[46] The proposed name: Young University.[47]

Think of it: just months after the Manifesto had been issued, the Church barely rescued from the jaws of utter destruction, Utah not yet a state, and already a network of Church academies in place and those Saints in their poverty wanted to create a genuine university. This early plan was shattered by the Panic of 1893, but the dream lived on. In the 1920s and 1930s, the Church withdrew from higher education, creating a system of institutes of religion and offering to state governments all of its academies except for our very own Brigham Young Academy, which the First Presidency determined to keep in order to develop one genuine university.[48] The dream was still alive.

Sixty years later, the Lord's Church of the twenty-first century is expanding miraculously all across the globe. Never again will we see a Church-wide network of colleges, but there is still one "genuine Church university" that has demonstrated its capacity to bless and be worthy of *all* the Saints—every one who pays a dollar of tithing. Some voices in today's winds claim that BYU will never achieve intellectual respectability as long as it is controlled by the Church. But in the twenty-one years since I joined the faculty, I have watched the faculty, the staff, and the students of this university take an astonishing leap in the quality of their teaching, learning, and scholarship. I can bear firsthand witness that BYU's recent emergence onto the national and international stage is winning the honest admiration of a society desperate for educational leadership because of that society's moral decay and intellectual confusion. And this leadership role is being thrust upon the university not *in spite* of its lifeline to the Church but precisely *because* of it.

I pay tribute to the thousands of women and men in the BYU community who match and exceed their rich professional achievements with lives of uncompromising faithfulness to the gospel, offering "in sacrifice all that [they have] for the truth's sake, not even withholding [their lives]," because they seek to know the mind and do the will of God.[49]

The dream of James E. Talmage has become a consuming vision: "a truly great university [that is] absolutely . . . faithful to the gospel of Jesus Christ." Its name is Brigham Young University. Pray for us, abba, for the dream is ours to fulfill. To this end I pray, in the name of Jesus Christ, amen.

NOTES

1. Alma 13:23.

2. See Paul B. Pixton, "History Department Memo," memorandum to Brigham Young University Department of History, April 1992. Memorandum in author's possession.

3. Richard L. Bushman, BYU commencement address, 15 August 1991.

4. Marilyn Arnold, Robert H. Daines, and Dennis L. Thomson, "Summary of the Discussion of the Religious Mission of Brigham Young University," 25 November 1991. Memorandum in author's possession.

5. See Chaim Potok, "Scholars Real and Imaginary in Culture Confrontation," paper presented at the Third Annual Tanner Academy Lecture, Utah Academy of Sciences, Arts, and Letters, Utah State University, Logan, Utah, 19 May 1989.

6. Potok, "Scholars Real and Imaginary," 4.

7. Potok, "Scholars Real and Imaginary," 3.

8. Potok, "Scholars Real and Imaginary," 3.

9. Potok, "Scholars Real and Imaginary," 4.

10. Potok, "Scholars Real and Imaginary," 5.

11. Potok, "Scholars Real and Imaginary," 6.

12. Potok, "Scholars Real and Imaginary," 3.

13. See John S. Tanner, "One Step Enough," BYU devotional address, 30 June 1992.

14. See C. Terry Warner, "An Open Letter to Students: On Having Faith and Thinking for Yourself," *New Era,* November 1971.

15. William James, "Is Life Worth Living?" *Essays on Faith and Morals,* sel. Ralph Barton Perry (Cleveland: Meridian Books, World Publishing, 1967), 25.

16. Parker J. Palmer, *To Know as We Are Known: A Spirituality of Education* (San Francisco: Harper and Row, 1983), xiv; see also xi–xii.

17. Palmer, *To Know,* 10.

18. Palmer, *To Know,* xi.

19. Robert Frost, "Two Tramps in Mud Time" (1936); quoted in Palmer, *To Know,* xi.

20. Palmer, *To Know,* xii.

21. Alan F. Keele, "All Truth Circumscribed in One Great Whole," *Student Review* 6, no. 27 (24 June 1992): 4.

22. David O. McKay, "The Church University," *Messenger* 11, no. 10 (October 1937): 3; emphasis added.

23. Theodore J. Marchese, "Getting a Handle on TQM," Editorial, *Change* 24, no. 3 (May/June 1992): 4.

24. Alma 23:6.

25. Alma 30:7.

26. Alma 30:42.

27. Doctrine and Covenants 59:5; emphasis added.

28. Mosiah 23:13–14.

29. See Thomas G. Plummer, "Diagnosing and Treating the Ophelia Syndrome," BYU faculty lecture presented to Delta Phi Alpha, 5 April 1990: "Ophelia [says], 'I do not know, my lord, what I should think.' Polonius answers, 'I'll teach you. Think yourself a baby'" [William Shakespeare, *Hamlet,* act 1, scene 3, lines 104–5].

30. Alma 5:46; emphasis added.

31. Mosiah 23:14; emphasis added.

32. Mark 10:17.

33. Michael Polanyi, *Personal Knowledge: Towards a Post-Critical Philosophy* (Chicago: University of Chicago Press, 1962), 53.

34. Mosiah 23:17–18.

35. Palmer, *To Know,* 51.

36. Spencer W. Kimball, "Education for Eternity," pre-school address to BYU faculty and staff, 12 September 1967.

37. Clayne L. Pope to author, August 1992.

38. See James Tunstead Burtchaell, "The Decline and Fall of the Christian College (I)," *First Things* no. 12 (April 1991): 25.

39. Palmer, *To Know,* 41.

40. "Felix," *The Desert Christian: Sayings of the Desert Fathers: The Alphabetical Collection,* trans. Benedicta Ward (New York: Macmillan, 1975), 242; quoted in Palmer, *To Know,* 41; punctuation and capitalization modernized.

41. Palmer, *To Know,* 43.

42. Alma 18:22.

43. See "Statement on Symposia," *Ensign*, November 1991; see also "Statement," *Church News*, 31 August 1991, 3.

44. Jeffrey R. Holland, "A School in Zion," BYU annual university conference address, 22 August 1988.

45. John R. Talmage, *The Talmage Story: Life of James E. Talmage—Educator, Scientist, Apostle* (Salt Lake City: Bookcraft, 1972), 108.

46. Talmage, *Talmage Story*, 108.

47. Talmage, *Talmage Story*, 108.

48. See Harold B. Lee, "Special Committee Report," Church Board of Education (Salt Lake City: The Church of Jesus Christ of Latter-day Saints, 1964).

49. *Lectures on Faith*, comp. N. B. Lundwall (Salt Lake City: N. B. Lundwall, n.d.), 58 (6:7).

The Snow-White Birds

Boyd K. Packer

⬦ *BYU University Conference Address, August 29, 1995*

INTRODUCTION

 When he gave this talk, Boyd K. Packer had just been released as a member of the BYU Board of Trustees, having served for thirty-four years. He spoke from long experience and with a long view of the challenges that "seem to cycle back each generation" (page 230). The title comes from a dream that President George H. Brimhall shared with Horace Cummings during one such crisis in the early twentieth century—a crisis that dealt with a deliberate effort to undermine faith. (See endnotes 3 and 4 on pages 232–233 for a fuller account of the administration's concerns.) Elder Packer noted that properly blending faith and reason is a perennial challenge for each generation. In Church education, "there must [always] be a feeling and a dedication and a recognition and acceptance of the mission of our Church schools" (page 230).

This talk has been excerpted; for the full text, visit speeches.byu.edu/envisioning-BYU.

219

*May you be blessed in all that
you do, that the Spirit of the
Lord will be in your hearts,
and that you will have the
inspiration combined with
knowledge to make you equal
to the challenge of teaching the
snow-white birds who come
to you to learn how to fly.*

—Boyd K. Packer

:❧:

I GREET YOU tonight with the blessings and good wishes of the First Presidency of the Church, who serve as the officers of the board of trustees and represent them in this assignment. With the faculty, staff, and administration present, only the students are missing. It is in their interest that I have entitled my message "The Snow-White Birds."

A few days ago President Lee asked me to substitute for Elder M. Russell Ballard, who is recovering from heart surgery and is doing very well. President Lee urged me to reminisce about my years of association with Brigham Young University.

My preparation, of necessity, has been limited to small blocks of time pried open in an already solid schedule—mostly when you were asleep. I have been shaken by the thought that my presentation this evening might bring you to that same condition!

President Harold B. Lee told me once that inspiration comes easier when you can set foot on the site related to the need for it. With a very sincere desire to be guided in preparing what I should say to you, early Sunday morning, before you were about, I stood in the Maeser Building, and I found that President Lee was right!

In one sense, this is a graduation [for President Rex Lee].

In one sense, I too am graduating tonight. After thirty-four years on the board of trustees for BYU, most of it on the executive committee, I have been released.

Members of the Quorum of the Twelve will now be rotated on the board. That is as it should be, for the Twelve, under the direction of the First Presidency, are responsible to watch over and "set in order"[1] the Church in all the world.

Since the future of the Church rests with our youth and since the budget for their education is the second largest of all Church appropriations (the budget for BYU alone is in the hundreds of millions of dollars), you deserve the responsible attention of all of the Twelve. And I am sure you will have that.

It has been said that *young* men speak of the future because they have no past, and *old* men speak of the past because they have no future. Responding to President Lee's request, I will act my age and reminisce. Our first visit to this campus was 48 years ago this month. Donna and I were returning from our honeymoon. Seven years later I walked into the Maeser Building, then the administration building, to an office I was to occupy as chairman of a summer school for all seminary and institute personnel. There were problems, and so we had been called in for some reinforcement, some shaping up.

Our instructor was Elder Harold B. Lee of the Quorum of the Twelve Apostles. He invited guest lecturers. President J. Reuben Clark Jr. came more than once; President Joseph Fielding Smith, Elders Spencer W. Kimball, Mark E. Peterson, Marion G. Romney, LeGrand Richards, Delbert L. Stapley, and Richard L. Evans, President Belle S. Spafford of the Relief Society (one of the greatest women of our time), and others came. For two hours a day, five days a week, for five weeks we were taught at the feet of the apostles. The influence of those days is still evident in our lives and in Church education.

The following year, as a supervisor of seminaries and institutes, I returned to the Maeser Building. I occupied an office there until the administration moved to the newly completed Smoot Building.

In 1958, A. Theodore Tuttle, the other supervisor of seminaries, was called as a member of the First Council of the Seventy.

In October 1961, I was called as an assistant to the Twelve. One of my first assignments was to the Church Board of Education, the BYU Board of Trustees, and the executive committee.

I can remember Presidents Franklin S. Harris, Howard McDonald, and Acting President Christen Jensen. I have had a close association with Presidents Wilkinson, Oaks, Holland, and Lee.

I remember as well Sunday, January 8, 1956. To understand why that is memorable to me, we must go back to 1910.

George Brimhall, having already served nineteen years as president of BYU, determined to establish a recognized teachers college. He had hired three professors: one with a master's degree from

Harvard, one with a doctorate from Cornell, and the other with a doctorate from Chicago. They hoped to transform the college into a full-fledged university. They determined that practicality and religion, which had characterized the school, must now give way to more intellectual and scientific philosophies.

The professors held that "the fundamentals of religion could and must be investigated by extending the [empirical] method into the spiritual realm," and they "considered evolution to be a basic, spiritual principle through which the divinity in nature expressed itself."[2] The faculty sided with the new professors and the students rallied to them.

Horace Cummings, superintendent of Church schools, became concerned because they were "applying the evolutionary theory and other philosophical hypotheses to principles of the gospel and to the teachings of the Church in such a way as to disturb, if not destroy, the faith of the pupils," and he wrote, "Many stake presidents, some of our leading principals and teachers, and leading men who are friends of our schools have expressed deep anxiety to me about this matter."[3]

Superintendent Cummings reported to the board that

> *1. The teachers were following the "higher criticism". . . , treating the Bible as "a collection of myths, folk-lore, dramas, literary productions, history and some inspiration."*
>
> *2. They rejected the flood, the confusion of tongues, the miracle of the Red Sea, and the temptation of Christ as real phenomena.*
>
> *3. They said John the Revelator was not translated but died in the year A.D. 96.*
>
> *4. "The theory of evolution is treated as a demonstrated law and their applications of it to gospel truths give rise to many curious and conflicting explanations of scripture."*
>
> *5. The teachers carried philosophical ideas too far: (1) "They believed sinners should be pitied and enlightened rather than blamed or punished," (2) and they believed that "we should never agree. God never made two things alike. Only by taking different views of a thing can its real truth be seen."*
>
> *6. . . . .*
>
> *7. The professors taught that "all truths change as we change. Nothing is fixed or reliable."*

8. *They also taught that "Visions and revelations are mental suggestions. The objective reality of the presence of the Father and the Son, in Joseph Smith's first vision, is questioned."*[4]

Superintendent Cummings concluded his report by saying that the professors "seem to feel that they have a mission to protect the young from the errors of their parents."[5]

President Brimhall himself defended the professors—that is, until some students "frankly told him they had quit praying because they learned in school there was no real God to hear them."[6]

Shortly thereafter President Brimhall had a dream.

He saw several of the BYU professors standing around a peculiar machine on the campus. When one of them touched a spring a baited fish hook attached to a long thin wire rose rapidly into the air. . . .

Casting his eyes around the sky he [President Brimhall] discovered a flock of snow-white birds circling among the clouds and disporting themselves in the sky, seemingly very happy. Presently one of them, seeing the bait on the hook, darted toward it and grabbed it. Instantly one of the professors on the ground touched a spring in the machine, and the bird was rapidly hauled down to the earth.

On reaching the ground the bird proved to be a BYU student, clad in an ancient Greek costume, and was directed to join a group of other students who had been brought down in a similar manner. Brother Brimhall walked over to them, and noticing that all of them looked very sad, discouraged and downcast, he asked them:

"Why, students, what on earth makes you so sad and downhearted?"

"Alas, we can never fly again!" they replied with a sigh and a sad shake of the head.

Their Greek philosophy had tied them to the earth. They could believe only what they could demonstrate in the laboratory. Their prayers could go no higher than the ceiling. They could see no heaven—no hereafter.[7]

Now deeply embarrassed by the controversy and caught between opposing factions, President Brimhall at first attempted to be conciliatory. He said, "I have been hoping for a year or two past that harmony could be secured by waiting, but the delays have been fraught with increased danger."[8] When an exercise in *administrative diplomacy* suddenly became an *issue of faith,* President Brimhall acted.

And now to Sunday, January 8, 1956. President David O. McKay came to Brigham City to dedicate a chapel built for students of the Intermountain Indian School. I stood next to him to introduce those who came forward to shake his hand.

A very old man, a stranger to me, came forward on the arm of his daughter. He had come some distance to speak to President McKay. It was impossible for me not to hear their conversation. He gave President McKay his name and said that many years ago he had taught at BYU. President McKay said, "Yes, I know who you are." Tears came as the old man spoke sorrowfully about the burden he had carried for years. President McKay was very tender in consoling him. "I know your heart," he said. That old man was one of the three professors who had been hired by President Brimhall in 1910.

In 1966, BYU underwent an accrediting evaluation. The evaluation of the College of Religion by two clergymen from differing faiths was thought to offer a fresh insight into the role of religion at BYU.

These two "outsiders" expressed concern over the intellectual climate and the "revelational and authoritarian approach to knowledge." They recommended that, for the purpose of intellectual ferment and free inquiry at BYU, the university should have one or two atheists on the faculty.

President Wilkinson wrote a response to the accreditation report and asked for corrections. He pointed out that "there were no limitations on teaching about these philosophies, but there were cautions about advocating them!"

Although the chairman of the commission invited a response to President Wilkinson's letter, none was ever received.

Perhaps the answer came from the 1976 Accreditation Committee. They explained in the introduction of their report:

*Institutional evaluation, as practiced by the Commission on Colleges, begins with an institution's definition of **its own nature and purposes;** and a declaration of **its goals and objectives** pursuant upon that definition. The institution is then evaluated, essentially in **its own terms,** from the point of view of how well it appears to be living up to **its own self-definition;** and how well its goals and objectives fit that definition, as well as the extent to which they appear to be carried out and achieved in practice.*[9]

That 1976 accreditation report was highly favorable. They found BYU "to be a vibrant and vital institution of genuine university caliber."[10]

Perhaps young men do speak of the future because they have no past, and old men of the past because they have no future. However, there are fifteen old men whose very lives are focused on the future. They are called, sustained, and ordained as prophets, seers, and revelators. It is their right to see as seers see; it is their obligation to counsel and to warn.

Immediately ahead is the appointment of a new president of BYU. A search committee has been appointed. Elder L. Tom Perry of the Quorum of the Twelve has been named chairman of that committee. Members of the committee are Elders M. Russell Ballard and Henry B. Eyring of the Quorum of the Twelve Apostles, Presiding Bishop Merrill Bateman, and President Elaine Jack of the Relief Society.

They are now at work. The appointment of the next president of Brigham Young University is a crucial one. During the next ten years, 59 percent of the faculty will retire. That comes about because of the enormous growth during the Wilkinson years. Imagine a 60 percent turnover in faculty!

The board has long since charged the administration to refine the hiring process to ensure that those who will come to replace you will be of the same quality of worthiness, spirit, and professional competency as you were at the beginning of your careers.

It is not always possible to give the watch care that you deserve. When things come to us a piece at a time, without an explanation of how they fit together, we may fail to see overall changes that are taking place.

Several years ago, the then president of the Relief Society asked why the name of one of the colleges at BYU was changed. It concerned her. She had watched the establishment of the College of Family Living, a decision that was far ahead of its time. The Joseph F. Smith Family Living Center, one of the largest buildings on campus at the time, was built to house the college. BYU stood unique in all the world in organizing such a college.

Why, she asked, did they change the name of the College of Family, Home, and Social Sciences? Her concern was that family would be lost to *social* and to *science.* The names of the courses were changed, things were shifted about, and their objectives shifted toward the professional and theoretical.

I thought that the Relief Society president asked a very insightful question, and I shared her concern. She was told that, since there was no counterpart in other universities to a college that concentrated on the family, there were academic reasons for the changes.

When researchers are too focused on what *is,* they may lose sight of what *ought* to be. A kitchen then may be regarded as a research lab, and a family as any group of unrelated people who spend the night under the same roof—defined that way because experts in the world convince the government that it is supposed to be that way.

Has something like that happened in the other colleges as well? Is the teaching of religion given a preeminent place, and are those who teach religion full-time recognized for the vital contribution they make to every other discipline? Has there been a drift in the College of Education? Has the responsibility to prepare teachers been divided up and parceled out and lost? Have words such as *training, instruction,* and *values* been brushed aside in favor of loftier theoretical and intellectual considerations? Consider these lines:

Today a professor in a garden relaxing
Like Plato of old in the academe shade
Spoke out in a manner I never had heard him
And this is one of the things that he said:

Suppose that we state as a tenet of wisdom
That knowledge is not for delight of the mind
Nor an end in itself, but a packet of treasure
To hold and employ for the good of mankind.

A torch or a candle is barren of meaning
Except it give light to men as they climb,
And thesis and tomes are but impotent jumble
Unless they are tools in the building of time.

We scholars toil on with the zeal of a miner
For nuggets and nuggets and one nugget more,
But scholars are needed to study the uses
Of all the great mass of data and lore.
And truly our tireless and endless researches
Need yoking with man's daily problems and strife,
For truth and beauty and virtue have value
Confirmed by their uses in practical life.
[Anonymous]

If students are going to partake of the fruit that is "desirable to make one happy," yeah, "desirable above all other fruit,"[11] which Lehi saw in his vision, they had better have their ladder leaning against the right tree. And they had better hold onto the iron rod while they are working their way toward it.

Now, in an absolutely remarkable consensus, leaders in politics, government, law enforcement, medicine, social agencies, and the courts recognize that the breakdown of the family is the most dangerous and frightening development of our time, perhaps in all human history. They are casting around for answers.

There is a desperate need for stable families and teachers who know how to teach values. Were we not better equipped a generation ago to produce them? Have some among us measured themselves against the world and its sophisticated intellectual standard? Have they "cast their eyes about as if they were ashamed"[12] and let go of the iron rod of Lehi's vision?

The prophet Jacob spoke of wasting one's time by following those who, "when they are learned they think they are wise." "To be learned is good," he further said, "*if* they hearken unto the counsels of God."[13]

Your faculty committees are now at work on the self-evaluation of the university. We have heard good reports of their progress. Those committees might well look thoughtfully and long and prayerfully at these issues.

Surely you will remember that the board of trustees has directed that in order to contribute to the central mission of the Church, "BYU is a Church-related [and I might say parenthetically totally owned], very large, national, academically selective, teaching-oriented, undergraduate university offering both liberal arts and occupational degrees, with sufficiently strong graduate programs and research work to be a major university, but insufficient sponsored research and academic doctoral programs to be a graduate *research* institution."[14]

Let them honor this direction from the minutes of the board of trustees: "Boards make policy and administrators implement policy.

"Boards must be informed of *all* proposed changes in basic *programs* and *key personnel* in order to achieve better understanding with the administrators."[15]

Your committee, indeed all of you, would do well to read carefully Jacob's parable of the olive vineyard in the Book of Mormon. You might stand, as the Lord of the vineyard did, and weep when he saw that some branches "grew faster than the strength of the roots, taking strength unto themselves."[16] You might ask with him, as we have asked, "What could I have done more in my vineyard? Have I slackened mine hand, that I have not nourished it?"[17] And yet some branches bring forth bitter fruit. And you might do as the lord of the vineyard did and as Brother Brimhall did. They pruned out those branches that brought forth bitter fruit and grafted in cuttings from the nether most part of the vineyard.

And by so doing, "the Lord of the vineyard had preserved unto himself the natural fruit, which was most precious unto him from the beginning."[18]

Now I must speak of the snow-white birds that Brother Brimhall saw in his dream or vision. I say *vision* because another old man, Lehi, told his son Nephi, "Behold, I have dreamed a dream; or, in other words, I have seen a vision."[19]

They need our help, these snow-white birds who now must fly in an atmosphere that grows ever darker with pollution. It is harder now for them to keep their wings from being soiled or their flight feathers from being pulled out.

The troubles that beset President Brimhall were hardly new. Paul told Timothy that, even in that day, they were of ancient origin:

"As Jannes and Jambres withstood Moses," he told Timothy, "so do these also resist the truth: men of corrupt minds, reprobate concerning the faith."[20]

Paul prophesied plainly that those challenges would face us in the last days. They seem to cycle back each generation. They emerged in the early '30s. The Brethren called all of the teachers of religion together for a summer school at Aspen Grove. President J. Reuben Clark Jr., speaking for the First Presidency, delivered the landmark address "The Charted Course of the Church in Education" (1938). That address should be read by every one of you every year. It is insightful; it is profound; it is prophetic; it is scripture.

That opposition emerged again in the institutes of religion in the early '50s, and the Brethren called the summer session of which I spoke earlier, with Elder Harold B. Lee of the Twelve as our teacher.

We need to be alert today. Although there are too many now in our schools for us to call all of you together, here at BYU much is being done to reaffirm standards. You yourselves have helped refine the credentials for one who will influence these snow-white birds of ours. That standard is temple worthiness, with a recommend in hand for members and a respect for our standards by those who are not.

But that is not all. There must be a feeling and a dedication and a recognition and acceptance of the mission of our Church schools. Those standards will and must be upheld. The largest block of the tithing funds spent at BYU goes for teaching salaries. We cannot justify spending the widow's mite on one who will not observe either the letter or the spirit of the contract he or she has signed. Every department chair, every director, every dean and administrator has a sacred obligation to assure that no one under their care will pull the snow-white birds from the sky or cause even one to say, "Alas, we can never fly again!" or to "believe only what could be demonstrated in a laboratory" or to think that "their prayer could go no higher than the ceiling, or to see no heaven—no hereafter."

We expect no more of anyone than that you live up to the contract you have signed. We will accept no less of you. The standards of the accreditation agencies expect no less of us. It is a matter of trust, for we are trustees.

I have said much about teachers. Many of you look after housing and food services or maintain the libraries, the museums, or the sports fields or keep the records, protect law and order and safety, service equipment, keep up the campus, publish materials, manage the finances, and a hundred other things. Without you this institution would come apart in a day. You are absolutely vital to the mission of Brigham Young University.

Your obligation to maintain standards is no less, nor will your spiritual rewards fall one bit below those who are more visible in teaching and in administration.

All of you, together with the priesthood and auxiliary leaders from the community who devote themselves to these snow-white birds of ours, are an example, an ensign to the whole Church and to the world. The quality of your scholarship is unsurpassed, your service and dedication a miracle in itself. There is not now, nor has there ever been, anything that can compare with you. Much in the future of the restored Church depends on you. Your greater mission lies ahead.

The prophet Isaiah said:

> He giveth power to the faint; and to them that have no might he increaseth strength.
> Even the youths shall faint and be weary, and the young men shall utterly fall:
> But they that wait upon the Lord shall renew their strength; they shall mount up with wings as eagles; they shall run, and not be weary; and they shall walk, and not faint.[21]

President Brigham Young told Karl G. Maeser: "I want you to remember that you ought not to teach even the alphabet or the multiplication tables without the Spirit of God. That is all. God bless you. Good-bye."[22]

Now I would, as one standing among those who hold the keys, do as President Young did, and that is invoke a blessing. I invoke the blessings of the Lord upon you, as teachers, as administrators, as members of the staff, as husbands and wives, brothers and sisters, parents and grandparents. May you be blessed in all that you do, that the Spirit of the Lord will be in your hearts, and that you will have the inspiration combined with knowledge to make you equal to the challenge of teaching the snow-white birds who come to you to learn how to fly. I say this in the name of Jesus Christ, amen.

NOTES

1. Doctrine and Covenants 107:58.

2. Ernest L. Wilkinson, ed., *Brigham Young University: The First One Hundred Years*, 4 vols. (Provo: BYU Press, 1975), 1:415.

3. Wilkinson, *Years*, 1:419. Cummings's report detailed that, in addition to teaching evolution, these professors also taught the following:

> *Miracles are mostly fables or accounts of natural events recorded by simple people who injected the miraculous element into them, as most ignorant people do when things, strange to them, occur. . . .*
>
> *. . . Sin is ignorance—education or knowledge, is salvation. . . . Ordinances may be helpful props to weak mortals, but knowledge is the only essential. . . .*
>
> *. . . Memory gems are immoral, since fixing the words fixes the thought and prevents growth. I was told that one teacher, before his class, thanked God he could not repeat on[e] of the Articles of Faith and another took his children out of Primary Association because they were taught to memorize. . . .*
>
> *. . . As we grow or change our attitude toward any truth, that truth changes. . . .*
>
> *. . . To get the real truth in any vision or revelation, modern as well as ancient, the mental and physical condition of the prophet receiving it must be known. After eliminating the personal equation, the remainder may be recognized as inspiration or divine.* [Report of General Superintendent Horace H. Cummings to President Joseph F. Smith and Members of

the General Church Board of Education, January 21, 1911, Brigham Young University Archives, Provo, Utah, 1–2]

Moreover, Cummings reported:

> ... *While these teachers extol the living oracles, it came to me from several sources that if their teachings are to be investigated they will demand that the ones who do the investigating shall be men of the same learning as themselves; none others could understand them and do them justice....*
> ... *Faith now seems to be regarded with pity as a superstition and is not a characteristic of the intellectually trained.* [Report of Cummings to Smith, 3]

4. Wilkinson, *Years*, 1:423. Cummings also confirmed:

> *These teachers have been warned by the presidency of the school and by myself, and even pleaded with, for the sake of the school, not to press their views with so much vigor. Even if they were right, conditions are not suitable; but their zeal overcomes all counsel and they seem even more determined, if not defiant, in pushing their beliefs upon the students.* [Report of Cummings to Smith, 4]

5. Wilkinson, *Years*, 1:423.
6. Wilkinson, *Years*, 1:421.
7. Wilkinson, *Years*, 1:421–22.
8. Wilkinson, *Years*, 1:430.
9. Wilkinson, *Years*, 4:112; emphasis added.
10. Wilkinson, *Years*, 4:113.
11. 1 Nephi 8:10, 12.
12. 1 Nephi 8:25.
13. 2 Nephi 9:28–29; emphasis added.
14. Adopted by Board of Trustees, June 1990; emphasis added.
15. Executive Meeting Minutes, April 27, 1982; emphasis added.
16. Jacob 5:48.
17. Jacob 5:47.
18. Jacob 5:74.
19. 1 Nephi 8:2.
20. 2 Timothy 3:8.
21. Isaiah 40:29–31.
22. Reinhard Maeser, *Karl G. Maeser: A Biography by His Son* (Provo: Brigham Young University, 1928), 79.

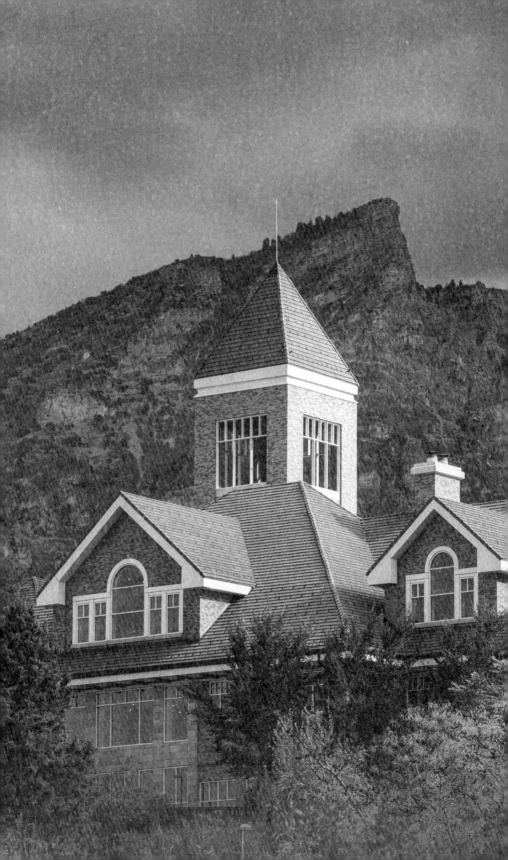

A House
of Dreams

John S. Tanner

◆ *BYU University Conference Address, August 28, 2007*

INTRODUCTION

John S. Tanner was academic vice president when he gave this address. In it, he argued that BYU is not only "built of brick and mortar" but of "dreams and ideals" (page 237). He recounted many inspired dreams that had come to BYU's leaders, analyzing in particular how BYU was doing in realizing President Kimball's vision for BYU in "Education for Eternity" (pages 159–184), which had been delivered forty years before.

This talk has been excerpted; for the full text, visit speeches.byu.edu/envisioning-BYU.

The lofty dream of BYU provides no occasion for pride or smug self-congratulation— only a clear call to try humbly to be the best we can be. We are indeed blessed to work and teach in a house of dreams.

—John S. Tanner

: ❦ :

Byu is built of brick and mortar. It comprises libraries and labora-tories, classrooms and cafeterias, well-groomed grounds and clut-tered faculty offices. It is built of impressive financial resources and of remarkable human capital. But, above all, BYU is and ever has been built of dreams and ideals. Our house of learning is also a house of dreams.

In the early days of Brigham Young Academy, the building that housed the school burnt to the ground. Many thought the fire signaled the end of the academy. Reed Smoot lamented to Karl G. Maeser that the school had been destroyed. But Brother Maeser knew better.

> *On Sunday, January 27, 1884, flames erupted from the second floor of the building. The cause of the fire was never determined, but it didn't matter. Provo had no fire department and the acad-emy had no insurance. Townspeople rushed to form a bucket bri-gade, but their efforts were futile. They removed what books and furniture they could, then they just stood and watched the building burn. Reed Smoot, one of the school's first 29 students, was among them. He would later become a U.S. senator and an apostle of the Lord. He approached Karl Maeser grief-stricken that the academy had burned down. But Karl set his jaw. "No! Fire has destroyed the house, but the academy lives on."[1]*

Brother Maeser knew that BYU, like Zion, exists as an idea, an aspiration, and indeed a prophetic injunction to "seek learning, even by study and also by faith"[2] and to "not . . . teach even the alphabet or the multiplication tables without the Spirit of God."[3] Such ideals are hardy; fire cannot destroy them, for they reside not in buildings alone but in the minds and hearts of the Latter-day Saints.

Even so, it took a prophetic dream regarding BYU's future to persuade Brother Maeser to stay here during those difficult days and years that followed the fire.

> *Nevertheless, despite Karl's determination, the next eight years were dark indeed. The school occupied several temporary buildings, including the Smoot Drugstore, and finally settled into a warehouse leased from ZCMI. But facilities were makeshift and supplies depleted. Karl struggled to pay the rent. At first the faculty were fiercely loyal, but then their families began going hungry. There was talk of closing the school. Even Karl himself wrote of giving up the cause: "I am **worn out and sick in spirit,** . . . and with all my love for this academy, I feel that I owe it to my very life, which is needlessly wearing itself out here in an apparently hopeless task, to accept any change that will promise me opportunities for permanent usefulness."*
>
> *With that he told his wife and his daughter that because there seemed to be no real support or future for a school here, he was going to accept a position at the University of Deseret, where he could get a regular salary and at least adequately provide for his family. Accordingly, his wife and daughter got things packed and then sat on their trunks for several days, until his daughter finally mustered enough courage to ask her father when they were moving. His response was: "I have changed my mind. I have had a dream—I have seen Temple Hill filled with buildings—great temples of learning, and I have decided to remain and do my part."*[4]

Such divinely sent dreams have punctuated our history, and the dream that BYU will become in time a great Latter-day Saint university if it remains true to its mission is woven throughout our institutional history. This dream preceded us. It overarches our current imperfect attempts to realize it. And it will outlast our brief contribution to it. Though all else changes, this dream endures. As Karl G. Maeser observed near the end of his tenure here:

> *Amid the ever-changing scenes of development which Brigham Young Academy has passed through, whether holding forth in one*

single room under makeshift arrangements, or enjoying the ben-
efits of more suitable facilities: whether in rented premises . . . , or
in her own palatial habitation; . . . there must go through it all, . . .
"one thing constant": the spirit of the latter-day work. As long as
this principle shall be the mainspring of all her labors, whether
in teaching the alphabet or the multiplication tables, or unfold-
ing the advanced truths of science and art, the future of Brigham
Young Academy will surpass in glory the fondest hopes of her most
ardent admirers.[5]

BYU's history abounds in such seemingly hyperbolic, visionary statements about its future. Such visionary hopes for BYU can seem daunting as well as exhilarating, especially when bogged down in the mundane tasks of grading, resource allocation, assessment, rank advancement, and the like. Yet even amid the quotidian cares and controversies that beset us, the extraordinary truth persists that great expectations envelop this university. The halls here echo with pro-phetic utterances, such as John Taylor's prophecy:

You will see the day that Zion will be as far ahead of the outside
world in everything pertaining to learning of every kind as we are
today in regard to religious matters. You mark my words, and write
them down, and see if they do not come to pass.[6]

Such statements are the stars that must guide the good ship BYU as it tacks across academic seas. Quoting Carl Schurz:

Ideals are like stars; you will not succeed in touching them
with your hands. But like the seafaring man on the desert of waters,
you choose them as your guides, and following them you will reach
your destiny.[7]

Over the years thousands of individuals have contributed to the dream of BYU. Every year new students and faculty add their particu-lar hopes and dreams to our collective vision.

As important as our contributions to the dream are, it is proph-ets who have ever provided the fundamental vision that guides our course at BYU. Our theme this year comes from one such prophetic statement, a remarkable talk entitled "Education for Eternity"[8] given by then Elder Spencer W. Kimball forty years ago at an annual faculty conference just like this. Subsequently, as president of the Church, President Kimball explicitly returned to and developed themes in "Education for Eternity" for "The Second Century of Brigham Young University,"[9] delivered in 1975 for BYU's centennial, and then again in the charge given to President Holland upon his inauguration in 1980.[10] Taken together, these three visionary discourses span three BYU administrations and thirteen years. They constitute a major prophetic pronouncement upon the unfolding dream of BYU.

So on this, the fortieth anniversary of "Education for Eternity," I want to consider our current accomplishments and challenges in light of President Kimball's talks, which articulate dreams that remain ours to fulfill. In doing so I recognize, of course, that we take our direction now from our living prophet and our current board and from the president they have selected. President Kimball himself frequently reminded us of our duty to follow the directions and policies set by the prophet and board if BYU is to fulfill its mission.[11] Nothing I shall say should be interpreted to diminish our duty to look to current prophets or their right to set the course for BYU. This said, I believe President Kimball's call to excellence is consistent with President Hinckley's challenge to "be excellent" and President Samuelson's exposition of our "quest for excellence" this morning. In addition, we can learn much by reflecting on the words of a former prophet who had so much to say about BYU's mission and destiny.

Today I shall simply cherry-pick a few ideas for consideration, which for purpose of analysis I have organized under three broad areas: students, programs, and faculty.

STUDENTS

A Refining Host for Brilliant Stars

I was not here when "Education for Eternity" was given in 1967, but I have spoken with those who were. The effect was electric. It was as if

Elder Kimball lifted the veil on a destiny few had dared even to dream when he launched into the second half of his talk with these words:

> *In our world, there have risen brilliant stars in drama, music, literature, sculpture, painting, science, and all the graces. For long years I have had a vision of the BYU greatly increasing its already strong position of excellence till the eyes of all the world will be upon us.*[12]

He then proceeded to enumerate at great length the names of notable men and women whom Latter-day Saints ought to emulate. And I use *emulate* here in its root meaning: "to strive to equal *or surpass.*" President Kimball believed that Latter-day Saint artists, scholars, statesmen, and scientists ought to outdo those who lack the grand doctrines of the Restoration and whose lives are sometimes unworthy of the companionship of the Holy Ghost. He said we should seek to emulate, among others, Wagner, Verdi, Bach, Handel, Paganini, and Liszt in music; da Vinci, Raphael, Michelangelo, Rembrandt, and Thorvaldsen in art; Goethe, Shakespeare, and Shaw in letters; Lincoln in statesmanship; and Pasteur, Curie, and Einstein in science. President Kimball's words were so audacious as to seem almost unbelievable. Yet he repeated this extravagant expectation as Church president in his talk "The Second Century of Brigham Young University." He expected "brilliant stars" to arise from BYU. "This university can be the refining host for many such individuals who will touch men and women the world over long after they have left this campus."[13]

As I reread "Education for Eternity" and the now-familiar charge to become a "refining host" for "brilliant stars," it struck me that President Kimball was thinking primarily about the accomplishments of BYU students, not faculty. After all, it is our students whose achievements will bless the world "long after they have left this campus." Likewise, it is our students who make up BYU's orchestras, orchestras that President Kimball predicted will one day rival in quality the Philadelphia Orchestra and the New York Philharmonic.[14] This does not mean that President Kimball lacked high expectations for faculty scholarship and creative work, as we shall see. It does mean that he anticipated that BYU's greatest contributions will come through its students.

This fact can serve as a salutary reminder for us about the fundamental purpose of scholarship at BYU. It is not, and must never be, to satisfy our own vainglory nor to advance our own careers. Nor even is it solely to advance truth and knowledge, though this is a worthy purpose and one specifically endorsed by BYU's institutional objectives. The primary purpose for the Church's large investment in faculty scholarship and creative work at BYU is to enable us to be a refining host for our students. Hence, we must strive for excellence, as President Kimball says, "not in arrogance or pride, but in the spirit of service."[15]

Quality Teaching and Learning

President Kimball felt that "the true measure of an institution of learning [is] the impact it makes on the total lives of its students" and that BYU stood preeminent "when measured with the true measuring rod" of greatness.[16] Note that even forty years ago President Kimball adduced student outcomes as the best measure of success at BYU. He also cautioned BYU to continue to foster quality teaching and learning:

> While the discovery of new knowledge must increase, there must always be a heavy and primary emphasis on . . . quality . . . teaching at BYU. Quality teaching is a tradition never to be abandoned. It includes a quality relationship between faculty and students. . . .
> We must be certain that the lessons are not only taught but are also absorbed and learned.[17]

I think about this injunction often. I quoted it to Russ Osguthorpe when giving him his charge as director of the Center for Teaching and Learning. The center is charged to work with faculty to support quality teaching and quality learning in the spirit of President Kimball's injunction. Our students deserve quality teaching in *every* class! I am troubled when evaluations are consistently low for a course or for a teacher for years and no remedial action is taken. We can do better. We must do better than this.

John Taylor's prophecy refers to the day when Zion will lead the world "in everything pertaining to *learning*."[18] Note the emphasis on "learning." Calling attention to this phrasing, Russ Osguthorpe has suggested that there may be deeper meaning in this prophecy about BYU's destiny as a house of learning than we have heretofore considered.

PROGRAMS

Peaks and Planks

President Kimball urged BYU to become an "educational Everest."[19] He felt that, while BYU was a great university, "a much greater one it can yet become!"[20] Such aspirations for BYU to get better coincide with President Hinckley's charge for BYU to be the best it can be.

Yet neither then nor now should the need for BYU to grow in stature be confused with a mandate for BYU to grow in size. Even in 1967 there were enrollment caps. President Kimball predicted that these will actually help BYU channel "energy formerly given to growth and expansion" into "making our dreams come true."[21] The same principle holds today. If BYU is to become an educational Everest, it will not be by getting bigger but by getting better. We must do more by doing less.

The metaphor President Kimball repeatedly used for the painful work of reallocation is that of a ship that must be kept seaworthy by taking out old planks:

> *The BYU must keep its vessel seaworthy. It must take out all old planks as they decay and put in new and stronger timber in their place. It must sail on and on and on.*[22]

I have used the metaphor of pruning.[23] Whether the metaphor is planks or pruning, BYU must engage in the discipline of ongoing reallocation of resources. "These changes do not happen free of pain, challenge, and adjustment,"[24] President Kimball remarked, commending the university for its efforts to change the academic calendar, manage the curriculum, and realign disciplines.

I commend you, too, for your efforts to reallocate and focus.

Such work is not "free of pain," but, wisely done, it can produce much good. Limits force us to think seriously about what we do best and where we must do better. They force us to focus, which is the necessary prelude to developing what President Kimball called "peak[s] of educational excellence"[25] on an educational Everest.

Not an Educational Factory

President Kimball admonished, "We do not want BYU ever to become an educational factory."[26] This is another phrase that frequently comes to my mind as I observe trends at BYU and in the academy generally. The warning seems ever more timely as higher education drifts toward consumerism and commodification. Education is no mere commodity, nor are students merely consumers. President Kimball quoted President McKay, who observed that "a university is not a dictionary, a dispensary, nor is it a department store. It is . . . an exercise in thinking, preparing, and living."[27] Similarly, President Kimball observed that BYU "must concern itself with not only the dispensing of facts but with the preparation of its students to take their place in society as thinking, thoughtful, and sensitive individuals."[28]

It is difficult to resist a mass production mentality when we must teach so many students. But resist it we must. Elder Ballard forcefully admonished chairs and deans just yesterday to remember in all we do the worth of the individual. Each soul is precious. Somehow we must attend to the one while we also serve the many. As President Kimball said:

> We can do much in excellence and, at the same time, emphasize the large-scale participation of our students, whether it be in athletics or in academic events. We can bless many and give many experience, while, at the same time, we are developing the few select souls who can take us to new heights of attainment.[29]

Frankly, I do not quite know how to bless the many and the one. I am impressed by faculty who teach large sections well and somehow find a way to connect with struggling individual students. My daughter had such faculty in her introductory physiology and chemistry courses. I know of faculty who teach the masses yet still manage to know students by name and make time to meet with them individually out of class. This is truly commendable. I don't know how to solve all the problems of scale at BYU, but I'm persuaded that remembering President's Kimball's warning that BYU must never become "an educational factory" will help. We must never forget that education is "not the filling of a pail but the lighting of a fire."[30] We must never forget the one as we teach the many.

FACULTY

In Pursuit of Excellence

President Kimball held out high expectations for the faculty as scholars, teachers, and citizens. His vision admits no place for mediocrity.

> As [Latter-day Saint] *scholars you must speak with authority and excellence to your professional colleagues in the language of scholarship, and you must also be literate in the language of spiritual things.*[31]

We must be "bilingual." Religious commitments "do not excuse you from reasonable achievement in your chosen field."[32] In "pursuit of excellence" at BYU, "we must do more than ask the Lord for excellence. Perspiration must precede inspiration; there must be effort before there is excellence."[33] "We must be professional, . . . reaching out to the world of scholars . . . who share our concerns" while remaining "willing to break with the educational establishment" where it has lost its way.[34]

Likewise, as previously noted, faculty must be superb teachers. We should care deeply enough about our students to pray for them daily.[35] As those with dual citizenship in the academy and Church, we should be examples of "individuals who have blended successfully things secular and things spiritual in a way that has brought to you earned respect in both realms."[36] President Kimball spoke pointedly and at great length about our responsibility as citizens to be faithful, devout, and loyal to the Church and its leaders: "Here there should be loyalty at its ultimate best."[37]

You get the point. For President Kimball the dream requires excellence in every area of faculty responsibility.

Bathed in the Light of the Gospel

President Kimball also challenged "every professor and teacher [to] keep his subject matter bathed in the light and color of the restored gospel."[38] This challenge still needs attention. Few of us come to BYU knowing how to fulfill the prime directive issued by Brigham Young to Karl Maeser to teach our subject matters with the Spirit. Graduate school certainly does not prepare us to teach our subjects with the Spirit. It often does not prepare us to teach at all. So where do we learn, and what does it mean, anyway, to teach the alphabet and multiplication tables with the Spirit of God?

We need to mentor each other in teaching with the Spirit and have more sustained and serious conversations about this fundamental dimension of BYU.

Beyond this, however, every faculty member can do at least two simple things urged by President Kimball to fill our classrooms not just with facts but with faith and testimony: (1) We can "teach the gospel . . . by example";[39] (2) We can "grasp the opportunity occasionally to bear formal testimony of the truth"[40] in our classes. I invite all of us to put into practice this counsel this semester.

No Place for Mercenaries

Finally, let me say something about salaries and sacrifice. President Kimball is clear and direct about faculty salaries: they should be "adequate" but "incidental [to] your grand and magnificent obsession [for] the youth and their growth."[41] "This university is not the place for mercenaries,"[42] he asserted. At the same time he quoted approvingly John Taylor's statement: "Some people say, we cannot afford to pay [teachers]. You cannot afford not to pay them."[43]

We are continuing to monitor and, where possible, make adjustments to faculty salaries.

Whatever we do regarding salaries, however, we will not entirely keep up with the Joneses in the academic marketplace, especially in the full-professor ranks. Nor should we try. The spirit of sacrifice and consecration must continue to attend our employment at BYU. When I think of the sacrifices made by the founding generation of faculty, who sometimes got paid—if they were paid at all—in turnips, I am deeply grateful for the generous and stable financial support we receive. I have always felt at BYU that I am paid more than I'm worth to do things I love—like teach and learn. And I am sobered by President Kimball's prophecy that "it will take just as much sacrifice and dedication in the second century of BYU—even more than that required to begin this institution in the first place."[44] For BYU to meet this impending test, we must keep alive the spirit of sacrifice and consecration.

CONCLUSION

Let me end these remarks by recounting three remarkable visions of BYU. The first is the well-known story of Alfred Kelly, the student commencement speaker who was asked to promote a scheme to sell Upper Campus. Here is a dramatization of his remarkable vision, which altered the destiny of BYU by preserving the land on which we sit—then called Temple Hill—from being sold for a subdivision.

By 1913, a new wave of [financial] *problems was threatening the university's future. BYU faced mounting debt. Faculty salaries were so low the teachers ran farms to survive, returning home to irrigate between classes.* [Its cornerstone laid in 1907,] *the Maeser Memorial Building sat silent and unfinished for years. Finally, it seemed, the only way to finance its completion was to divide the land on Temple Hill into housing lots and sell them. A student named Alfred Kelly was selected to promote this idea during a commencement speech, but the assignment troubled him. Early one morning he walked to the top of Temple Hill to pray. What he saw that morning as he looked out across the valley left an unforgettable impression upon all who heard him relate it the day of his address, because what Kelly saw was you.*

"Gradually the morning light advanced across the valley floor toward the spot where I stood. I closed my eyes partially to the advancing light and was startled by the strange vision that seemed to appear before me. The advancing sunlight took on the appearance of people, thousands of young people who approached me, their arms laden with books. I turned around to find the area behind me illuminated as well. In that light I saw hundreds of buildings, large and beautiful temples of learning. Those young people passed by me and entered in. Then, with cheerfulness and confidence, they turned toward the east and lifted their eyes heavenward, where, again becoming part of the sunlight, they gradually disappeared from my view."

Kelly sat down to a stunned silence. Suddenly Jesse Knight leaped to his feet, pledging several thousand dollars to BYU. Others followed [suit.] Eventually, under the direction of President Joseph F. Smith, the Church assumed the school's remaining debt. Finally, the future of the university had become secure.[45]

The Lord evidently had a plan for the ground the campus now occupies—as He always had for BYU. He would not let even its leaders prevent its divine destiny. Such divine intervention on the things that matter most to the Lord is a comfort to me, knowing He can intervene to correct my lapses in judgment or vision.

Also deeply comforting to me is a less well known but equally dramatic vision that came to President John Taylor during another financial crisis in our early years. Zina P. Young Williams Card, the dean of women at Brigham Young Academy and daughter of Brigham Young, came to President Taylor very distraught because the financial troubles of the school were so severe that they threatened to close it.

After listening to Sister Williams's plea for help, President Taylor took her hand "in a fatherly way" and said:

"My dear child, I have something of importance to tell you that I know will make you happy. I have been visited by your father. He

came to me in the silence of the night clothed in brightness and,
with a face beaming with love and confidence, told me things of
great importance and, among others, that the school being taught
by Brother [Karl G.] Maeser was accepted in the heavens and was
a part of the great plan of life and salvation; . . . there was a bright
future in store . . . and that Christ Himself was directing and had a
care over this school."[46]

I earnestly hope that BYU today is still accepted in the heavens! It
is frankly astonishing to me to think that BYU has a place in the "great
plan of life." And it is deeply consoling to learn that Christ Himself
has "a care over this school." Gratefully, from time to time I have had
sacred personal experiences that have reassured me that heaven still
directs this school. These moments of grace have renewed my sense of
love and hope for BYU.

I know many of you have had similar moments of vision and grace.
These may have led you here or kindled your love for BYU and hope
for its future. Let me share one final such sacred experience. It happened to one of our faculty only weeks ago—again near the Maeser
Building, on what seems to be sacred ground. With permission, I
quote from a note the president and I received a week ago Friday from
an admired faculty colleague:

It is just about 8:30 p.m. on Friday evening. I have enjoyed
watching from my office the brief thunderstorm that passed over
campus . . . and thought I would write you a short note. I recently
met with my department chair and received my letter of appoint-
ment. This occasion always makes me feel grateful and introspective
about my weaknesses and failings.

Not too many weeks ago I was working late and left the Grant
Building to walk to my car parked by the former presidents' home.
As I left the Grant Building I walked past the Karl G. Maeser
statue. It was a beautiful night, and the Maeser Building looked
spectacular as it stood on the edge of our campus highlighted by the
lights that make it almost glow as a sort of beacon.

My wife's great-great-grandparents . . . hosted the Maeser
family during their very first months in Utah. Later, my wife's

great-grandfather . . . worked on campus and helped build the Maeser Building and initiated student employment on campus. His daughter . . . was one of the first women to receive an MA at BYU. As a result, I always feel a special feeling when I see this building because of her family connection to this place.

I do not think there was anyone nearby—it was almost 1:30 a.m.—yet I felt a presence of many people. I do not know what exactly I was experiencing, but there seemed to be other people present. Past students, faculty and staff, or future students? I do not know.

As I stopped at that very moment and looked at Karl G. Maeser, I was overcome and began to weep. I felt happy to be at BYU. I know there are many people who could replace me (someday someone will, and they will sit in my office and not even know that I ever sat there), but, for whatever reason, I am at BYU now, and I feel like I need to do better. . . .

My heart was full that night, and I feel some of that right now.[47]

May all of us be filled with a renewed sense of gratitude to be here and a determination to do better. The lofty dream of BYU provides no occasion for pride or smug self-congratulation—only a clear call to try humbly to be the best we can be. We are indeed blessed to work and teach in a house of dreams. Let us resolve to do our part to put a foundation underneath so that the dreams that have inspired generations may become realities.[48]

NOTES

1. Excerpt from DVD *Passport to Destiny*, BYU history documentary, September 2005 update; taken from Ernest L. Wilkinson and W. Cleon Skousen, *Brigham Young University: A School of Destiny* (Provo: BYU Press, 1976), 74–76.

2. Doctrine and Covenants 88:118.

3. Brigham Young, quoted in Reinhard Maeser, *Karl G. Maeser: A Biography by His Son* (Provo: Brigham Young University, 1928), 79.

4. Excerpt from DVD *Passport to Destiny*; taken from Wilkinson and Skousen, *School of Destiny*, 84–85; emphasis in original.

5. Karl G. Maeser, "History of the Academy," first Founders Day exercises, 16 October 1891, in Reinhard Maeser, *Karl G. Maeser*, 131–32.

6. John Taylor, *Journal of Discourses*, 26 vols. (London: Latter-day Saints' Book Depot, 1854–86), 21:100 (13 April 1879); quoted in Spencer W. Kimball, "The Second Century of Brigham Young University," BYU devotional address, 10 October 1975.

7. Carl Schurz, address in Faneuil Hall, Boston, 18 April 1859; quoted in Kimball, "Second Century."

8. Spencer W. Kimball, "Education for Eternity," pre-school address to faculty and staff, Brigham Young University, 12 September 1967.

9. Kimball, "The Second Century of Brigham Young University."

10. See Spencer W. Kimball, "Installation of and Charge to the President," *Inaugural Addresses*, 14 November 1980, Brigham Young University, 9–10.

11. See Kimball, "Education for Eternity," "Second Century," and "Installation of and Charge."

12. Kimball, "Education for Eternity."

13. Kimball, "Second Century."

14. See Kimball, "Education for Eternity."

15. Kimball, "Second Century."

16. Kimball, "Education for Eternity."

17. Kimball, "Second Century."

18. Taylor, *Journal of Discourses* 21:100; quoted in Kimball, "Second Century."

19. Kimball, "Second Century."

20. Kimball, "Education for Eternity."

21. Kimball, "Education for Eternity."

22. Kimball, "Education for Eternity"; cf. "Second Century."

23. John S. Tanner, "Pruning," in *Notes from an Amateur: A Disciple's Life in the Academy* (Provo: Religious Studies Center; Salt Lake City: Deseret Book, 2011), 50–2.

24. Kimball, "Second Century."

25. Kimball, "Second Century."

26. Kimball, "Second Century."

27. David O. McKay, *Gospel Ideals* (Salt Lake City: Improvement Era, 1953), 346; quoted in "Second Century."

28. Kimball, "Second Century."

29. Kimball, "Second Century."

30. Attributed to William Butler Yeats; cited in Scott Evenbeck and Sharon Hamilton, "From 'My Course' to 'Our Program,'" *Peer Review* 8, no. 3 (Summer 2006): 17.

31. Kimball, "Second Century."

32. Kimball, "Education for Eternity."

33. Kimball, "Second Century."

34. Kimball, "Second Century."

35. See Kimball, "Education for Eternity."

36. Kimball, "Education for Eternity."

37. Kimball, "Education for Eternity."

38. Kimball, "Education for Eternity."

39. Kimball, "Education for Eternity."

40. Kimball, "Education for Eternity."

41. Kimball, "Education for Eternity."

42. Kimball, "Education for Eternity."

43. Taylor, *Journal of Discourses* 24:169 (19 May 1883); quoted in Kimball, "Second Century."

44. Kimball, "Second Century."

45. Excerpt from DVD *Passport to Destiny*, BYU history documentary, September 2005 update; taken from B. F. Larsen, "Fifty Years Ago," speech given at a BYU alumni meeting, 25 May 1962, B. F. Larsen biographical file, BYU Archives, 4–5.

46. John Taylor, in Leonard J. Arrington, ed., *The Presidents of the Church* (Salt Lake City: Deseret Book, 1986), 109 ; see also Zina P. Young Williams Card, "Short Reminiscent Sketches of Karl G. Maeser," typescript, undated, Zina Presendia Young Williams Card Collection, MSS 1421, box 2, folder 20, L. Tom Perry Special Collections, Harold B. Lee Library, Brigham Young University, Provo, Utah.

47. Faculty email sent to John S. Tanner, 17 August 2007.

48. See Kimball, "Education for Eternity": "Can we not build dream castles in the air and build foundations solidly under them?"; see also Henry David Thoreau, "If you have built castles in the air, your work need not be lost; that is where they should be. Now put the foundations under them" (*Walden* [1854], Conclusion).

EDUCATION IN ZION

Education in the kingdom of God
is different because it operates on the
Zion principle of love.

— C. Terry Warner

I GET MY LIGHT
FROM GOD

Learning in the Light

John S. Tanner

• *BYU University Conference Address, August 26, 2008*

INTRODUCTION

John S. Tanner was serving as academic vice president when he delivered this address. The exhibit *Education in Zion* had just opened in the newly completed Joseph F. Smith Building. Tanner encouraged faculty to visit the exhibit, which recounts the story of education among Latter-day Saints with a focus on BYU. In a sense, it functions as a visual companion to *Envisioning BYU*. During his speech, Tanner took the faculty on a virtual tour of the exhibit. He concluded with an image from Lord of the Rings, reminding faculty that they, too, must light fires that rally those who will fight with the King when He returns. The first section of the talk, which deals primarily with administrative matters, has been omitted.

This talk has been excerpted; for the full text, visit speeches.byu.edu/envisioning-BYU.

We are light bearers
in a precious tradition
of learning in the light.

—John S. Tanner

: ✤ :

THIS PAST WEEK the university (at long last!) opened an exhibit in the Joseph F. Smith Building called *Education in Zion*. It is housed in stunning exhibit space that has not been accessible to the campus or public until now. The gallery is bathed in light, with spectacular views of the campus and mountains. [Let me] share personal reflections about learning in the light prompted by visiting this light-filled exhibit that tells the story of how the Latter-day Saints have sought to see the light of truth both by the natural light of reason and by the spiritual light of revelation. I'll give you a sort of virtual tour. You can take your own actual tours starting immediately after this meeting and thereafter on any weekday.

THE SAVIOR AS THE SOURCE OF LIGHT

When I visit the exhibit, I am reminded by its very structure that the Savior is the source of light and truth as well as the Master Teacher whose example must ever guide us here. Even the courtyard fountain consisting of water gushing from massive rocks reminds me of Christ, as does the oculus set in the exact center of the exhibit hall ceiling. Both the sunlight streaming through the oculus and all spatial relationships in the exhibit radiate from this point of light. One enters the exhibit via a circular stairway, literally climbing toward the light radiating from the oculus. As I climb up the stairs, I think of a passage from a poem by the seventeenth-century poet John Donne about his struggle to find the true church:

On a huge hill,
Cragged, and steep, Truth stands, and he that will
Reach her, about must, and about must go.[1]

257

The ascent reminds me that learning by the light of study and faith requires strenuous effort—mental and spiritual. The Lord taught Latter-day Saints this from the first. Yet too often many assume that the Lord will reveal truth merely for the asking—as if Latter-day Saints were somehow excused from the rigorous effort required of others just because we have the gospel. Not so. There must be strenuous effort. Latter-day Saint scientists, poets, composers, artists, and scholars must pay the same price as anyone else. Likewise, we are deeply indebted to those from all faiths and walks of life who have toiled away in behalf of truth and beauty. The Light of Christ is available to all people, and Latter-day Saints are expected to learn from all those who have brought light into the world. As I ascend the stairs to the gallery, this thought humbles me, inspiring gratitude and determination to work hard.

Later in the exhibit I observe replicas of textbooks used in the School of the Prophets, reminding me that even a mighty seer and translator submitted himself to the difficult discipline of language study to acquire Hebrew, German, and Greek. I am also moved by the accompanying bowl, towel, and clean linen—reminders that those who entered the School of the Prophets were to be clean. Worthiness and work: in the Lord's curriculum, these twin virtues have ever been prerequisites for learning in the light. Those who would receive light by study and faith must work and must be worthy.

As I enter the hall, I am drawn to the spectacular view of Y Mountain through a two-story glass wall and to a quiet grouping of furniture in the center of the exhibit. The furniture surrounds a small, graceful statue of Christ as shepherd, set on a table standing on a carpet designed with a vine motif. I recall President Hinckley's admonition to us, as BYU faculty, to be shepherds to our students and the Savior's injunction to graft our lives into the true vine.[2] All these elements of the main gallery—the oculus, the stairway, the carpet, the figure of Christ—attest to the centrality of the Savior in the Latter-day Saint quest to learn in the light.

LIGHT FROM TEMPLES AND TOWERING FOUNDERS

Dominating the exhibits in the side halls are two huge murals facing each other: one depicting the Kirtland Temple and the other illustrating Brigham Young Academy and the Maeser Building. These murals introduce the respective themes in the south and north wings. The south wing recounts the story of establishing schools in Zion— starting from the Midwest through the migration of the Saints to these mountains—while the north-wing mural tells of the rise of Brigham Young Academy and the early history of BYU. Seeing the murals together, facing each other, causes me to contemplate the relationship between Latter-day Saint temples and schools. The Kirtland Temple was used as a school and is specifically referred to in scripture as "a house of learning."[3] Likewise, the Academy buildings and the Maeser Building, along with other campus edifices, were regularly referred to in our early days as "temples of learning." There are, and ought to be, deep continuities between these houses of learning—Latter-day Saint temples and Church universities. Note that the Church has always located its colleges and universities near a temple. May the day never come when it appears oxymoronic to think of BYU as a temple of learning bearing a familial resemblance to Latter-day Saint temples.

Reflecting on the relationship between temples and the university, I recall a lesson learned through a sacred experience many years ago when I was working on the academic freedom committee. We put this question to the BYU Board of Trustees: Should a temple worthiness standard apply to BYU faculty as it does for all other Church employees? The answer came back emphatically yes in spite of the complications this might create around academic freedom–related employment issues. As I pondered the answer, I had the strong spiritual impression that the Lord wanted a consecrated faculty at BYU. He was, after all, entrusting large numbers of the youth of Zion to us. Yes, He wanted faculty who would keep the Honor Code. But if they were Latter-day Saints, He wanted a consecrated faculty who had made temple covenants—the very covenants that our students are learning to make and keep. This would be critical for BYU to shine with a special light and to play a role in the ongoing rolling forth of the kingdom.

As I continue to orient myself to the exhibit space, I note that the exhibits in the south wing are introduced by a display about Joseph Smith as God's student while the north wing features a display on Karl G. Maeser. By implication, the stories told in each wing seem to be part of the long shadow of these towering founding figures. Their influence on Church education continues to unfold. This reminds me that the history of education in Zion is not primarily about buildings but about people, such as Brother Joseph and Brother Maeser. Within the exhibit I discover stories, many stories, of people who have given their lives to educating Zion. I am told that these stories are not intended to idolize the founders nor to inflate their accomplishments but to make each observer feel "I can do that" and "I should do that." That is the effect on me.

LIGHT FROM OUR PIONEER HERITAGE

As I walk through the south wing, which tells of the Saints' heroic efforts to establish schools in Kirtland, Nauvoo, and the Great Basin, I am overwhelmed with the epic story of struggle and sacrifice to educate the Saints according to the pattern and principles revealed to the Prophet Joseph. It inspires me to remember the legacy of learning in the light bequeathed us by the early pioneers. After leaving the comfortable red-brick world of Nauvoo—where seemingly every home, store, and community building doubled as a school—the Saints were faced with the challenge of educating the rising generation in barren sagebrush valleys. In such circumstances, one would expect the pioneers to concentrate on mere survival. Instead, from the very first, Latter-day Saint pioneers focused their energies on culture, civilization, and education as well as on the requirements of mere subsistence. Their aim was not merely to survive but to raise up a Zion people, which meant educating and refining a rising generation. They knew, as Elder Holland put it, that

this Church is always only one generation away from extinction. . . .
All we would have to do . . . to destroy this work is stop teaching our
children for one generation.[4]

So they taught their children in the light.

They taught the gospel out of the scriptures, yes, but they also taught "out of the best books."[5] They taught "of things both in heaven and in the earth, and under the earth . . . ; [and of] wars and the perplexities of the nations."[6] They taught of "languages, tongues, and people."[7] At first they taught arithmetic and grammar in lean-to tents and around campfires, later in log homes and rudimentary schools, and eventually in impressive stake academies that rose high above treeless sagebrush valleys and red sand deserts. These academies would in time form the foundation of both the state and Church systems of higher education. Weber State, Utah State, Snow College, Dixie College, and even the University of Utah all began as Church schools.

As I take in the displays on education in pioneer Utah, I recall research that I did a few years ago for an article on Shakespeare among the early Latter-day Saints.[8] No other western pioneers were so committed to promulgating not only Shakespeare but also all the arts and sciences. Wallace Stegner, who grew up in a small frontier town on the Canadian prairie, tells of finding his family's two-volume edition of Shakespeare's collected plays tossed unceremoniously in the town dump. He ruefully saw this as a symbol of how much had to be discarded, how much left behind, to settle the West.[9]

By contrast, Latter-day Saints brought with them into the wilderness not only Shakespeare but all the best books they could carry, not to mention musical and scientific instruments. All these would be needed to build up Zion. Upon arriving in the Valley of the Great Salt Lake, the pioneers quickly formed the Deseret Musical and Dramatic Society, built the Social Hall, and later built the finest theater between the Mississippi and San Francisco. Within a few years you could see more Shakespeare in Salt Lake City than anywhere between the Mississippi and the West Coast. Moreover, virtually every Latter-day Saint village in the hinterlands had a school stocked with the *McGuffey Reader*—containing quotes from Shakespeare and other famous writers—and many towns sponsored community musical and dramatic associations. I discovered that within two years of settling Cedar City, Latter-day Saint pioneers staged *The Merchant of Venice* in a log fort using blankets for curtains—a remarkable pioneer prelude to the replica Globe Theater that now stands in the shadow of the red cliffs of the old Iron Mission. This is but one example of how seriously our forebears took the scriptural injunction to seek light and wisdom out of the best books. What would they think of our opportunities to learn in the light?

LEARNING IN THE LIGHT OF TESTIMONY

Knowing the extensive research required for me to uncover the history of Shakespeare in pioneer Utah, I am impressed by the research that informs the displays I peruse. To my knowledge, never before has the story of education in the Church been told in such a comprehensive way. Remarkably, the research, graphic designs, and artwork in the exhibit were executed largely by students. Student researchers sometimes appear in the short videos in the displays, sharing their perspectives on the topic at hand. This format works especially well for me in a video about a well-known academic freedom controversy during the Brimhall administration.[10] It is illuminating to see this controversy presented from a student point of view. The student commentators clearly sympathize with President Brimhall and with the students in the early 1900s caught up in the event—the beautiful white birds Brimhall dreamed of, lured to the ground and rendered incapable of flight. Our current students' reflections on this episode make me realize what was most at stake in the controversy. It was not simply what was being taught but whether it was being taught with testimony or in a cynical attempt to undermine faith. Then and now, BYU students expect to be taught with testimony. They can tolerate significant diversity of viewpoint if they know and feel that their professors are deeply devoted to the Lord and His Church.

This imperative to teach with testimony hasn't changed over the years. The same fundamentals apply. Students expect to be taught with testimony, no matter the subject, by faculty who are themselves happily grounded in the gospel, no matter their disciplines. Within these parameters, there is considerable room for viewpoint diversity. Walking through this display brings back memories of my days working on BYU's academic freedom statement and of reading the recent biography of Henry Eyring, whose example of integrating science and faith inspired generations of Latter-day Saints. Henry Eyring, though not a BYU faculty member, is exemplary of many faculty here who have taken seriously the integration of one's life as a scholar and saint.[11]

MAESER'S ENLIGHTENED PLAN FOR CHURCH SCHOOLS

Chief among these at BYU is Karl G. Maeser, whose influence shaped a whole generation of Latter-day Saint academics: Widtsoe, Talmage, Edwin Hinckley, Alice Louise Reynolds, and a host of others who then went on to extend the Maeser influence across the Church and the generations. The exhibit properly emphasizes Maeser's influence on others. His key contribution was imparting light to others.

I have long known that Maeser's educational philosophy included welding character and academics. I have often heard anecdotes from his life. What I did not know until visiting the exhibit is that—after receiving the famous charge from Brigham Young to teach nothing, not even the alphabet or times tables, without the Spirit of God[12]— Maeser set down his educational philosophy for Brigham Young Academy in writing, and his plan included a strong commitment to active student learning. The written plan is now lost, but the exhibitors located the desk where Maeser composed it and have sketched out what can be inferred about the contours of Maeser's plan. They wrote the following:

> *In the late spring of 1876, shortly after his arrival in Provo, Maeser received word that in a few days Brigham Young would be visiting him. President Young wanted to learn how Maeser planned to implement the charge he had given him.*
>
> *Maeser sat at his desk that night to work out his ideas. Nothing came. Through the next day and the day after, he paced his*

office and scribbled notes. The third day, in the late afternoon, he dropped, exhausted and disheartened, to his knees.

"O Father," he pleaded, "show me the way, help me to make the plans for this great work. I cannot do it of myself."

Immediately the confusion of the preceding days was lifted, and within a few hours Maeser had written out the plan for the new school. It had come to him as an answer to prayer.[13]

The model Maeser developed featured mentoring by faculty who were to be role models of academic rigor and moral rectitude. Maeser's model also featured active learning by students who were expected to take responsibility for their own education and for helping other students learn. Again the exhibitors write:

As "the guiding rule for the teacher," [Maeser] believed that "whatever can be done by the pupils, the teacher should never do himself." The system engaged the students in the Academy's daily operations, including maintaining department or classroom order, recording student performance, and mentoring younger students. Maeser instructed faculty to identify students who needed help so that competent tutors could be assigned to work with them. . . . Maeser called this the "monitorial system." It helped the students become "responsible for something outside of their own individual concerns, but . . . essential for the comfort and well-being for the whole of the little community (the school or class) of which each of them form a part."[14]

Maeser formalized student peer teaching in the following way:

Once a week, [students met in] small groups to discuss what [they had studied]. Each [discussion] group was led by an older student called a repetitor. One BYA instructor observed the effectiveness of this approach: "A free-for-all discussion now took place which did more to arouse interest and rivet conviction than ten times the amount of passive listening would have done."[15]

In the run up to this meeting, a phrase kept coming to me from section 88 of the Doctrine and Covenants: "teach one another," "teach one another," "teach one another."[16] As I learn about Maeser's system, I feel confirmed in my mind that there is more we can and should do to foster active learning. This appears to be part (albeit an all-but-forgotten part) of our institutional patrimony. In both the School of the Prophets and in Brigham Young Academy, learners were expected to teach one another. The BYA instructor said that students learned ten times as much by discussing and teaching each other than they would have learned by passive listening. Interestingly, this figure just about duplicates the findings of educational researchers who have evaluated the effectiveness of teaching others on retention rates.[17]

Now I do not regard students teaching other students, or any other mere technique for that matter, as a magic bullet for improving learning. Indeed, I have experienced some pretty ineffective classes where faculty devolved almost all responsibility for instruction to the students. Moreover, I personally still prefer to mix lecture and discussion along with other pedagogical strategies. Nor will it surprise you that, as an English teacher, one of the strategies I use is writing. I am a strong believer in requiring students to put their ideas into writing and to present them orally for class discussion and critique. Writing and discussing what one thinks—these constitute highly effective, time-tested active learning strategies. As Sir Francis Bacon said of education: "Reading maketh a full man; conference [i.e., conversation] a ready man; and writing an exact man."[18]

I know of no substitute for writing and conversation for teaching critical thinking. But I also know that I learn by teaching. I learned best how to write by teaching others to write. My understanding of literature and scriptures has been immeasurably enhanced by teaching them. And I first learned to appreciate many great books of the Western tradition and many great issues that have engaged the modern world by being invited as a senior at BYU to proctor classes in these subjects for new freshmen. We learn by teaching. It is a powerful way to capture and communicate the light. So I come away from the Maeser displays thinking about how to strengthen peer tutoring, teaching assistantships, and other opportunities for students to learn by teaching.

MENTORING: THE MEANS FOR PASSING ON THE LIGHT

The final display I want to discuss immediately follows the display on Brother Maeser. This may be my favorite room in the exhibit. It contains rotating displays of faculty and staff at BYU up through the mid-twentieth century who have augmented and transmitted the light of the Y to students and colleagues. As I peruse some of the panels in the room, I see some names that I recognize, like James Talmage, who called Karl G. Maeser "my second father,"[19] and Alice Louise Reynolds, who at first feared Maeser but with her sister later came to "love him as we have seldom loved anyone else."[20] I am reminded by these comments that *mentor* comes from the name of the surrogate father Odysseus appointed to care for his son Telemachus. To be a mentor can involve a profoundly personal and transformative relationship, comparable to that of a surrogate parent.

I also see the names of others whom I have not heard of such as Brigham Thomas Higgs, who introduced the student employment program on campus, and Delbert Brigham Brown, a custodian in the Smith Fieldhouse who became a wise counselor to hundreds of students. Delbert Brown once found a student's wallet with a risqué picture in it. When a young boy came to claim it, Brother Brown took out his own wallet and showed him pictures of his wife and daughters, encouraging the boy with a budding pornography problem to tuck these kinds of pictures into his wallet and into his mind. As I read such stories, I am reminded that many unnamed individuals have kindled the light of the Y, including administrators and staff. As Joseph B. Keeler, one of Maeser's first twenty-nine students and himself an unsung hero of our tradition, observed: "Deep down in the heart of this great school, there are noble deeds untold."[21] I reflect, with gratitude, on the noble deeds of our current staff and administrators who influence students for good. These include secretaries, counselors, bookkeepers, managers, advisors, custodians, and on and on. So many have played and do play formative roles in the lives of students. They brighten the light that emanates from the Y. As I think of this, I am filled with gratitude that the support side of BYU has embraced the "Big, Hairy, Audacious Goal" of giving up their slots to be used to hire additional faculty. This is simply unheard of in the academy, but it falls squarely within the tradition of mentoring honored in this room, which celebrates all mentors, great and small, who have made BYU what it is.

On the far wall is displayed "Mentoring: The Lifeblood of Our Tradition." The panels remind me that our initiatives in mentoring are not new. BYU has long been blessed by the likes of mentors such as Joseph K. Nicholes, who built a chemistry department of doctorally prepared faculty though he himself was prevented by circumstance from finishing his own PhD at Stanford; and by little Tommy Martin, who began his life as a coal miner in the English midlands and went on to excel as a teacher in the field of soil science. Tommy would select students of high potential and say, "Look here, young man, don't you know that you have some great intellectual possibilities?"[22] and then help them plan their careers and win fellowships. Of his former students, one hundred and fifty earned advanced degrees in agronomy[23] and seventy-five were on faculties at universities throughout the United States and Canada.[24] His students became known across the country as "the Thomas L. Martin boys."[25] Reading about Joseph Nicholes, Tommy Martin, Harvey Fletcher, Florence J. Madsen, and many others confirms that we are on the right track in pursuing a mentoring model. Mentoring is a part of our patrimony.

On the way out of the exhibit, I see video clips of current faculty discussing their experiences at the Y. One particularly touched my heart. It is Mary Farahnakian, from Theatre and Media Arts, telling how she found God at BYU. She said, "I came to BYU not knowing anything, but BYU taught me not the secular education; instead I got my spiritual life. I learned who I am. BYU gave me my God." Her story captures the experience of countless students and faculty alike, whose relationship to God has been deepened by learning in the light at BYU.

I GET MY LIGHT FROM GOD

As I walk out of the Joseph F. Smith Building and back across campus, I recall a sundial that once stood near the stairs leading down to the fieldhouse. It was a gift from the class of 1916. Engraved on one side were the words "I get my light from God." For BYU to remain true to its finest traditions, we too must get our light from God. His is the light we are instructed to hold up to the world.[26] Consequently, if BYU is to shine as a city on the hill, it must ever be with reflected glory. We must get our light from God.

Lost in these thoughts, I look up at the mountains and recall a Scouting event I participated in years ago. Scout troops from all across Utah climbed peaks with large mirrors. In the early morning light, each troop watched for a signal from a troop on another peak. When they saw the light flash, they deployed their own mirror to pass on the signal to other Scouts on other peaks. It was a thrilling sight: light flashing from peak to peak all across the state—much like the image depicted in the movie *The Return of the King,* when Pippin lights the beacon in Gondor to rally the Riders of Rohan.

Brothers and sisters, we are like those who stand upon mountain peaks, responsible for transmitting light in these last days darkening with signs of battle before the return of the King. Having seen the light from others who have scaled similar peaks, our task is to reflect light to those on the next peak—over and over, from peak to peak, across the miles and the years until the King returns. We are light bearers in a precious tradition of learning in the light.

I use the word *tradition* deliberately, keenly aware of its etymology. Tradition literally means something that is handed off, from the Latin *traditio,* "to hand over." As we have seen in the recent Olympic relay races, handoffs can be muffed. Batons are sometimes dropped, just as footballs are sometimes fumbled. So are traditions. Some deserve this fate, but others do not. It takes wisdom, attention, and deliberate effort to identify which traditions to preserve and to successfully pass them on to the next generation. The consequences of failure can be dire. Dropping the baton disqualifies the relay team; fumbling the football turns the initiative over to the opposition. Likewise, intergenerational institutions are always but one generation away from extinction. A successful intergenerational institution, like a four-hundred-meter relay team or a football team, requires good handoffs. The exhibit offers an important means to pass on the best traditions of education in Zion, to keep the flame alive that has lighted the Y over the years. We plan to build it into new faculty and new student orientations and, where appropriate, into the curriculum. I again encourage you to find time to visit the exhibit and learn about our traditions, for we are all players in handing off the BYU tradition to succeeding generations.

I don't want to muff the handoff. Not infrequently I wonder how I am doing in preserving the traditions at BYU that most deserve preservation, in casting aside unproductive traditions, and in developing new traditions consistent with our mission. Have I seen clearly what needs to be passed on, what should be developed and what should be discarded in order to burnish BYU as an institution of light? We all occupy our positions on the peaks at BYU for only a brief time. May we use our moment in the sun here at BYU to learn in the light and pass on that light to others. In the name of Jesus Christ, amen.

NOTES

1. John Donne, *Satire III,* lines 79–81.

2. See John 15:1–6.

3. Doctrine and Covenants 88:119, 109:8.

4. Jeffrey R. Holland, "That Our Children May Know," BYU Campus Education Week devotional, 25 August 1981.

5. Doctrine and Covenants 88:118.

6. Doctrine and Covenants 88:79.

7. Doctrine and Covenants 90:15.

8. See John S. Tanner, "Shakespeare Among the Saints," *Journal of Mormon History* 32, no. 1 (Spring 2006): 82–115.

9. See Wallace Stegner, "The Dump Ground," in Stegner's memoir *Wolf Willow: A History, a Story, and a Memory of the Last Plains Frontier* (New York: Viking Press, 1962), 31–36.

10. See Ernest L. Wilkinson, ed., *Brigham Young University: The First One Hundred Years,* 4 vols. (Provo: BYU Press, 1975–76), 1:412–33.

11. See Henry J. Eyring, *Mormon Scientist: The Life and Faith of Henry Eyring* (Salt Lake City: Deseret Book, 2007).

12. See Brigham Young, quoted in Reinhard Maeser, *Karl G. Maeser: A Biography by His Son* (Provo: Brigham Young University, 1928), 79.

13. Joseph F. Smith Building (JFSB) exhibit, *Educating the Soul: Our Zion Tradition of Learning and Faith,* quoting Ida Stewart Peay, "A Story Dr. Maeser Told," *Improvement Era,* January 1914, 194–95; also "That Master Teacher,"

Improvement Era, April 1952, 218; see also Alma P. Burton, *Karl G. Maeser: Mormon Educator* (Salt Lake City: Deseret Book, 1953), 29–30.

14. JFSB exhibit, quoting Karl G. Maeser, "The Monitorial System," Church School Department, *Juvenile Instructor,* 1 March 1901, 153; see also Maeser, *School and Fireside* (Salt Lake City: Skelton and Co., 1898), 272.

15. JFSB exhibit, quoting Nels L. Nelson, "Theology in Our Church Schools," *Improvement Era,* September 1900, 850.

16. Doctrine and Covenants 88: 77, 118.

17. See David A. Sousa, *How the Brain Learns: A Classroom Teacher's Guide,* 2nd ed. (Thousand Oaks, California: Corwin Press, 2001), and Melvin L. Silberman, *Active Training: A Handbook of Techniques, Designs, Case Examples, and Tips,* 3rd ed. (San Francisco: Pfeiffer, 2006).

18. Francis Bacon, "Of Studies," *Essays* (1625).

19. James E. Talmage, journal, 11 January 1893, in *Papers, 1876–1933,* James E. Talmage Collection, MSS 229, box 25, reel 2, L. Tom Perry Special Collections, Harold B. Lee Library, Brigham Young University, Provo, Utah.

20. "Autobiography of Alice Louise Reynolds to 1919," *Faculty Biographical Files (1900–2000),* UA 909, L. Tom Perry Special Collections, BYU; quoted in Amy Brown Lyman, *A Lighter of Lamps: The Life Story of Alice Louise Reynolds* (Provo: Alice Louise Reynolds Club, 1947), 16.

21. Joseph B. Keeler, in *Collection* (ca. 1840–1935), address given in honor of Susa Young Gates, undated spelling tablet manuscript, MSS 2016, box 1, folder 11, L. Tom Perry Special Collections, BYU.

22. Thomas L. Martin, *My Life Story* (s.l., n.d.), 68; in L. Tom Perry Special Collections, BYU.

23. See "Thomas L. Martin," in Jean Anne Waterstradt, ed., *They Gladly Taught: Ten BYU Professors,* 3 vols. (Provo: Brigham Young University and the Emeritus Club, 1986–88), 1:109.

24. See Leonard J. Arrington, *The Mormon Experience: A History of the Latter-day Saints* (Urbana: University of Illinois, 1992), 318.

25. See *They Gladly Taught,* 1:110.

26. See 3 Nephi 18:24.

An Education
of the Whole Soul

C. Terry Warner

❖ *BYU Devotional Address, November 11, 2008*

INTRODUCTION

C. Terry Warner gave this beautiful devotional address as he was about to retire, having served for many years at BYU. He had been chair of the philosophy department, director of the Honors Program, and dean of the College of General Studies. At the end of his career, he was the founding curator of the *Education in Zion* exhibit in the Joseph F. Smith Building. Warner's devotional provides an inspiring perspective on the university drawn from his years at BYU and his work on the exhibit. He reminds us of the vision of BYU's founders and calls on BYU to remain true to its heritage.

I have learned from the lives of our founders that this school does indeed deserve the name "A Temple of Learning." I pray this may continue to be so.

— C. Terry Warner

: 🌿 :

Across the eastern face of the new Joseph F. Smith Building, which was dedicated three years ago, runs a two-hundred-foot curved glass curtain. This curtain encloses a grand gallery on the second and third floors. In this gallery, a permanent multimedia exhibit opened its doors this fall. The exhibit is entitled *Education in Zion,* and its theme is how our Zion tradition of learning and faith has always been focused on the education of the whole soul.

For dozens of us who worked on the exhibit—all but a few were BYU students and recent graduates—this project has been like a secret passageway to a remarkable treasure. I think of it as an inheritance that we did not know was ours. We discovered this treasure in the stories of the people who founded this school. Under the guidance of God, these people created a kind of education that in certain very important ways is different from anything the world has to offer. To tell you more about this inheritance, I will share a few of their stories with you.

A CHARGE TO TEACH WITH THE SPIRIT OF GOD

At some point after the Saints had begun settling in the Mountain West, Brigham Young foresaw the need for schools that would cover the primary grades up through what we now call high school and would teach both the academic subjects and the principles of our religion.[1]

In the spring of 1876, Brigham Young called Karl G. Maeser to preside at the first of these schools, Brigham Young Academy in Provo—which, at that time, was already in its first term under the interim principal, Warren Dusenberry. During his interview with Maeser, President Young gave Maeser the now famous charge "that you ought not to teach even the alphabet or the multiplication tables without the Spirit of God."[2]

Maeser could scarcely have been better prepared for the job. He had obtained a world-class education in his native Saxony, served three missions after his conversion, and administered and taught in schools in Salt Lake City for about a decade and a half.

Maeser took over the academy at the beginning of its second term in late April. Before he left Salt Lake City for Provo, the Territorial School Association gave him a magnificent desk in recognition of his service[3]—a desk that will figure importantly in our story.

On a Friday afternoon at the end of the first week of school, Maeser received word that in three days President Young would be in Provo. The prophet wanted to see Maeser's plans for a program that would fulfill the charge to teach every subject by the Spirit of God.

So under the pressure of the prophet's pending arrival, Maeser sat at his desk through that Friday night trying to develop an educational plan that would incorporate President Young's momentous conception of the Spirit's role in true education. Nothing came. All through Saturday he worked, into the night, and then again on Sunday until the afternoon turned into evening. Finally he dropped, disheartened, to his knees, pleading, "O Father, show me the way, help me to make the plans for this great work. I cannot do it of myself."[4] Immediately the confusion of the preceding days was lifted, and within an hour or two Maeser had written out the plan for the new school. It had come to him as an answer to prayer.

Maeser's plan ingeniously worked out many ways in which the students would grow morally and spiritually in the very same educational process that developed them intellectually.[5] One of the factors that would make this process work was Maeser's determination to have the teachers do nothing that the students were able to do. Students participated in the academic planning meetings, conducted discussion sessions following the theology classes, assisted administratively, and looked out for one another in a program much like our home and visiting teaching programs today. In this school each would serve the others, and all would progress together.

This educational program became the model for a great system of Church schools, many of which were called *academies*. Over a span of more than forty years, this system produced tens of thousands of

Latter-day Saint leaders and faithful members. By and large, those who first developed the seminary and institute programs all over the world came from these schools.

I love to contemplate these two momentous steps in the development of what is today the worldwide Church Educational System of seminaries, institutes, and schools of higher education. The first of these steps was a prophet's instruction for the operation of a school he was founding, which was to give place to the Spirit of God in everything, and the second was a revelation in answer to the prayer of a very good and able servant, which that servant gratefully wrote down while sitting at the desk that he had been given for faithful service to the children of Zion.

Whatever the details of the plan Maeser recorded that day, they included the Spirit of God. As James E. Talmage wrote while still a student, "all our discipline, all our studies are conducted according to the spirit of the living God."[6] Student recollections of the period suggest that the Spirit was most noticeably manifest in the love and unity that prevailed in the school and that this love emanated especially from Brother Maeser. Many stories describe how he lifted and nurtured people. "He knew how to touch a boy's heart like no one else that I've ever known," said Bryant S. Hinckley. "I have seen men come from the farm and ranch and stay there six months and go home with an entirely new light in their eye."[7]

AN EDUCATIONAL GENEALOGY

Maeser had not always possessed this gift of love, at least not in such abundance. Apparently it came to him when President Young called him to preside at the academy. George S. Reynolds, the First Presidency's secretary, was present and said that he would never forget the Spirit that filled the office that day. Prior to his calling, Maeser had a wide reputation in Salt Lake schools for severity; for example, he once boxed young Reed Smoot on the ear for coming to school unprepared. But it was this same Reed Smoot who later, and gratefully, attended Brigham Young Academy as one of Maeser's first students and who as an older man said that Maeser's "whole nature changed" at the time of his calling.[8] Without this transformation, it is doubtful that Maeser could have instilled a nurturing spirit in his students, which surely he did. I'll tell you about a few of them.

Joseph B. Keeler, one of Maeser's first students, later managed the school's finances and physical facilities while teaching eight classes per term. He was widely known for his splendid example, for listening, and for finding ways to help students in need.[9] One day he overheard BYU's fourth president, George H. Brimhall, expel a very uncooperative repeat offender. As the student was leaving, Keeler drew him into his office in order, he said, to "take care of the details." He asked about the young man's plans, which included going into business. Then, explaining that withdrawing from school would take a few days, Keeler offered the young man work in the office "to finish out the week." The week became a month, and then more. The young man stayed in school. He graduated with honors and became an upright business-man. Years later, he attributed his "success in life to that great man."[10]

As a faculty member, Alice Louise Reynolds obtained most of her advanced education studying with some of the world's finest litera-ture teachers during leaves from her teaching position. She brought back and shared with her students, who flocked to her classes, what-ever she had discovered that had enriched her life.[11] She was a person of uncommon intellectual standards who taught her students to bring together "all the beauty and all the uplift there is in art" with "all the reverence and all the holiness and beauty there is in religion."[12] I think she was able to awaken both the faith and the intellect of her students because she had blended them so well in her own life. Similarly she could build the confidence of her students because she believed in them so much herself.

Brigham T. Higgs taught carpentry classes and supervised the school's maintenance. He was the first to hire students for this pur-pose. Though he arrived at the academy too late to work under Brother Maeser, he quickly came to exemplify the school's nurturing spirit. He would meet with the student workers daily before dawn and instruct them not only in their duties but also about the value of work and virtuous living. "Don't be a scrub,"[13] he would say, meaning someone who does less than his best. He believed a father should "be the kind of man he would be proud to have his son become."[14] Higgs would visit the students' boarding houses to make sure their living conditions were adequate and bring food to the ones who were struggling. President George H. Brimhall once said that no one had been more valuable to the university than B. T. Higgs, and a number of Higgs's students praised him as their greatest inspiration.

Partly because of the influence of these and other educational pioneers as the years rolled by, more Latter-day Saint students who went to major universities for advanced schooling stayed in the Church, and many of these returned to build up Zion, rear their own families, and become leaders among their people. Many taught in the Church's quorums, auxiliaries, and schools. Then these faithful ones' students, who were even more numerous, did the same. Each succeeding generation was better prepared academically and spiritually than its predecessors. Thus a branching, expanding, educational genealogy runs through our history as well as the history of other Church educational schools and programs. Sadly, we have records of relatively few individuals kindling in others the flame of learning, but I am sure that this lighting of others' lamps happened many thousands of times in our history and that all the stories are written in the book of life.

A ZION TRADITION OF LEARNING

The stories I have shared clearly illustrate two of the characteristics of education in the kingdom of God that make it different from anything to be found in the world.

First, as already indicated, it is an education of the whole soul. We saw in the story of Brother Maeser the limitations of a person with extraordinary talent whose development was deficient in some essential respect.

Second, if we are living as the gospel requires, when we ourselves are learning, we are unwilling to leave others behind. An essential part of our growth comes in helping others grow. And then those we help in turn help others—among them, in many instances, our own posterity. This draws us close to one another, even across generations, and we become united, a Zion people. Fundamentally, education in the kingdom of God is different because it operates on the Zion principle of love.

The Zion tradition of learning did not begin with Brigham Young and Karl G. Maeser. In this dispensation, it goes back to Joseph Smith. His was truly an education of the whole soul, divinely orchestrated. Heavenly teachers were his instructors and models.[15] His scriptural translations and revisions gave him great knowledge of God's dealings with Israel and developed his ability to obtain revelation. In the tribulations he passed through, he grew in virtue, leadership, compassion, and wisdom. God was developing not just Joseph's mind but his whole being.

Joseph also exemplified the second characteristic of a Zion education in that his constant labor was to help the Saints come to gain the same knowledge and enjoy the same holy experiences that he had obtained. He did not reserve any privileges for himself alone. The instructions for the first School of the Prophets were given by the Lord, and they are in all respects expressive of Joseph's heart. They outline the way the participants were to build each other up and thus advance together.

The school met in Kirtland in an eleven-by-fourteen-foot room above Newell Whitney's store and included the most seasoned Church leaders. They were instructed to study subjects that would develop all their gifts and talents, from the doctrines of the kingdom to the affairs of the world, so that they, like Joseph, could be prepared to help build up a Zion people. And they were told how to conduct themselves in the school, which brought a dimension to their learning and growth that otherwise would have been absent. For example, everyone was to come repentant; humble; reverent; invigorated after a good night's sleep; clean and wearing fresh clothing; fasting; free of pride, envy, and faultfinding; and bonded together by love. The learning itself was to be collaborative, with each given a chance to teach the others and then listen carefully while the others taught, so "that all may be edified of all, and that every man may have an equal privilege."[16] The pattern of their preparation and study together, which is rooted in the order of the priesthood, would enable them to grow in many directions.

You can see that in these instructions the Lord was building up His beloved servants by asking them to build up one another. Following this divine example, Joseph, Brigham Young, and their successors sought diligently to bring the kind of education that began in the School of the Prophets to as many Latter-day Saints as possible. I haven't time to speak of details, but I will just say that throughout the next century, as the Church grew, they established priesthood quorums,[17] priesthood auxiliaries, community schools, stake academies, colleges, a university, and eventually the seminaries and institutes. They kept at the work even in desperately impoverished circumstances, when many others thought education should be postponed.

They understood very clearly the urgency that Elder Jeffrey R. Holland expressed when he presided at this school in 1981. "This Church," he said, "is always only one generation away from extinction. . . . All we would have to do . . . to destroy this work is stop teaching our children for one generation."[18] It was not primarily for themselves but for the children of the future, for Zion, that these visionary leaders and their faithful associates worked so hard. There's almost nothing we can name that has absorbed as much of the latter-day prophets' attention, energy, and care as the education of this people.

A CRUCIAL TASK

You may have thought that you are here at this university to take a certain series of courses, obtain a degree, and then leave learning behind. If so, you do not fully understand. God desires the flourishing of your whole soul for the glories He has in mind for you, including an eternal family with children who will shine as jewels in His crown and yours, and that is why He intends to bless you, if you will exert yourself, with a soul-stretching education.

It is also why He has provided this school, together with all the rest of Church education. I caution you against making the mistake of supposing these resources to be merely human institutions. In 1885, when Brigham Young Academy's financial challenges were particularly trying, a faculty member, who also happened to be Brigham

Young's daughter, sought President John Taylor's help. President Taylor told her that her father, who had passed on some years before, had come to him "in the silence of the night" and said "that the school being taught by Brother Maeser was accepted in the heavens and was a part of the great plan of life and salvation; . . . and that Christ himself was directing, and had a care over this school."[19]

Brigham Young founded the academy because he was alarmed that educational institutions were rapidly forgetting their religious heritage and rearing children to embrace an increasingly secular and increasingly atheistic culture. Only a different kind of school could avoid this fate—a school in which all teaching and learning would be done by the Spirit of God. Maeser once put it this way: the new academy simply had to have "the spirit of the latter-day work" running through it "like a golden thread."[20]

Maeser's successors shared that conviction. Our fourth president, Franklin S. Harris, said at his inauguration in 1921, "There has grown out of the history of [this] institution . . . a certain fire that must be kept burning. . . . The first task of the future is to preserve . . . this spirit that comes to us from the past."[21]

This is our task also.

We should not expect this task to be easier than what the founders had to do. As in Brigham Young's time, we live surrounded by a secular culture that seems more and more threatening. I suppose that most of us unwittingly bring elements of this culture into our community of learning. We import tinges of its contempt for simple religious faith, its frivolous and often angry mental life, its demand for rights without responsibility, its tolerance for wasted time, its sickening vulgarity, its pride in gaining advantage over others, and much more. When we help or allow such attitudes to encroach upon this community, we subtly but surely lend ourselves to the devil's project of making this school over in the image of the world, which is something President Spencer W. Kimball said must not happen.[22]

We can overcome such dangers not by becoming a cultural police force but by actively building up a far better way of life. When men and women are "anxiously engaged in a good cause, and do many things of their own free will [to] bring to pass much righteousness,"[23] they make it very hard for the attitudes and habits of a carnal and violent world to get a foothold. By building others up and thus building Zion, we overcome evil with good.

I think of Florence Jepperson Madsen, who had gained great prominence as a contralto soloist in Boston and New York. When she came to BYU in 1920, she and her husband, Franklin, established a great musical tradition by hiring fine faculty and mounting splendid productions. Beyond that, she organized and directed over two thousand groups of singing mothers throughout the Church. We cannot count the students who carried their enhanced musical talents and enthusiasm wherever they went. It was said that no Latter-day Saint woman did more to bring beauty and harmony into this world.

I think of Sidney B. Sperry, who, beginning in the late 1920s, helped to pioneer the blending of scholarship with the teaching of scripture. It was a time when the faith of young Latter-day Saints was being shaken by scholars' naturalistic explanations of spiritual events recorded in the Bible. Sperry used these scholars' findings, though not their irreligious speculations, to deepen religious understanding. By this means, over the course of nearly forty years, he brought gospel scholarship into the lives of Church education teachers and students and a wide audience of Church members. Among those who learned from him were many who later shaped religious instruction in the Church Educational System.

I ask myself, what if people such as these had not built up this school and the rest of the Church Educational System? What would we be learning? Would our attitudes, aspirations, and relationships be at all different from those who are part of the secular culture around us? Would we care about God? Would we have any idea of His plan of happiness? What would we be like if the teachers of our teachers, going back very far, had not been men and women such as Karl Maeser, Alice Louise Reynolds, and Sidney Sperry? Remember, the way "to destroy this work"—and to cheat the children of the future of everything we hold dear—"is [to] stop teaching [them the gospel, our precious way of life,] for [just] one generation."

A TEMPLE OF LEARNING

Today I have spoken of the importance to us of our educational ancestors. So many of us have given this topic so little thought that I supposed it helpful to tell you that for many of us who have learned about their lives, they have become an unexpected treasure. We soon realized as we worked on the exhibit that we were not just recounting the stories of bygone men and women. We were coming to know these people, as if in person. Even across the years we could feel their influence spiritually. Their example seemed to gently pull us aside and show how we could be doing better. They became part of our work.

In the process, we sought the Lord's Spirit so that our efforts, like theirs, might enlighten, edify, and encourage others. Thus we joined our hands and hearts with theirs, and we became part of their work.

This has seemed to me a very real inheritance in Zion. We have been given a place among eternal friends who did eternal work for souls they had yet to meet. I learned from these noble people that laboring *in* Zion *for* Zion, in whatever capacity, gives us the privilege of using all our talents, gifts, and learning to build up a Zion way of living together, a holy culture, a desperately needed alternative to a perishing world! In that Zion culture, the major formative influence upon our posterity will come from well-prepared, good, and faithful people.

I have been closely associated with three great universities and can tell you that, for me, the life of learning does not get any sweeter than this. The inheritance I have described is also yours to claim if you desire.

On two high, facing walls, one on the north and the other on the south of the exhibit gallery, are two remarkable, eighteen-foot-high murals painted by one of our students. The one on the south depicts the Kirtland Temple, the first temple of the dispensation, which, like all temples, was to be a house of learning. It is labeled *The Temple, a Holy School.* The mural on the north depicts Brigham Young University in President George H. Brimhall's time, with the Academy Building in the foreground and the newly constructed Maeser Building further in the background on Temple Hill. Its title is *The School, a Temple of Learning*.

I have learned from the lives of our founders that this school does indeed deserve the name "A Temple of Learning."

I pray this may continue to be so. I bear witness in the name of Jesus Christ that the work of this university and of the entire Church Educational System is His work, for He commanded, "Feed my lambs. . . . Feed my sheep."[24] Amen.

NOTES

1. See Brigham Young Academy Deed of Trust, 16 October 1875, in *Deeds and Indentures of the Brigham Young Academy, 1872–1903*, Manuscript Collection, UA 399, L. Tom Perry Special Collections, Harold B. Lee Library, Brigham Young University, Provo, Utah; also in appendix 1 of *Brigham Young University: The First One Hundred Years* (Provo: BYU Press, 1975–76), 1:523–25.

2. Brigham Young, quoted in Reinhard Maeser, *Karl G. Maeser: A Biography by His Son* (Provo: Brigham Young University, 1928), 79; see also Karl G. Maeser, "History of the Academy," address delivered on 16 October 1891 at Brigham Young Academy's first Founders Day exercises, in *Karl G. Maeser: A Biography*, 130.

3. See Presentation, in "Local and Other Matters," *Deseret News*, 24 December 1873, 748.

4. Karl Maeser, quoted in Ida Stewart Peay, "A Story Dr. Maeser Told," *Improvement Era*, January 1914, 195; also "That Master Teacher," *Improvement Era*, April 1952, 218; see also Alma P. Burton, *Karl G. Maeser: Mormon Educator* (Salt Lake City: Deseret Book, 1953), 29–30.

5. See Karl G. Maeser, "The Monitorial System," Church School Department, *Juvenile Instructor*, 1 March 1901, 153–54. (In this reference, Maeser stated that although he called his system by the name commonly used among educators, he altered his version of the system to discourage student abuses, such as bullying and tattling, and to encourage "cultivation of a public spirit among the pupils.") See also "Brigham Young Academy of Provo," *Deseret News*, 30 January 1878, 829.

6. James E. Talmage, "Incidental Instructions," 13 October 1879, recorded by M. J. John, page 9 in *Theological References*, book 2, in *Papers, 1879*, Manuscript Collection, UA 238, L. Tom Perry Special Collections, BYU.

7. Bryant S. Hinckley, quoted in Beatrice Maeser Mitchell, page 3 of oral history interview by Hollis Scott, 29 September 1980, Manuscript Collection, UA OH 38, L. Tom Perry Special Collections, BYU.

8. Reed Smoot, BYU assembly address, autumn 1930, page 3 of typescript in *Papers, 1930, 1932*, Manuscript Collection, UA 290, L. Tom Perry Special Collections, BYU; see also Smoot, BYU Founders Day address, 17 October 1932, page 1 of typescript in *Papers, 1930, 1932*; see also Smoot, *Conference Reports of The Church of Jesus Christ of Latter-day Saints*, October 1937, 19.

9. See Amos N. Merrill, "In Remembrance of President Joseph B. Keeler," typescript, undated, 8, UA 909, L. Tom Perry Special Collections, BYU.

10. In Beulah May Keeler McAllister, "Treasured Heritage," typescript, 1958, 143–44, Joseph B. Keeler Collection, MSS 2016, L. Tom Perry Special Collections, BYU; see also Daniel M. Keeler, *Build Thee More Stately*, 1989, 324–26, MSS 2016, Joseph B. Keeler Collection, L. Tom Perry Special Collections, BYU.

11. See Alice Louise Reynolds, "Autobiography of Alice Louise Reynolds," 39 pages, BX 8670.07 R331a, L. Tom Perry Special Collections, BYU; see also Amy Brown Lyman, *A Lighter of Lamps: The Life Story of Alice Louise Reynolds* (Provo: Alice Louise Reynolds Club, 1947), 37–46.

12. Alice Louise Reynolds, in Lyman, *Lighter of Lamps*, 69.

13. See "'Don't Be a Scrub,' He Told His Boys," Church News, 13 September 1975, 16; see also B. T. Higgs, "A Talk Given by B. T. Higgs to a Group of College Students Who Are Doing Janitor Work in the Brigham Young University," 18 December 1936, Manuscript Collection, L. Tom Perry Special Collections, BYU.

14. Emma Higgs Wakefield, "Brigham Thomas Higgs—Builder of Houses and Men," *Improvement Era*, August 1940, 474.

15. See Wilford Woodruff, *Journal of Discourses*, 26 vols. (London: Latter-day Saints' Book Depot, 1854–86), 16:265 (8 October 1873); see also Alexander L. Baugh, "Parting the Veil: Joseph Smith's Seventy-Six Documented Visionary Experiences," in John W. Welch and Erick B. Carlson, eds., *Opening the Heavens: Accounts of Divine Manifestations, 1820–1844* (Provo: BYU Press, 2005), 265–326.

16. Doctrine and Covenants 88:122.

17. See William G. Hartley, "The Priesthood Reorganization of 1877: Brigham Young's Last Achievement," *BYU Studies* 20, no. 1 (Fall 1979): 3–36; see also William G. Hartley, "Brigham Young and Priesthood Work at the General and Local Levels," in Susan Easton Black and Larry C. Porter, eds., *Lion of the Lord: Essays on the Life and Service of Brigham Young* (Salt Lake City: Deseret Book, 1995), 338–70; see also John A. Tvedtnes, *Organize My Kingdom: A History of Restored Priesthood* (Bountiful, Utah: Cornerstone, 2000), 219–30.

18. Jeffrey R. Holland, "That Our Children May Know," BYU Campus Education Week address, 25 August 1981.

19. Zina P. Young Williams Card, page 3 of "Short Reminiscent Sketches of Karl G. Maeser," typescript, undated, Zina Presendia Young Williams Card Collection, MSS 1421, box 2, folder 20, L. Tom Perry Special Collections, BYU.

20. Maeser, "History of the Academy," 131.

21. Franklin S. Harris, address given at his inauguration in 1921.

22. See Spencer W. Kimball, "The Second Century of Brigham Young University," BYU devotional address, 10 October 1975.

23. Doctrine and Covenants 58:27.

24. John 21:15–17.

The Tie Between Science and Religion

Russell M. Nelson

◆ *BYU Life Sciences Building Dedication, April 9, 2015*

INTRODUCTION

President Russell M. Nelson, an apostle at the time that he gave these touching remarks, recounted in this talk how the gospel had "provided the undergirding foundation" for his remarkable educational journey (page 292). His journey had taught him, among other things, that "all truth is part of the everlasting gospel" (page 291) and that "when the laws of God are obeyed, wanted blessings will *always* result, not just *maybe* or *sometimes*" (page 293). President Nelson's sterling example reminds us that we are blessed as we become disciples in the disciplines. Indeed, the Lord expects all of His people to be consecrated covenant keepers who are following the covenant path, no matter their worldly occupation.

The great privilege of studying God's creations builds in its students a reverence for life and a testimony that we are literally created by Deity.

— Russell M. Nelson

: ⚜ :

THIS UNIVERSITY IS committed to searching for truth and to teaching the truth. All truth is part of the gospel of Jesus Christ. Whether truth comes from a scientific laboratory or by revelation from the Lord, it is compatible. All truth is part of the everlasting gospel. Brigham Young so taught: "If you can find a truth in heaven, earth or hell, it belongs to our doctrine. We believe it; it is ours; we claim it."[1] There is no conflict between science and religion. Conflict only arises from an incomplete knowledge of either science or religion— or both.

Research and education become religious responsibilities for members of The Church of Jesus Christ of Latter-day Saints, for we know that "the glory of God is intelligence."[2] And our perspective is enlarged by knowing that "whatever principle of intelligence we attain unto in this life, it will rise with us in the resurrection."[3]

Meanwhile, there will always be more to learn, especially when studying topics that relate to the Creation, physiology, and the laws of life. Why? Because life comes from God. There will always be a gap between what He knows and what we now know.

He has revealed the following promise, which may bring comfort to those who cannot find answers to all of their questions at this point in time. He said:

> Yea, verily I say unto you, **in that day when the Lord shall come,** he shall reveal all things—
> Things which have passed, and hidden things which no man knew, things of the earth, by which it was made, and the purpose and the end thereof—
> Things most precious, things that are above, and things that are beneath, things that are in the earth, and upon the earth, and in heaven.[4]

In the BYU Life Sciences Building, the focus will be centered on learning from and about God's living creations. Now I will confess a personal prejudice: I think that a person can learn more by studying God's creations than by studying the works of people, even by the most erudite and educated scholars. Job felt the same way when he wrote:

> But ask now the beasts, and they shall teach thee; and the fowls of the air, and they shall tell thee:
> Or speak to the earth, and it shall teach thee: and the fishes of the sea shall declare unto thee.[5]

In my early days of research into the workings of the human heart, very little was known. There was no field of heart surgery. In fact, we were taught in medical school that one must never touch the beating heart. To do so would cause the heart to stop beating. So little by little we began to tread into uncharted waters. For me, those early exploratory experiments were buttressed by this sure word of the Lord from the Doctrine and Covenants:

> All kingdoms have a law given;
> And there are many kingdoms; for there is no space in the which there is no kingdom; and there is no kingdom in which there is no space, either a greater or a lesser kingdom.
> And unto every kingdom is given a law; and unto every law there are certain bounds also and conditions.[6]

This knowledge, coupled with one other revelation, provided the undergirding foundation I needed for my work. The other revelation is well known to you:

> There is a law, irrevocably decreed in heaven before the foundations of this world, upon which all blessings are predicated—
> And when we obtain any blessing from God, it is by obedience to that law upon which it is predicated.[7]

By learning for the kingdom of the heart what laws must be obeyed for the heart to beat, eventually we were able to turn the heartbeat off and turn it on again. This enabled surgery of the heart to be predictable and dependable. Even educated and experienced doctors would wonder, Can you really do that?

The answer is simply this: When the laws of God are obeyed, wanted blessings will *always* result, not just *maybe* or *sometimes*. Divine law is dependable! Divine law is incontrovertible!

The great privilege of studying God's creations builds in its students a reverence for life and a testimony that we are literally created by Deity. That reverence for our Creator represents true religion. The meaning of the word *religion* is literally "to ligate" or "to tie us once again" back to God.

For students, there is nowhere better to confront the questions shared between science and religion than in the College of Life Sciences at Brigham Young University.

NOTES

1. Brigham Young, "Remarks," *Deseret News*, 4 May 1870, 152; *Journal of Discourses*, 26 vols. (London: Latter-day Saints' Book Depot, 1854–86), 13:335 (24 April 1870).

2. Doctrine and Covenants 93:36.

3. Doctrine and Covenants 130:18.

4. Doctrine and Covenants 101:32–34; emphasis added.

5. Job 12:7–8.

6. Doctrine and Covenants 88:36–38.

7. Doctrine and Covenants 130:20–21.

Photo Credits

PAGE 2. Joseph Smith statue: Bradley Slade/BYU, 2022.

PAGE 10. Brigham Young statue: Nate Edwards/BYU, 2017.

PAGE 11. Reinhard Maeser: L. Tom Perry Special Collections, UA 244.

PAGE 16. Academy Building on October 16, 1900, for a Founders Day celebration: L. Tom Perry Special Collections, UAP 2 Folder 031.

PAGES 17, 147. Karl G. Maeser: Charles Roscoe Savage/The Church of Jesus Christ of Latter-day Saints.

PAGE 22. J. Reuben Clark Building: Aaron Cornia/BYU, 2016.

PAGE 23. J. Reuben Clark: The Church of Jesus Christ of Latter-day Saints.

PAGE 42. Centennial Carillon Tower on BYU campus: Jaren Wilkey/BYU, 2020.

PAGES 43, 159. Spencer W. Kimball: Eldon Keith Linschoten/The Church of Jesus Christ of Latter-day Saints.

PAGE 62. Students at a BYU devotional: Ryan Campbell/BYU, 2019.

PAGE 68. Student studying: Rebekah Baker/BYU, 2018.

PAGE 84. Student researching: Jaren Wilkey/BYU, 2019.

PAGE 85. Kevin J Worthen: Mark A. Philbrick/BYU, 2014.

PAGE 102. Joseph Smith Building: Nate Edwards/BYU, 2017.

PAGES 103, 199. Bruce C. Hafen: Craig W. Dimond/The Church of Jesus Christ of Latter-day Saints, 2007.

PAGE 128. Y Mountain: Nate Edwards/BYU, 2020.

PAGES 129, 193. Jeffrey R. Holland: Leslie Nilsson/The Church of Jesus Christ of Latter-day Saints, 2018.

PAGE 144. BYU campus: Nate Edwards/BYU, 2018.

PAGE 145. John Taylor: Charles Roscoe Savage/The Church of Jesus Christ of Latter-day Saints.

PAGE 146. Karl G. Maeser statue: Nate Edwards/BYU, 2017.

PAGE 152. *Tree of Wisdom* sculpture: Nate Edwards/BYU, 2019.

PAGE 153. Zina P. Young Williams Card: The Church of Jesus Christ of Latter-day Saints.

PAGE 158. Staircase to Education in Zion Gallery: Nate Edwards/BYU, 2016.

PAGE 186. Provo Utah Temple: John Snyder/BYU.

PAGE 192. Karl G. Maeser Building: Nate Edwards/BYU, 2016.

PAGE 198. BYU graduation: Nate Edwards/BYU, 2017.

PAGE 218. Student walking on BYU campus: Jaren Wilkey/BYU, 2021.